TAKING OWNERSHIP OF ACCREDITATION

To my dear friend Joseph — With admiration and affection for you and your work, I look forward to years of friendship and professional collaboration. Amy

TAKING OWNERSHIP

OF ACCREDITATION

Assessment Processes that
Promote Institutional Improvement
and Faculty Engagement

Edited by

Amy Driscoll and

Diane Cordero de Noriega

Preface by Judith A. Ramaley

Sty/us

STERLING, VIRGINIA

COPYRIGHT © 2006 BY STYLUS PUBLISHING, LLC

Published by Stylus Publishing, LLC
22883 Quicksilver Drive
Sterling, Virginia 20166-2102

Library of Congress Cataloging-in-Publication Data
Taking ownership of accreditation : participatory
approaches to promote engagement in assessment and
ongoing institutional improvement / edited by Amy
Driscoll and Diane Cordero de Noriega.
p.   cm.
ISBN 1-57922-175-0 (alk. paper)—ISBN 1-57922-176-9
(pbk. : alk. paper)
1. Accreditation (Education)—United
States.   2. Universities and colleges—United
States—Evaluation.   3. California State
University—Accreditation.   I. Driscoll,
Amy.   II. Noriega, Diane Cordero de, 1943–
LB2810.3.U6D75   2005
379.1'58—dc22
2005020541

ISBN: 1-57922-175-0 (cloth) / 13-digit   ISBN: 978-1-57922-175-1

ISBN: 1-57922-176-9 (paper) / 13-digit   ISBN: 978-1-57922-176-8

Printed in the United States of America

All first editions printed on acid-free paper
that meets the American National Standards Institute
Z39-48 Standard.

Bulk Purchases

Quantity discounts are available for use in
workshops and staff development.

Call 1-800-232-0223

First Edition, 2006

10 9 8 7 6 5 4 3 2 1

Dedication

This book is dedicated to our colleague and dear friend, Linda Stamps. As the Senior Associate for Accreditation and Policy Development, Linda provided leadership and guidance to the campus for the entire accreditation process. Linda was relentless in her pursuit of integrity and the highest standards for our documentation. She was meticulous in her attention to detail and transparent in her commitment to a true process of inquiry. Linda brought both mischief and brilliance to our processes. Our best memories are filled with her deep laughter, her unwavering enthusiasm, her sincere search to "get it," her passionate intolerance of less than our best, and her patience with our most convoluted thinking.

Linda was a perfect fit for the energy and impassioned inquiry of the campus. Linda Stamps left her signature on California State University Monterey Bay's successful accreditation and the ongoing improvement we describe in this book. We dedicate our work to her with affection and admiration.

CONTENTS

USING ACCREDITATION TO IMPROVE PRACTICE

Judith A. Ramaley

I t has been a privilege to be an outside insider as California State University Monterey Bay (CSUMB) has developed over the past several years. Usually, the role of the chair of a site-visit team is to support a group of visitors who come to a campus during the accreditation process to study the evidence that an institution has prepared to demonstrate its "accreditability" and to test some of the assertions by direct observation. In this instance, however, as chair of three different teams that visited CSUMB during its initial accreditation process, I became a collaborator in a grand experiment designed to demonstrate how an institution could embody and advance its vision and demonstrate its institutional capacity and effectiveness in new ways, while, at the same time, advancing those goals in the very process of demonstrating them to its accreditors. As Amy Driscoll explains in chapter 2, this was a joint venture between CSUMB as it prepared for its first institutional accreditation and the Western Association of Schools and Colleges (WASC) as it worked on introducing a new way of approaching the process of accreditation. Since the whole thing was an experiment, it will not come as a surprise that the role of the site visit team was an experiment also.

Accreditation as an Example of Design Research

In the past decade, a new approach to linking scholarship to practice has begun to emerge in education research. The analogy between this model, called *design research*, and the experimental accreditation process undertaken by CSUMB in cooperation with WASC is instructive. As in design research, we all invented as we went, and the process got better and the product more useful as we moved from one phase of the accreditation process to the next. Burkhardt and Schoenfeld (2003) divide the field of educational research into three domains based on the cognate disciplines in the humanities, science, and engineering. The humanities approach is judged by its internal consistency, its fit with prevailing wisdom, and its plausibility. There is no requirement that the assertions be subject to empirical test. In contrast, the scientific approach does require empirical observations and testing of assertions. However, neither approach can close the gap between research and practice unless it becomes linked functionally to the practical experiences and needs of the education system. This is what design research seeks to do, based on an engineering design paradigm. This is also what the innovative approach to accreditation undertaken by CSUMB and WASC sought to do, to link assessment, reflection, and institutional improvement to the process of accreditation itself. However, in the absence of an agreed-upon way to test assumptions and claims, the design research field remains an interesting but not yet compelling approach to bridging the research-practice gap (Kelly, 2004). According to Eamonn Kelly, the question that design research cannot yet answer is, "Can this new set of methods establish boundaries (demarcations) between sound and unsound claims about learning and teaching" (p. 12). In our joint venture, we set out to solve that problem for the accreditation process and explore ways to distinguish between sound and unsound claims, both on the basis of documents and on the basis of direct interaction and observation.

In 1992, Ann L. Brown wrote about her research "in the blooming, buzzing confusion of inner-city classrooms" (1992, p. 141). She described her attempt "to engineer innovative educational environments and simultaneously conduct experimental studies of those innovations (p. 141.)" The resulting design research model seeks to contribute simultaneously to the advancement of theory and practice through an iterative process in which the starting theory and interpretation of research findings become design elements for an intervention, the results of which test the starting design and the theory that underlies it and advance a growing body of knowledge in what Burkhardt and Schoenfeld (2003) call a process of "cumulativity." The results of this linkage of research and practice are "key products . . . tools and/or processes that work well for their intended uses and users, with evidence-based evaluation" (p. 5). The conceptual model is comparable to the approach taken in engineering design research, where research is directed toward knowledge that will have a practical impact, combining "imaginative design and empirical testing of the products and processes during development" (p. 5). That is just what we were setting out to do at CSUMB.

A New Approach to Accreditation: Design Research in Action

The new WASC process for accreditation was in the design stages as CSUMB moved into the preparation for its first full accreditation review. The process had two components, institutional integrity and educational effectiveness, to be assessed in two separate phases a number of months apart. The two core commitments upon which the entire accreditation process was to be based were defined by WASC as follows:

1. Institutional Integrity: The institution functions with clear purposes, high levels of institutional integrity, fiscal stability, and organizational structures to fulfill its purposes.
2. Educational Effectiveness: The institution evidences clear and appropriate educational objectives and design at the institutional and program level, and employs processes of review, including the collection and use of data, that assure delivery of programs and learner accomplishments at a level of performance appropriate for the degree or certificate awarded.

The role of the WASC evaluation team was to work with the institution's own evidence and exhibits (e.g., documents, databases) to determine if they accurately and fairly described the institution and then, using the commission's standards, to determine if the institution had made a convincing case that it had met the two components (i.e., core commitments) of the review. In addition, the site visit team chose to ask itself whether the institution had sufficient capacity and systems of quality assurance and improvement in place to demonstrate educational effectiveness at the time of the review and whether these conditions were likely to continue.

One of the distinctive features of the entire evaluation was that it resembled design research, a process through which, with careful experimentation and testing, a stronger and more effective institutional model would emerge. WASC was very clear about its intentions and invited both the campus community and the site visit team to work out ways to advance these goals and to invent ways to demonstrate that the process was, in fact, producing these results. The expectations were challenging. The list consisted of seven elements.

1. The development and more effective use of indicators of institutional performance and educational effectiveness to support institutional planning and decision making
2. Greater clarity about the institution's educational outcomes and criteria for defining and evaluating these outcomes
3. Improvement of the institution's capacity for self-review and of its systems of quality assurance
4. A deeper understanding of student learning, the development of more varied and effective methods of assessing learning, and the use of the results of this process to improve programs and institutional practices
5. Systematic engagement of the faculty with issues of assessing and improving teaching and learning processes within the institution, and with aligning support systems for faculty more effectively toward this end
6. Validation of the institution's presentation of evidence, both to assess compliance with accreditation standards and to provide a basis for institutional improvement
7. Demonstration of the institution's fulfillment of the Core Commitments to Institutional Capacity and Educational Effectiveness

Specific Tasks of the Preparatory Review Team

Unlike other site visits that I have led, this one was more like an anthropological field trip, or at least, my understanding of what my colleagues in anthropology tell me goes on during field trips. We invented a way to audit and verify the information provided in the institutional presentation and to assure ourselves that the evidence fairly and accurately portrayed the state of the institution at the time of the review. We did this by examining the self-study materials as well as by observing how people on campus interacted, worked on problems, and explored issues. The team served as participant-observers, interacting with members of the campus community in problem-solving mode rather than solely in interview mode.

When examining the documentary evidence, we applied the same criteria that any scholar would use to evaluate a work of scholarship. Were the objectives clear? Had explicit indicators and metrics of achievement and/or specific bodies of evidence been provided that could help the institution determine to what degree its objectives have been met? Had action been taken on the basis of evidence in order to improve performance? What had been the results of those actions? This may remind the reader of the criteria for scholarship articulated by Glassick, Huber, and Maeroff (1997).

Using the Glassick, Huber, and Maeroff (1997) model as a guide, the case for institutional effectiveness must have *clear goals* and must be firmly grounded in knowledge about the institution and the context in which it operates (*adequate preparation*). The warrant must be built upon a solid body of evidence gathered and interpreted in a disciplined and principled way (*appropriate methods*) and shown to be significantly related to the challenges at hand (*significant results*). The case must be presented effectively (*effective presentation*) and be studied reflectively (*reflective critique*), with a clear and compelling sense of responsibility for the effects of the ideas and proposed actions on the community that will be affected, both inside and outside the institution (*ethical and social responsibility*) (qualities in italics taken from Glassick, Huber, & Maeroff, 1997).

This list of standards leads to a more finely grained set of expectations for how an institution and its leadership can most effectively approach institutional development and improvement at a transformational level. Change must be intentional and must affect a significant part of the institutional mission; for example, general education, undergraduate majors, research, and outreach. Change must be supported by a culture of evidence that documents the consequences of the steps undertaken. A community must have a way to learn from its experiences.

It is very important to start out with a clear sense of the stages of organizational change. Since everything is always connected to everything else, it helps to be mindful that one thing will lead to another—what I have learned to call the "ripple effect" and to examine how this set of interactions may spread and what happens when it does. No matter where a campus starts and what change it introduces, the experience will set in motion a chain reaction of adjustments and realignments necessary to support and maintain the desired outcome. These kinds of reactions are hard to capture in a document, but they can be studied directly if a site visit team interacts in authentic collegial mode with members of a campus community. For this reason, the site visit teams developed the idea of an on-campus audit to sample specific administrative processes and procedures to verify that they are followed and in place, to select a set of important and challenging questions that are authentically relevant to the campus in its current stage of development, and to engage in as realistic an exploration of these questions as possible while on campus. This allowed the team to see how the campus worked, how people talked with each other, how they dealt with difficult and often complex issues, whether they really did approach the work of institutional design and development in the ways that they attested to in their self-study. The questions that were used for this test probe were developed in cooperation with the institution and are outlined in Amy Driscoll's chapter 2. Another campus in a different stage of development would have generated different questions. The interactions that arose from a consideration of these questions (e.g., is there a continuous process of inquiry and engagement by the institution to enhance educational effectiveness?) offered everyone an opportunity to observe the campus community in action. At the same time, the issues that framed the interactions of the campus and the team were important to the campus and merited their serious attention. One might call this inquiry-based or problem-based learning, embedded in the accreditation process itself.

In my opinion, this new design research model of accreditation worked extremely well. The site team learned a lot about the institution, and the institution, I believe, learned a lot about itself, both during its own self-study process, whose design is described in wonderful detail in this book, and through its interactions with the site visit teams. By approaching both the self-study and the site visits as an act of scholarship, CSUMB demonstrated that it did, indeed, engage in a continuous process of inquiry and engagement with a resultant advance in educational effectiveness while, at the same time, contributing to the scholarly literature on assessment and institutional change. I have no doubt that you will learn a lot from CSUMB about putting a compelling vision into action, about maintaining and enhancing a sense of common purpose and a community of interest, and about making progress visible. This is indeed a university that practices what it teaches.

References

Brown, A. L. (1992). Design experiments: Theoretical and methodological challenges in creating complex interventions in classroom settings. *Journal of the Learning Sciences, 2*(2), 141–178.

Burkhardt, H., & Schoenfeld, A. H. (2003). Improving educational research: Toward a more useful, more influential, and better-funded enterprise. *Educational Researcher, 32*(9), 3–14.

Glassick, C. E., Huber, M. T., & Maeroff, G. I. (1997) *Scholarship assessed: Evaluation of the professoriate.* San Francisco: Jossey-Bass.

Kelly, A. E. (2004). Design research in education: Yes, but is it methodological? *Journal of the Learning Sciences, 13*(1), 115–128.

I

ASSESSMENT AND ACCREDITATION

Productive Partnerships

Amy Driscoll

I n the opinion of the editors of this book, it could not have been written fifteen years ago—it would not have fit in the scene of higher education, would not have made sense to our colleagues, and it probably would have gathered dust on a shelf had anyone ordered it. In today's context of assessment and accreditation in higher education, we intend this book to be useful and usable, offering strategies for the documentation process of accreditation.

The chapters of this book are authentic descriptions of the processes of assessment used by our campus to demonstrate educational effectiveness. Our campus, California State University Monterey Bay (CSUMB), dedicated our accreditation self-study to ongoing improvement processes rather than one-time strategies. The processes and strategies that we describe here are practical—ready to use or adapt for most campuses. Our approach also reflects the fact that both processes (assessment and accreditation) have undergone a significant shift in terms of form and function, and even more important, a welcome change in perspective.

Setting the Stage

This chapter sets the stage for the strategies and processes that our colleagues will present in the following chapters by tracing the paradigm shift in assessment and in accreditation. This description is intended to make it easier to understand and apply the ideas that follow. Both of those *A* words along with a close relative, accountability, have not been popular on campuses. Sherril Gelmon (1997) once said that the three terms are capable of "provoking responses ranging from religious fervor to extreme distaste to complete cynicism" (p. 51). In fact, all three *A* words have been misunderstood, considered suspect, and viewed as unconnected from the work of faculty and student learning. From the perspective of faculty, assessment, accreditation, and accountability have been the responsibility of "someone else." That someone else has typically been an administrator, often in an office of institutional research.

The current state of all three *A*s is that they are very much part of the mainstream of higher education, a shared responsibility of administration and faculty across several offices or centers, and are integral to teaching and learning. Fortunately for you, and us, perspectives about and responses to assessment and accreditation have changed, as we will describe in the sections that follow.

Assessment of the Past

Not so very long ago in higher education, assessment was a data-gathering process assigned to an institutional office. Faculty were involved in assessment only in so far as they engaged in informal formative assessment (quizzes, question-and-answer sessions, homework assignments) or in formal summative assessment (exams, final reports, projects), typically in the privacy of their own classrooms. The campus assessment or research offices were not connected to their processes and were seldom used or accessed by faculty.

Resistance to Assessment

When the pressure to change assessment began to be heard and felt on campuses, it generated enormous resistance on the part of faculty (Palomba & Banta, 1999). Our experiences tell us that there were two reasons for that resistance—fear that assessment would be used to evaluate faculty, and faculty's discomfort with their own lack of expertise. In addition, Trudy Banta (Palomba & Banta, 1999) points out that "some faculty view assessment as a threat to their academic freedom" (p. 71). The lack of experience or expertise is not as publicly acknowledged but few faculty will claim skill or take the lead in assessment work. Both of us have advanced degrees in education, yet we acknowledge that our preparation for assessment was limited or almost nonexistent.

Ongoing Resistance

Over and above faculty and administrators' resistance to assessment, another barrier has been the issue of assessment costs, in terms of money, resources, and faculty time. Resentment about the allocation of resources to assessment was exacerbated by the perception that the process was externally driven, as indeed it generally was.

Peter Ewell (2002) described a range of state mandates that left public colleges and universities scrambling to develop assessment capacity in the late 1980s and early 1990s. Institutions of higher education took a reactive role, much to the chagrin of faculty. Assessment began with the taint of being part of a corporatist vision, and as a means for governmental interference in the academic business of colleges and universities. This was followed by debate about higher education's public purposes and ensuing calls for statewide outcomes testing. Assessment was viewed as a mechanism for assuring quality for external audiences. It was received with emphatic resistance—faculty felt huge pressures "put upon them."

Indications of Change

These external pressures did little to reduce faculty resistance even as thinking about assessment began to change. External forces may have added to the resistance, but they also accelerated the momentum of assessment without giving it form or substance. However, it wasn't until assessment was seen as higher education's "means to examine its educational intentions on its own terms" (Maki, 2004, p. 15) that the resistance began to break down. With this breakdown came the perception of faculty responsibilities and roles in assessment and an engagement that would be mutually rewarding for them and their institutions. Our readers will hear descriptions of those rewards in the chapters that follow, chapters written by our coauthors, colleagues at California State University Monterey Bay.

When you study this book, it will be clear that faculty have shifted their responses to assessment. They no longer have to be cajoled to engage in assessment. Many of the authors (chapters 6, 7, 10, for example) initiated major assessment projects themselves out of interest and commitments. They found value and used assessment to improve student learning and their own teaching. How did this change happen? What prompted the shift in assessment in higher education? What forces finally broke down the resistance? A look at the history of assessment's shift will help answer those questions.

From Resistance to Responsibility

Peter Ewell (2002) traces the "birth" of assessment as the movement we know today to 1985 with the first National Conference on Assessment in Higher Education cosponsored by the National Institute of Education (NIE) and the American Association for Higher Education (AAHE). Not surprisingly, the conference forums were marked by conflicting political and intellectual themes. In spite of conflicts, the conference was focused on a unifying theme, student learning, and included recommendations from research to improve achievement. An interesting message was communicated at the conference, one that has remained a strong theme of the assessment movement to today. The message was that there was much to "learn" from assessment data and "feedback on student performance" for both faculty and institutions (Ewell, 2002, p. 7). That learning potential prompted a number of the assessment projects described in the later chapters.

Related reports that focused on undergraduate curriculum and pedagogy were disseminated around the time of the conference, and they extended the message of the conference to not only learn from assessment but to use it to become learner-centered. That theme has gathered strength and followers and continues to nurture campus commitments to assessment today as we write this chapter (Driscoll, 2005).

The resulting movement went beyond supporting the commitment to assessment; it produced assessment with forms and functions that are authentic and meaningful, embedded in or integrated with teaching and learning, and well aligned with the professional role and intentions of faculty. Gardner, Csikszentmihalyi, and Damon (2001) speak of the importance of alignment, or the fit, with our professional values as essential to "high quality" work and responsibility. Hence, the changes in assessment have not only eased the resistance, they have moved assessment to a "collective responsibility" of faculty at many institutions. The changes also take the form of significant advances in the quality of assessment.

Remaining Challenges

Ewell (2002) reminds us of the challenges of developing commitment to and responsibility for assessment:

- Defining assessment in ways that promote its use for improvement
- Identifying and ultimately developing "credible and useful" (p. 10) ways of assessing student learning and related processes

- Widespread institutional inexperience and few examples for learning
(pp. 34)

Those of us who were caught up in the early stages of campus development of assessment turned to those few exemplars—Alverno College, Truman State University, Kings College, Ball State University—for inspiration and lessons on "how to." On our individual campuses, the momentum was not immediately evident as faculty resisted, administrators questioned, and we initiated our subtle beginnings almost in isolation. Assessment committees and, later, assessment centers emerged on campuses as a sign of growing involvement of institutions, but the momentum could only be described as sluggish. As a brand new director of teaching, learning, and assessment, this author spent an entire year able to entice very few faculty to collaborate on assessment projects or activities, even with generous funding as motivation.

As Peggy Maki (2004) reminds us, "there are no absolute places to start, but there are contexts, issues, or institutional developments that become opportunities to initiate the effort" (p. 14). Some of those possibilities for "jump-starting" assessment movement on a campus include times when a mission statement needs development or revision, a strategic plan is needed, curricular review or revision is imminent, or new programs are in process. Accreditation is clearly another one of those jump-starting factors, as our chapters will demonstrate. Ewell (1997a) calls these "triggering" opportunities and in his ongoing wisdom reminds us that faculty will embrace change when "they are unhappy with the quality of learning that seems to result despite their efforts, and unhappy with a particular instructional delivery system" (p. 4).

Gaining Momentum: From Triggers to Engagement

In my role as director of assessment I waited a year for the "trigger" and the possibilities for faculty involvement. For many faculty and institutions, their openness to assessment derived from inquiry about student achievement and the need for information to improve their approaches. The theme of improving student learning made it possible for many of us to slowly engage faculty on our campuses. The connections between assessment and pedagogy and curriculum reduced the original resistance and strengthened the engagement. In chapter 10 Swarup Wood describes faculty responses to those connections with a full range of resistance to acceptance.

From campus to campus, faculty began to move from distrust of assessment as they discovered assessment's potential for improving their teaching and courses. In many cases, faculty took charge and articulated the purpose(s) of assessment and even defined assessment to capture their philosophy and priorities. At CSUMB faculty unanimously agreed that they would not settle for any assessment that simply measured or described learning. They insisted that assessment must enhance or extend learning. Such collaborative processes for faculty to define and develop intentions for assessment significantly reduced most of the former fears about the potential use of assessment and increased faculty's level of engagement.

The Implications of New Roles

It must be noted that even when faculty take the lead to articulate purposes and definitions, they continue to need extensive training and development to carry out the associated responsibilities for assessment. Many of the chapters of this book will provide guidance to early campus efforts in assessment. Our work will contribute to the expanding effort to support faculty and entire institutions in assessment work. Betty McEady's chapter on surveying best practices in assessment as a public and visible learning process is a model for almost any campus or department. Such efforts have multiplied from campus to campus and at a regional and national level.

Trudy Banta (Palomba & Banta, 1999) describes the extensive materials produced in the last ten years—books, pamphlets, workbooks, newsletters and other publications, Web sites, resource guides, and bibliographies (p. 55). Conferences and large meetings at state, regional, and national levels attracted an increasing number of interested, or at least skeptical, participants including faculty and administrators. Campuses attended to Banta's recommendations to support faculty assessment efforts with three *R*s—clearly defined *Roles, Resources* for developing expertise in assessment, and *Rewards* such as stipends and recognition (Palomba & Banta, p. 53). A large number of campuswide forums have showcased individual faculty work in assessment. A few campuses including our own have articulated the importance of faculty assessment contributions as scholarship in promotion and tenure guidelines. In Banta and associates, 2002, Trudy Banta wrote about the emerging scholarship of assessment and encouraged campuses and faculty to view and configure their assessment with the qualities and criteria of scholarship.

Assessment Today

All of the supports and possibilities have worked together to ensure that assessment won't be a passing phase or a fad of our times. Richard Shavelson

(Shavelson & Huang, 2003) assures us that "the calls for assessment-based accountability are not going away any time soon" (p. 11). He describes the current momentum as a "frenzy" and urges us to respond responsibly so that our assessment frameworks are aligned with valued outcomes of higher education. Diane Cordero de Noriega's chapter 3 about vision, values, and mission demonstrates how those intentions can guide such alignment. Along with faculty across the country, Shavelson discourages the use of a "one size fits all" standardized testing response that would "reduce the diversity of learning environments that characterize and give strength to our national higher education system" (2003, p. 11). The strategies of *Taking Ownership of Accreditation* will demonstrate that high-quality assessment is possible with individualized approaches that consider varied student populations, unique curricula, and respond to meaningful inquiry of a campus while at the same time addressing questions of accountability.

Guidance for the Times

Peggy Maki, who has been such a mentor to many of us in the assessment movement, describes a significant kind of prescription for sustaining faculty engagement in high quality assessment. She says that "a dialog that focuses on teaching and learning is a sign that the assessment process is developing and maturing" (2004, p. 15). Much like Shavelson, she encourages us to respond responsibly and to build and nurture a collaborative community on our campuses, a community that engages in assessment work. Again, Swarup Wood's chapter 10 describes interviews he conducted with faculty who worked in such communities. Those communications began with the development of shared expectations of student learning, the articulation of shared criteria and standards, and the shared analysis and interpretation of student evidence. They found and embraced those connections between assessment and teaching and learning. Their interviews are examples of the kind of enthusiasm, commitment, inquiry, and innovation that faculty are expressing on campuses today. It's a stark contrast to the mistrust, disdain, and resistance of the past.

Maintaining the focus on teaching and learning is a key to the paradigm shift, and it will keep assessment from returning to a place of marginalization and from being an "empty and intellectually unfulfilling activity" (Maki, 2004, p. 15). All of the chapters that follow emphasize that focus and provide guidance to sustain the connection between assessment and student learning.

Looking to the Future of Assessment

That early message of the 1984–85 reports—for higher education to become learner-centered—has influenced the assessment movement to the extent that assessment is embraced by faculty and institutions as an integral part of the work of educating students. AAHE, Association of American Colleges and Universities (AACU), and several of the accrediting associations have sponsored or currently sponsor very popular workshops for campus teams to develop learner-centered approaches to learning and assessment. Many campus assessment designs are directed to "learner-centered assessment" for a better fit with the pedagogy and curriculum of today's institutions. Mary Huba and Jann Freed (2000) have articulated the many ways learner-centered assessment supports quality undergraduate education. The characteristics that demonstrate such support include the following:

1. Promotes high expectations
2. Respects diverse talents and learning styles
3. Promotes coherence in learning
4. Synthesizes experiences and integrates education and experiences
5. Involves students in learning
6. Provides prompt feedback
7. Fosters collaboration
8. Depends on increased student-faculty contact (pp. 22–24)

When we look at the list and recognize all of the supports for learning that are now integral to assessment, we are aware of the exciting developments that have occurred in the recent history of assessment in higher education. We can also sense that the movement is as healthy and solid as we could hope.

After reviewing the developments we conclude that the paradigm shift in one of the *A* words is stunning, but that the other *A* word, *accreditation*, has also changed. One has to ask, "Were the two shifts related?" Did one prompt the other? Which came first? Your editors chose to avoid the chicken-or-egg controversy and describe each of the histories separately while acknowledging that assessment and accreditation could not possibly have changed in isolation from each other.

Accreditation of the Past

Accreditation has a history of being viewed as a burden, an expensive and strenuous routine, a quality assurance process for the public, an external pressure by institutions of higher education. As Sherril Gelmon (1997) reminds us, "accreditation has had mixed perceptions of its identity and how it works" (p. 54). In addition, there has been significant variation across accreditation agencies, and some of that difference exists today in terms of specific procedures, expectations for documentation, schedules, and even visitation teams.

Seeds of the Paradigm Shift

In the early 1980s, as the states were demanding reform and performance funding, accreditation agencies became involved in the assessment movement. The effect of the 1984–85 national reports, state mandates, and dissatisfaction with higher education both internally and externally significantly influenced accreditation much like assessment.

By 1984, accreditation was described as a guided self-evaluation and self-improvement process, a peer review process to stimulate program evaluation, and a "facilitating, integrated, continuous assessment process" (Gelmon, 1997, p. 54; Millard, 1984). Most agencies continued to use complex sets of predetermined standards against which academic units and entire campuses were judged. Ideally, it was hoped that the processes of accreditation stimulated campus inquiry, data gathering, reflection, and, ultimately, improvement. And they probably did achieve those ends in many cases, but the rigidity of past accreditation processes and standards "presented a barrier to innovation, accreditation, and the natural process of program evolution (Gelmon, 1997, p. 54). Historical perceptions of accreditation may have limited the potential for a paradigm shift.

Another outcome of those traditional perceptions of accreditation was that related work on most campuses was assigned to a particular office much like assessment, or to someone with "release time" from teaching, or to a task force. It was rarely seen as the responsibility of an entire campus or entire department. With that isolation came a perception that accreditation had no implications for teaching and learning, and, thus, it prompted only peripheral or fleeting interest of faculty, or a paid development task prior to review.

Progress in Accreditation Shifts

Changes began to occur when the accreditation agencies became involved in assessment. Their role was prompted by the involvement of state legislatures in higher education. Those early efforts by agencies to require assessment, specifically outcomes assessment, were intended to curtail the states' influence and to discourage attempts to design standardized tests, common instruments, and/or pre/post testing.

In 1985–86 the Southern Association of Colleges and Schools took the lead with a standard that linked outcomes-based assessment to institutional effectiveness. In 1989 the North Central Association of Colleges and Schools required its affiliated institutions to institutionalize outcomes-based assessment within a specified time period. Many of the disciplinary associations (business, engineering, nursing, and teacher education) followed the lead and adopted an outcomes-based approach to their evaluation processes.

Continued Pressures Prompt Paradigm Shifts

Another event in the recent history of the assessment movement also added impetus to the paradigm shift in accreditation. The reports of dissatisfaction with higher education and calls for reform that were previously discussed in this chapter made no mention of any possible role for accrediting agencies in the improvement of higher education. Banta and Associates (2002) describe the reaction, "Accreditors were stung by this oversight," (p. 243) and attribute the situation to the invisibility created by policies of confidentiality espoused by the agencies. Their response was an immediate acceleration of their shift in priorities.

In 1988, the U.S. Department of Education called for a new focus on "educational effectiveness" in the accreditation process. The department stipulated that agencies require systematic documentation of the educational achievement of students as evidence of effectiveness. The new requirement was definitely one of those "triggering" opportunities—the accreditation community went beyond meeting those requirements and began a process of redefinition and refocus. Universities like CSUMB went beyond the accreditation requirements to an intense and engaged inquiry process that ultimately promoted long-term change and improvement.

Assessment and Accreditation on Parallel Tracks

The same flurry or frenzy that characterized the most recent activity in the assessment movement was also apparent in the accreditation movement of the late 1990s. Again the federal government added impetus with the founding of the Council for Higher Education Accreditation (CHEA) and spurred accreditation agencies to abandon traditional processes and take the lead in prioritizing assessment of student learning outcomes. Banta and Associates (2002) describe a strong relationship between the historical events of the late 1980s and early 1990s that mutually influenced assessment and accreditation. The initial growth of the assessment movement relentlessly pushed the accreditation agencies to acknowledge assessment as a major form of institutional accountability.

By the mid 1990s, reform of accreditation gained the same vigorous momentum we witnessed with assessment. However, in time, the tides reversed and accreditation agencies became the driving force with their expectations for assessment and their insistence that campuses "raise their level of assessment activity" (Banta & Associates, 2002, p. 243). In 1992 Ralph Wolff referred to the link between the two *A* words as neither a "shotgun marriage" nor a "match made in heaven." Instead, he encouraged an ideally productive partnership. Since then, the relationship has blossomed and campuses have taken advantage of accreditation reform to direct their own self-studies and identify priorities for review. Assessment was a common choice among those campuses that tailored their accreditation processes with institutionally specific themes, encouraged by agencies such as the Western Association of Schools and Colleges (WASC) and the North Central Association of Colleges and Schools.

WASC campuses and others around the country receive significant support and training in the development of documentation of educational effectiveness focused on student learning. That focus leaves no choice but to develop assessment strategies and processes. North Central Association campuses were also guided to focus on student learning in the "Statement on Assessment and Student Academic Achievement." One of the North Central Association's notable leaders, Cecilia Lopez (1999), urged campuses to avoid seeing assessment as an end in itself but rather as a means of gathering information for improvement (p. 5). The faculty at our campus took that message to heart and designed documentation processes to improve our institution, which is the theme of this book.

In addition to the pressure from regional agencies, leading thinkers in higher education reconceptualized educational effectiveness in ways that supported the shifts in thinking about assessment and accreditation. Barr and Tagg (1995) disturbed traditional campus responsibilities with their admonishment to move from teacher-directed to learner-directed education. Their seminal article prompted a whole new way of thinking about the work of campuses. The authors identified a range of modifications, restructuring, and reconfiguring of methods, courses, teaching, programs, and departments. Ultimately, the thinking and answers of higher education had to be focused on "what works in terms of students learning" (pp. 18–20). Their recommendations were seen in the redesign and refocus of accreditation.

Later, Ernest Pascarella (2001) addressed the concept of educational effectiveness, which was previously open to multiple interpretations. The lack of clear indicators left campuses floundering over how to achieve such effectiveness and how to document for accountability. Pascarella provided guidance for those efforts with the notion that effectiveness could be focused on two indicators—student learning evidence and use of "best practices." Institutions as well as their accreditation agencies had no choice but to attend to his indicators.

CSUMB found Pascarella's guidance helpful and focused much of its documentation of educational effectiveness on the two indicators.

Ongoing Challenges to a Complete Shift

Lopez and many of her assessment colleagues hoped that campuses would see assessment as a means of becoming learner-centered institutions, but her 1999 study of campus team reports found that most institutions were only partially achieving that goal. She identified some of the obstacles to assessment efforts:

- Lack of expertise in setting goals and outcomes, in developing assessment tools and strategies, and in data collection and interpretation
- Failure to review and use assessment results
- Lack of integration of assessment information with campuswide planning and decision making
- Few campus collaborations in assessment (Lopez, 1999)

Those obstacles sound similar to the challenges that Peter Ewell (2002) articulated for the shifts in assessment.

Lopez's study did indicate progress in that accreditation processes were modeling good practices in assessment and guiding campuses to a continuous improvement culture. The work of both accreditation agencies, WASC and North Central Association, were influential in the development of the processes and approaches described in this text. It is, in fact, the philosophy and goals expressed by Cecilia Lopez earlier in this section about the potential for accreditation and assessment that are the intentions of the editors and authors of this book. The documentation processes and strategies in the chapters that follow are the kind of assessment that leads to continued improvement of a campus, and are being used in that way for CSUMB's own culture of inquiry and innovation.

Evidence of the Accreditation Shift

A brief look at the standards and language of accreditation agencies across the country offers insight into the paradigm shift that made the accreditation process one of learner-centeredness. Their standards and requirements support faculty efforts to be learner-centered in pedagogy, curriculum, and assessment.

In 1992, the Northwest Commission on Colleges and Universities emphasized the centrality of outcomes assessment with professional judgments about student effects. Later, in the same spirit, the Southern Association of Colleges and Schools (1997) included language in their criteria that directed institutions to consider the quality of program and level of student achievement rather than focus on particular pedagogy or curriculum.

In Standard 4, the New England Association of Schools and Colleges (1992) requires that "The institution clearly specifies and publishes degree objectives and requirements for each program. Such objectives include the knowledge, intellectual skills, and methods of inquiry to be acquired" (p. 7).

The Middle States Association of Colleges and Schools (2002), in Standard 14, takes the connections further with "Outcomes assessment involves gathering and evaluating quantitative information that demonstrates the congruence between the institution's mission, goals, and objectives and the actual outcomes of the educational activities" (p. 65).

These statements are clear indications of the shift in accreditation and the significance of carefully assessing student learning in the context of campus identity.

Learning from Accreditation

If one browses the standards and policies of all of the agencies, it is clear that the accreditation process is indeed modeling and teaching about best practices in assessment. There is much to be learned from many of their recommendations:

> The institution conducts sustained, evidence-based, and participatory discussion about how effectively it is accomplishing its purposes and achieving its educational objectives. These activities inform both institutional planning and systematic evaluations of educational effectiveness. (WASC, 2001, p. 29)

> Assessment is evolutionary, ongoing, and incremental. Assessment efforts should be comprehensive, systematic, integrative, and organic . . . and

should be both qualitative and quantitative. (New England Association of Schools and Colleges, 2005, p. 2)

The North Central Association expanded the knowledge base about assessment with its study of team reports to assess the progress of assessment in accreditation (Lopez, 1999). Its findings highlighted common obstacles to implementation and institutional learning along with important recommendations for campuses to stay learner-centered. The study also found a rich array of good practices in assessment located in accreditation reviews. The study, with its purpose and findings, demonstrates how accreditation is truly focused on guiding assessment with the intent of improving student learning.

Assessment and Accreditation: Partners for Improvement

This book illustrates the connections and mutual support that assessment and accreditation can now provide for a campus. Each of the strategies and processes of our chapters blend assessment examples with documentation evidence for accreditation. Much of the work described was not achieved simply for accreditation, or in many cases, even primarily for accreditation. Our objectives were to improve the institution and to create frameworks that continue positive changes over time. Our work also demonstrates how well assessment and accreditation in their new forms create a synergy for learner-centered education. In chapter 2 Driscoll delineates the contextual status of both the institution (CSUMB) and the accreditation agency (WASC) as a way of setting the stage for the assessment processes that follow in chapters 3 through 11.

Chapter Previews: Integrating Assessment and Accreditation

At about the same time as the accreditation agencies were contributing to the knowledge base of assessment, the American Association for Higher Education developed *Principles of Good Practice for Assessing Student Learning* (1997), which continues to inform campus developments in assessment and indicators for accreditation. Those principles are included in chapter 8. As Betty McEady describes in chapter 8 on the best practices survey, such methods can serve as powerful self-assessment benchmarks for a campus and can drive ongoing improvement in assessment work. Many of the best practices provide a foundation of the approaches and thinking of this book.

By the time CSUMB began final documentation for its first accreditation review and visit, assessment practices had been embraced by many faculty and campuses, and accreditation was a supportive and reflective process to self-assess and to promote improvement as described in chapter 2. From our experience, and it may reflect the novelty and challenge of our institution's first accreditation, the process was demanding but rewarding. As Driscoll describes in chapter 2, both the institution and the accreditation agency were engaged in "high stakes" trial and error of innovative processes. As a result, it became an authentic and mutual learning process. It was not something "done to us" but, rather, a process in which faculty initiated and directed major components of our self-study. Our accreditation agency, WASC, provided support and logistics while encouraging us to design our own processes and forms. We did. In chapter 4 Salina Diiorio describes our preparation process and provides examples of our unique forms and strategies for mapping ongoing inquiry and documentation. Many of the forms promoted our learning process and were directed to campuswide involvement.

Our entire self-study process was unique to our culture and intentions. We approached assessment and accreditation with a clearly articulated mission, vision, and core values. Those statements of intention served as both guides and filters for our inquiry, data collection, documentation, reporting, and improvement efforts. Provost Diane Cordero de Noriega in chapter 3 describes that cultural context as an important foundation for the strategies and processes in the remaining chapters.

That foundation enabled us to design authentic assessment conducted in response to our unique inquiries well in advance of any documentation work. Our program review model described by Seth Pollack in chapter 5 is one example of an ongoing assessment that promotes continuous improvement. Our studies of how we support students' writing (chapter 6) and our capstone model (chapter 7), a summative project in which students integrate their learning, were initiated out of interest in determining effectiveness rather than for accreditation. Each demonstrates the kind of assessment espoused by the campus and attends to principles of good practice. Dan Shapiro's chapter 7 discusses the ongoing impact of the study of capstones from the initiation of the idea to recent developments. Annette March in chapter 6 shows how a study of one program can be methodologically designed and analyzed for campuswide implications so that improvement potential is maximized.

The importance of individual departmental cultures and intentions is an equally important consideration in the assessment of student learning. Brian

Simmons's chapter 9 describes a case study of an individual program using a comprehensive, long-term, and multimethod approach to document effectiveness from a disciplinary perspective as well as a guide for ongoing improvement of a new academic program.

Current accreditation standards emphasize the "growing inclusion of administrative units" (Nichols & Nichols, 2000, p. 14) in the assessment expectations of self-study. In chapter 11, Diane Cordero de Noriega and Salina Diiorio describe a decision-making model that aligns priorities, processes, and benchmarks of administrative units with their impact on student learning.

The Future of Accreditation and Assessment

When describing the future of the accreditation and assessment movements, Nichols and Nichols (2000) predicted that the accreditation associations would be expecting comprehensive and complete assessment plans from campuses "in the next several years" with "full implementation and use of results within five years" (p. 14). Those expectations are realistic at the time of this writing and they highlight one more very important aspect of the paradigm shift, that is, the "use of results." Current accreditation and assessment thinking call for moving beyond data collection and analysis to use of the information. The current phrase is "closing the loop," and as Mary Allen (2004) defines it, it's a process of "determining implications for change" (p. 166) from the data and making those changes happen. Closing the loop is the major theme of this book, with the idea that the closing process can go on well after accreditation is complete. The improvements that result from assessment and accreditation can be ongoing and long term, and can have a significant impact for the entire campus.

For our campus, assessment and accreditation have been learning processes as well as prompts for improvement. Our hope is for our readers to experience some of the insights, implications, and improvements that emerged from our processes and strategies, and to use and adapt them for their institutions.

References

Allen, M. J. (2004). *Assessing academic programs in higher education*. Bolton, MA: Anker Publishing.

American Association of Higher Education (1992). *Principles of good practice for assessing student learning.* Washington, DC: Author.

Banta, T., & Associates. (2002). *Building a scholarship of assessment.* San Francisco: Jossey-Bass.

Barr, R., & Tagg, J. (1995). From teaching to learning: A new paradigm for undergraduate education. *Change, 12*(6), 12–25.

Driscoll, A. (2005, January). *Learner-centered assessment.* Paper presented at the forum of the American Association of Higher Education and the Western Association of Schools and Colleges, Glendale, CA.

Ewell, P. T. (1997a). Organizing for learning: A new imperative. *AHHE Bulletin, 54*(4), 3–6.

Ewell, P. T. (1997b). Accountability and assessment in a second decade: New looks or same old story? In American Association for Higher Education Conference Proceedings, *Assessing Impact: Evidence and Action.* Washington, DC: AAHE.

Ewell, P. T. (2002). An emerging scholarship: A brief history of assessment. In T. Banta (Ed.), *Building a scholarship of assessment* (3–25). San Francisco: Jossey-Bass.

Gardner, H., Csikszentmihalyi, M., & Damon, W. (2001). *Good work: When excellence and ethics meet.* New York: Basic Books.

Gelmon, S. (1997). Intentional improvement: The deliberate linkage of assessment and accreditation. In American Association for Higher Education Conference Proceedings, *Assessing Impact: Evidence and Action.* Washington, DC: AAHE.

Huba, M., & Freed, J. (2000). *Learner-centered assessment on college campuses.* Boston, MA: Allyn & Bacon.

Lopez, C. L. (1999). *A decade of assessing student learning: What have we learned; What's next?* Chicago: North Central Association of Colleges and Schools Commission on Institutions of Higher Education.

Maki, P. L. (2004). *Assessing for learning: Building a sustainable commitment across the institution.* Sterling, VA: Stylus and American Association for Higher Education.

Middle States Commission on Higher Education. (2002). *Standards for accreditation and characteristics of excellence in higher education.* Philadelphia, PA: Author.

Millard, R. M. (1984). The structure of specialized accreditation in the United States. *Journal of Education for Library and Information Science, 25,* 87–97.

New England Association of Schools and Colleges. (2005). *Policy on institutional effectiveness.* Bedford, MA: Author.

Nichols, K. W., & Nichols, J. O. (2000). *The department head's guide to assessment implementation in administrative and educational support units.* New York: Agathon Press.

Northwest Commission on Colleges and Universities. (1992). *Standards for accreditation.* Redmond: WA: Author.

Palomba, C., & Banta, T. (1999). *Assessment essentials: Planning, implementing, and improving assessment in higher education.* San Francisco: Jossey-Bass.

Pascarella, E. (2001). Identifying excellence in undergraduate education: Are we even close? *Change, 33*(3), 19–23.

Shavelson, R., & Huang, L. (2003). Responding responsibly to the frenzy to assess learning in higher education. *Change, 35*(1), 11–19.

Southern Association of Colleges and Schools (1997). *Standards for accreditation.* Decatur, GA: Author.

Western Association of Schools and Colleges (2001). *WASC handbook of accreditation: User's guide.* Alameda, CA: Author.

Wolff, R. (1992). Assessment and accreditation: A shotgun marriage? In *Achieving institutional effectiveness through assessment, a resource manual to support WASC institutions.* Oakland, CA: Western Association of Schools and Colleges.

CALIFORNIA STATE UNIVERSITY MONTEREY BAY AND THE WESTERN ASSOCIATION OF SCHOOLS AND COLLEGES

Understanding Their Cultures of Innovation

Amy Driscoll

The first chapter described the current context of assessment and accreditation, setting the stage for the strategies and processes that are the focus of the chapters that follow this one. As we assembled our approaches for easy adaptation and use on other campuses, we realized that our stage setting needed more specific contextual details. Our stage was set, but there were no props, no lighting, few backdrops, and the curtain had not been completely lifted. This second chapter emerged as a way of further illustrating the "big picture" of our accreditation decisions and intentions. This chapter sets the stage with scenery that elaborates a multifaceted context, a situation characterized by uniqueness, for the strategies and processes of the following chapters.

Descriptions from Two Perspectives

The scenery of understanding that we review here consists of descriptions of the accreditation process from two perspectives—from that of the accreditation agency, and from that of the campus being reviewed. In this chapter, we first describe information about accreditation, its stages, interactions, and the expectations set by our agency, the Western Association of Schools and Colleges. That information will provide a sequence of processes, direction, and specific requirements for understanding our documentation work. Next in this chapter, we provide descriptions of timelines, responsibilities, and unique aspects of our campus approaches. We encourage our readers to observe the preparation at California State University Monterey Bay. We invite you to listen to our thinking and intentions, to attend our work sessions as we planned and carried out the documentation processes of the chapters that follow.

An Important Caveat

Before describing the accreditation process from either perspective, it is important to note that CSUMB is a new campus, or at least was a new campus (seven years old) at the time of accreditation. It is important to note that WASC was also new in significant ways. The agency had been engaged in an intense rethinking of its accreditation process and was ready to introduce a new way of preparing for it. Thus, the campus and the agency were novices in accreditation. For the campus, accreditation processes were designed and conducted with tensions, enthusiasm, insecurities, and the freshness of a "first-time" situation. The agency experienced a similar newness and the same tensions, insecurities, and enthusiasm. A mutually reciprocal culture of inquiry reigned with new questions being posed and new strategies explored. The institution was innovating and creating itself as it developed documentation, and the campus needed affirmation, feedback, and critique regarding its attempts. WASC was also innovating even as it reviewed our campus, and, similarly, needed affirmation, feedback, and critique regarding its attempts. The situation provided freedom and opportunity for creativity from both directions even though the stakes were high.

Hopefully, revealing the newness, assets, and challenges for both institution and agency lifts the curtain on our stage allowing the reader to better understand the big picture that follows. The broad scan of this chapter begins with a paradigm for accreditation that emerged from the creative design process of the Western Association of Schools and Colleges.

Western Association of Schools and Colleges: Innovative Accreditation Thinking

As described in chapter 1, accreditation agencies across the country have engaged in a "process of redefinition and refocus" since the early 1990s. WASC approached the task of developing a new accreditation paradigm with a vigor and a drive that focused on student learning and assessment, insisting that accreditation processes be linked to improvement of the institution. Its current accreditation paradigm with its standards, processes, policies, and practices is the result of years of "active exploration and experimentation within their region involving hundreds of representatives of higher education and the public" (WASC, 2001, p. v).

As WASC explored learner-focused thinking and designed its innovative approaches, it simultaneously encouraged campuses to engage with the agency "in a series of experimental visits" and in the development of new approaches to both self-study and team visits. For some campuses, WASC's encouragement only served to raise the anxiety level and the insecurities. Fortunately, for CSUMB, WASC's thinking was a good fit for the campus culture of inquiry and its developing status as a new institution. WASC intended that its new standards and processes inform and contribute to the development of improved institutional practices. We echoed that intention as we often reminded ourselves, "Don't do it for WASC, do it to improve student learning . . . It was as if we were collaborating with WASC in a pilot of new procedures, and we both had the same intentions" (Driscoll, 2005). For this chapter, those new processes will be the context even though they may continue in a pilot phase or be recreated for other campuses. A look at the design principles that guided WASC's changes offers insights into the motivations, priorities, and direction of the agency.

Design Principles to Guide Development Processes

From the beginning, WASC staff and relevant task forces decided that revision of current standards was not the appropriate direction for serving their region. It was clear that a vigorous paradigm shift was in order, much like the shift in the national context of assessment and accountability. An intense learning process followed that decision, and a set of principles emerged to guide a "conscious development of new approaches to and models of accreditation" (WASC, 2001, p. v). Those principles included commitments to a new model that would reduce an unnecessary burden to institutions. The model would "function to the extent possible on institutional evidence with a central focus given to educational effectiveness and student learning" (p. v). The principles contained a pledge to collaborate with institutions so that the process could be "aligned with the institutional context and areas of needed development" (p. v). Those principles indicated a contrast to accreditation of the past and further affirmed the need for a new paradigm. As we review the steps of the process and the expectations of campus documentation, it will be helpful to keep those principles in mind.

We begin our review of the new WASC model with a brief description of the preliminary steps that institutions take toward initial or first-time accreditation. Most campuses would bypass those steps and begin with Proposal Review, described later.

Preliminary Steps for an Initial Accreditation

For the few campuses like CSUMB that are seeking accreditation for the first time, some preliminary steps should be achieved before moving into the three major steps of accreditation (both initial and reaffirmation processes). The first step is Eligibility Review, a process of focusing on institutional readiness. The campus submits a narrative-style report describing how the criteria are being met. Typically, a campus leadership group prepares the documents and gathers initial data to support the summary. There is no visit to the campus, but a review panel examines the submission and determines if the criteria are met and if the campus is indeed ready to begin the accreditation process. From there, with approval, the institution prepares for the steps of Candidacy Review and Extension of Candidacy. For the first process, the portfolio is expanded and a visit is conducted. For the Extension of Candidacy, the campus is urged to go forward and is directed to begin proposal development.

When CSUMB began these initial processes, WASC was in a transitional phase and the agency's old standards were addressed by the campus. By the time the campus was ready for Extension of Candidacy, the new processes were being adopted and the campus was caught in the middle. New WASC processes urge a campus to identify themes for the self-study, but the visiting team for CSUMB's Candidacy Review developed five questions based on previous documentation under the old standards. Those five questions became our themes for self-study of educational effectiveness:

1. Does the institution have effective means to review and evaluate the outcomes of its educational model?
2. Is there a continuous process of inquiry and engagement by the institution to enhance educational effectiveness?
3. Does the institution utilize good practices to assess student learning?
4. Are institutional resources aligned with activities designed to achieve educational effectiveness?
5. Does CSUMB's educational model yield better outcomes for students

and their employers than more traditional models and is there convincing proof of the value of this approach for student learning and talent development? (Ramaley, Desrochers, & Olsen, 2002)

These questions are listed again later in this chapter as we describe the campus content, and they are the focus of many of the chapters that follow. The questions became the core of our proposal for self-study (step one) that follows and for our documentation of educational effectiveness.

Preliminaries: Proposal for Self-Study: Submitted, Reviewed, and Approved

The majority of institutions begin with this step. The institution to be reviewed submits a proposal detailing its plan for preparation, self-study, and documentation, including the following:

- In-depth description of the institutional context
- Preliminary self-review using the accreditation standards
- Identification of institutional issues and themes for study
- Elaborate plan with methods, data, timeline, responsibilities, and resources available

Another important and unique component is a set of expected outcomes described by the campus for the accreditation process. This is a significant component that should be highlighted. By asking campuses to describe their expectations, WASC is reminding all of us to do this for the institution, not for WASC.

The proposal or plan is submitted about two and a half years prior to the next two stages of review. The chart of the WASC institutional review cycle provides the total sequence and time commitments in years between steps, thus framing the "big picture" for our readers (figure 2-1).

The proposal for self-study is reviewed by a Proposal Review Committee composed of representatives of other campuses and members of the WASC commission and staff. The committee may provide feedback, may accept or reject the plan, or may ask for revision intending to review it again. From the perspectives of the institution and the agency, this is a helpful, supportive step. From the campus perspective, the institution has the security of knowing that the agency deemed the plan appropriate to take forward and implement with a kind of assurance that the plan would be successful. In turn, the accreditation agency can feel secure that the institution is moving in the right

FIGURE 2-1
Preparation for WASC Interactions: An Overview

Interactions → / Preparation →	Eligibility Review	Candidacy Review	Initial Accreditation	--Reaffirmation of Accreditation--			Special Visits or Progress Reports	Substantive Change	Annual Reports
				Proposal	Capacity & Preparatory Review	Educational Effectiveness Review			
Focus	Institutional Readiness	Compliance w/ Standards	Compliance and Deep engagement	Identify Issues and Approach	Core Commitment to Institutional Capacity	Core Commitment to Educational Effectiveness	As specified by Commission action	Institution-desired change	Continuing Capacity and Effectiveness
Document(s) Submitted	**Narrative:** How the 23 Criteria are being met	**Self-study:** Meets all Standards, CFRs & Guidelines at least at *minimal* level (using the "Comprehensive" approach)	**Self-study:** Meets all Standards, CFRs, & Guidelines at a *substantial* level (using the "Comprehensive" approach)	**Proposal:** Institutional Context; Which approach; methods; issues; Plans for next stages (15 page max.)	**Self-Study:** Demonstrate Core Commitments to Institutional Capacity (35 page max.)	**Self-Study:** Demonstrate Educational Effectiveness: Evidence student/ institutional learning <50 pp	**Report:** As specified by Commission action	**Proposal:** As per the Substantive Change Manual	Annual Report Form (5 pages) due April 15 of each year
Data Required	Summary Data Form	Required Data Tables; other	Required Data Tables; other	Required Data Tables; other	Required Data Tables; other	Institutional portfolio	As specified	As specified	Audited financial statement

Preparation	Typically: Executive and Academic leadership	Self-Review Under the Standards; Plans in place for future development	Self-Review Under the Standards; Deep institutional engagement; (graduated one full class)	Preliminary Self-Review Under the Standards; Identify institutional issues	Review of Capacity and Infrastructure to Support student Learning; data portfolio and reflections	Faculty engagement w/ learning results and org. learning systems; data analysis	As specified	Typically: Related academic leadership	Typically: ALO; CFO, CEO
Peer Site Visit?	No	Yes: 2-stage	Yes: 2-stage	No	Yes	Yes	Visit: Yes Prog. Report: No	6 mos. after for new sites	No
Typical Time Period	N/A	Up to 3 years to prepare for Candidacy	Candidacy up to 4 years	Submitted 2½ years before Capacity Review	12 months before Edu. Effectiveness Review	Typically 12 months after C&PR Review	Per Commission action	As needed	Annually
Commission or Staff Action	Eligibility Committee Review Panel determines if criteria are met	Teams[1] report to Commission for both reviews, which acts to grant Candidacy	Teams[1] report to Commission for both reviews, which acts to grant Initial Accreditation for up to 7 years	Proposal Review Committee accepts or asks for revisions	Team[1] reports to Commission for action to continue with EE Review	Team[1] reports to Commission. Reviews both reports: Reaffirms, or with monitoring or sanctions. Sets schedule	Special Team[1] reports to Commission for action; Progress Report reviewed by Interim Report Committee	Sub Change Committee: Reviews and acts; reports to Commission	Staff: Receive and Review

[1]**Team:** Peer, volunteer educators, chosen for expertise and training, with reporting responsibilities to WASC Commission and Staff

Note: From *Preparation for WASC interactions: An overview*, by R. Winn, 2004, Alameda, CA: Western Association of Schools and Colleges. Reprinted with permission.

direction, should be successful, and that ultimately the review process should proceed smoothly. Again, like most good assessors, WASC is committed to high standards while supporting its learner campuses for successful reviews. The proposal review process represents a kind of formative assessment with its opportunities for improvement.

Once the proposal is approved, the institution is ready to go forward. If the proposal has been well designed, the next two processes have been framed for the work ahead. Although campuses typically begin working toward both of the stages that follow, the preparatory review will have more of a sense of immediacy since the related visit will be scheduled first.

Stage One: Preparatory Review—Assessing Institutional Capacity

The preparatory review is designed to assess whether an institution fulfills the core commitment to institutional capacity. That capacity is defined as follows:

> The institution functions with clear purposes, high levels of institutional integrity, fiscal stability, and organizational structures and processes to fulfill its purposes. (WASC, 2001, p. 41)

To prepare for this review, the institution develops a portfolio with specific reporting, primarily evidentiary, with sets of exhibits that support the claim that it meets the core commitment to capacity. Campuses are encouraged to limit accompanying narrative to concise explanations or reflections on the evidence. WASC also urges campuses to consider the portfolio as a "standing" document; that is, it will be used for succeeding reviews for efficiency reasons of effort and costs.

With respect to the evidence and narratives, WASC identified three priorities to guide campus preparation and to frame the preparatory review:

- Establishment of clear objectives
- Indicators and metrics of achievement to show that the objectives have been achieved
- Actions taken on the basis of evidence, "closing the loop" (WASC, 2001, p. 42)

The priorities again demonstrate the agency's commitment to modeling good practices of assessment in the accreditation processes. Speaking from experience, this author found that the three priorities served as a useful filter for checking progress, for selecting documentation examples, and for assembling the entire portfolio. WASC provides helpful and descriptive recommendations for this portfolio development in its *Handbook of Accreditation: User's Guide* (2001).

A brief site visit is scheduled for a team review of the portfolio at this stage. The team conducts the review much like an academic audit: sampling specific administrative processes to verify their adherence, or reviewing documentary evidence followed by conducting interviews probing the data provided. In addition to surveying institutional capacity, the visit is aimed at determining the clarity of objectives, adequacy of documentation, and readiness for the next step, the Educational Effectiveness Review.

Stage Two: Educational Effectiveness Review—Assessing Inquiry and Engagement

This second stage review is intended to be different from previous reviews. It encourages a process of inquiry and engagement by focusing on the following purposes:

- Review of the design and results of institutional efforts to evaluate the effectiveness of educational programs
- Examination of institutional practices for evaluating student learning, and use of good practices in using results to improve teaching and learning
- Examination of the alignment of institutional resources with activities designed to achieve the institution's educational objectives
- Promotion of sustained engagement with issues of educational effectiveness selected by and of importance to the campus (WASC, 2001, p. 45)

This review process encourages the kind of exploration, reflection, study, and tailored documentation described in the chapters that follow. Campuses have a choice of models to follow in preparing their review portfolio—special themes, a strategic-planning base, a comprehensive overview of educational quality, or an audit-based approach. CSUMB was asked to respond to five questions designed by a team that reviewed the campus readiness for accreditation. Those questions served as a framework for our study in lieu of self-selected themes. WASC urges campuses to focus on assessment and improvement of student learning, and the five questions directly addressed those priorities. Other campuses select their own themes to authentically represent their institutional uniqueness. For example, California State University Sacramento selected planning at its campus, academic programs, campus life, and community engagement as its foci for an upcoming WASC review.

While campuses have choices of models for preparing their documentation, the WASC process has consistent expectations for all campuses:

- A description of how the institution works to achieve educational effectiveness
- Deep engagement in and analysis of educational effectiveness
- Supporting evidence that shows that the campus engages in analysis of educational effectiveness and student learning
- Synthesis and integration of the varied approaches and implications of the self-review of educational effectiveness (WASC, 2001, p. 45)

The visiting team is larger for this review than for previous reviews, and the visit may be longer. Even when the documentation satisfies the expectations of WASC, the team will inquire about "next steps," will ask how current practices will be sustained, and will probe what was learned from the self-study and documentation process. The educational effectiveness visit is very much characterized by the "deep engagement and analysis" that is demanded of the campus prior to the visit.

In responding to the requirements of the Educational Effectiveness Review, CSUMB clearly intended to design and document its self-study in ways that went beyond satisfying the accreditation expectations and promoted ongoing and long-term improvement. That intention is the foundation for this book.

Summary of WASC Accreditation Processes and Philosophy

The three basic processes of WASC's accreditation model are all focused on self-study that flexes with the individual campus priorities and approaches while illustrating best practices in assessment. Student learning is at the heart of the model. Institutions cannot be satisfied with data collection that is not related to student learning and that is not used to improve that learning. As we discovered at CSUMB, taking WASC seriously in terms of "deep engagement and inquiry," focus on student learning, and "closing the loop" was a benefit to the campus—we gained much more than accreditation in the processes. Much of that value can be attributed to WASC's thinking and new model, and much of that value can be attributed to the way the campus approached the accreditation requirements and expectations. We describe those approaches in the remaining sections of this chapter and in the chapters that follow.

California State University Monterey Bay: Innovative Accreditation Thinking

CSUMB's institutional presentation begins:

> CSUMB has engaged in a collaborative, cross-functional, and evidence-based process that authentically reflects the institution in its current state of growth and development and is consistent with the new WASC model for accreditation. (CSUMB, 2003b, p. 1)

That statement describes well the campus process of inquiry and documentation for accreditation. The majority of the work that was done for the reviews consisted of processes the campus was already engaged in, either in further development or in improvement. Participation in the processes occurred as part of the regular work scope of most individuals. A look at the committee representation for each of the review processes will be helpful. Figure 2-2 provides that representation and suggests the kind of engagement each committee represented for the documentation processes.

Another description will help set the stage for our readers to understand the strategies used by our campus, which are described in the chapters that follow. The campus portfolio presented institutional evidence in three forms:

1. Bound copies of essays and data displays
2. Document room with extensive documentation and evidence
3. Online version of the essays and displays

Approaching the Preparatory Review: Capturing the Institution's Unique Commitment

Within the materials for the preparatory review were the essay, data displays, and an evidence map that was organized around the four standards and references in support of the criteria for review (see chapter 4). A look back at WASC requirements for institutional capacity will help our readers interpret how the campus approached this review. CSUMB was institutionally committed to clear purposes, well-described and consistently discussed vision, mission, and core values. As Diane Cordero de Noriega describes in chapter

FIGURE 2-2
Chart of Representation for Accreditation Review Committees

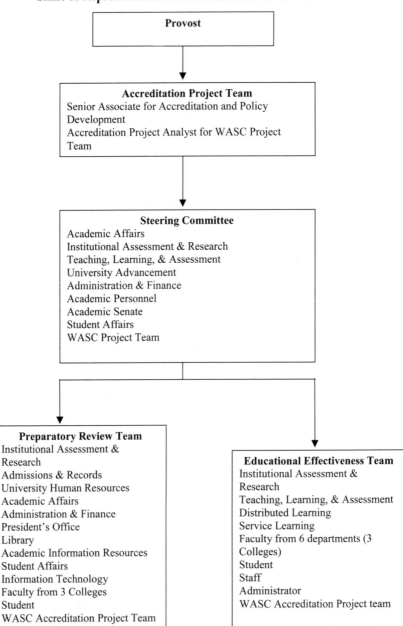

3, the campus intentions surround the institution, literally and figuratively. Framed copies of the vision hang in most offices; segments of the mission structure course syllabi; and core values consistently direct curriculum planning, budgetary allocations, and marketing/recruitment strategies for potential students and faculty. One of the external sources of data, the National Survey of Student Engagement (NSSE, 2003) and its related study, Project DEEP (Documenting Effective Educational Practice), provided strong support for the institutional integrity and focused commitment. "Administrators and faculty referred to the vision as an orienting device—a compass of sorts" (NSSE Institute for Effective Educational Practice, 2004, p. 13). The researchers described how faculty, staff, and "more than a few students" could articulate the vision in their own words and with personal meaning. Their conclusion was that "a strong, cohesive sense of purpose is present" and that "an unusually high level of energy is devoted to experimenting with ways to implement the vision" (p. 13).

The campus had an exceptional framework to build evidence of fiscal stability, organizational structures, and processes to fulfill its purposes—the newly designed strategic plan. In chapter 4, Salina Diiorio, member of the Preparatory Review Team, describes how well the plan supported alignment of the fiscal and organizational structures and processes with the outcomes articulated in the strategic plan. Diiorio described the strategic plan as "such a powerful factor that it could easily be a piece of evidence for the four standards as well" (personal communication, April 6, 2005).

Much of the success and clarity of the essay and materials for the preparatory review can be attributed to the selection of committee members. Those members were chosen to represent administrators, staff, faculty, and students who were actively involved in the processes to be documented. Their accreditation work was integrated into their university roles. Participation in the Preparatory Review Team had the immediate effect of studying, analyzing, and improving campus practices all through the documentation. Ultimately it had potential for long-term reflection and improvement. For example, Bill Robnett, director of the library, participated on the committee and was simultaneously coordinating a collaborative planning process for a new library facility. He took the accreditation focus on student learning into the planning process and used it as criteria for organizing and assigning space in the new building. "We went beyond the concept of programs being tenants in the library facility and looked for new ways to integrate programs for added value to student learning. We began to think of the building as a learning center" (B. Robnett, personal communication, April 20, 2005).

Many of the priorities and integration of accreditation processes into campus roles typified the participation of members of the Educational Effectiveness Team. Descriptions of their thinking and intentions will assist our readers in understanding the strategies and processes of the chapters that follow.

Approaching Educational Effectiveness: Capturing Uniqueness of Approaches

To prepare for the second stage of our review, we established the Educational Effectiveness Team, co-chaired by the director of teaching, learning, and assessment and members of the WASC Project Team for the campus. The committee members again represented faculty, administration, staff, and students who were actively engaged in the processes to be documented. Before beginning any agenda setting or work tasks, the committee spent a day in retreat away from campus. The intent of the retreat was to reflect and engage in inquiry before getting to the specifics of the documentation process. Committee members described their hopes for a process characterized by the qualities of collaboration, creativity, scholarship, trust, interaction with the campus, learning, and integrity. The committee members represented much of the thinking and approaches that are commonplace across the campus. By the end of the retreat, the committee agreed upon the following principles for its documentation work:

1. The work would intentionally be a learning experience for the committee as well as the campus.
2. The work would be public and visible through both methodology and dissemination.
3. The work would be achieved through scholarly means and would produce scholarly products.
4. The work would model "best practices" in teaching, learning, and assessment. (CSUMB, 2003a, p. 7)

We follow with some examples of how the committee followed those principles as it set about its responsibilities for demonstrating and documenting the educational effectiveness of the institution. Members often referred to the principles as they recommended strategies or designed processes or made choices about direction for the group's work agenda.

The first process of the committee focused on a literature review of "best practices" in assessment for the last ten years. The readings and literature summaries prompted both inquiry and a documentation process as described by Betty McEady in chapter 8. During the study of assessment literature, the committee members adopted two texts for the "learning experience" aspect of their intentions. *Learning That Lasts: Integrating Learning, Development, and Performance in College and Beyond* (Mentkowski & Associates, 2000) and *Assessment Essentials: Planning, Implementing, and Improving Assessment in Higher Education* (Palomba & Banta, 1999) were chosen for their emphasis on learning that most closely represented the thinking and prioritizing of the campus. Prior to the preparation for accreditation, the campus engaged in extensive deliberations about the meaning, purpose, and uses of assessment. For academic contexts, assessment was defined as a "dynamic pedagogy" and its purpose was to extend, enhance, and expand learning for students. The major use of assessment was to improve student learning. These views were consistent with the texts chosen for Educational Effectiveness processes of documentation as well as the priorities of our accreditation agency. That fit between the campus thinking and the accreditation expectations was a key factor in the success of the campus accreditation processes.

The principles of ensuring that the "work process would be a learning experience" for the committee and that of "using scholarly means" to achieve the work were well served by the committee's use of the texts just described. Each work session was initiated by a review and discussion of readings, sections of the texts, and other related material. In a spontaneous process, committee members consistently raised questions about, sought clarification of, and identified explanations of our work in the texts. On several occasions, the committee became a serious study group and had to be reminded of the documentation agenda of the work sessions. The study aspects of the committee's work were later reflected in the essays developed by each member—scholarly essays about our documentation processes. The campus work was consistently questioned and supported by scholarly references from the literature.

At this point it is important to note that committee members were consistently reminded to "produce scholarly products," not simply accreditation reports. The essays were produced as scholarship with attention to documenting the university's achievements in educational effectiveness and with potential for publication. By the time that the final essay was published for the Accreditation Team Review, several essays had been published and at least six had been presented at national and regional conferences. This book represents the final scholarly product produced by the committee members. In addition to reflecting the scholarly qualities of the university's work, the process was motivating to both students and faculty. Writing an accreditation report is not always the most enticing responsibility (what an understatement!), but writing for publication has several motivations especially for junior faculty, six of whom were preparing for tenure. The scholarship of assessment described by Banta and Associates (2002) was certainly relevant to the campus, and the essays prepared for review all qualified as scholarship. Those essays describe documentation practices that were "consistent with the tradition of robust, participatory and practice-oriented scholarship already established by the assessment movement" (Ewell, 2002, p. 25). Transformed into the chapters of this book, they make significant contributions to both theory and practice, again qualifying as traditional scholarship.

The principle of making the committee work "public and visible" was accomplished by a number of strategies included in this book: the best practices in assessment survey (chapter 8), the capstone survey and report (chapter 7), and the program review process (chapter 5) were clearly conducted in ways that involved the majority of the campus. Both the methodology of the processes as well as the dissemination of the findings were directed to being "public and visible."

Most of the processes involved large numbers of faculty, students, staff, and administrators in the actual data collection or documentation and provided learning experiences for those engaged in the processes. For example, when one of the departments completed its responses to the best practices in assessment survey in a departmental meeting, its administrator sent a response to the committee describing appreciation. She talked about the reflection and learning processes that occurred with the departmental discussions directed to answering the survey. Clearly the process of documentation extended the learning process to faculty beyond the committee members.

The Scholarship of Assessment: Enhancing Accreditation

One final note must be made concerning the origin of many of the documentation processes described in the chapters that follow. Much like the recommendations of Banta for the scholarship of assessment, those processes were originated by individual faculty and administrators out of interest, inquiry, and a commitment. Annette March undertook her comprehensive study of the campus writing support program because she cared deeply about the students' writing and questioned how to best support their writing achievement. She sought funding and campus support and was able to garner both, but her individual persistence and commitment to students were the primary stimuli for her extensive study. Dan Shapiro had coordinated student capstones for years and initiated his campuswide study, again with the intention to learn from and improve his work using the insights of the varied approaches of other departments. Swarup Wood passionately describes his own enthusiasm and wonder as the impetus for his interview study of faculty who participated in assessment design and analysis of student work. The efforts and documentation work of Annette, Dan, and Swarup were clearly not tasks that originated at an administrative level, the assessment paradigm of the past. They sought answers and ways to improve student learning, excellent models of contemporary assessment and its scholarship.

A few other aspects of the CSUMB approach to accreditation must be acknowledged for their contributions to its uniqueness of documentation. From its beginning, the campus was designated as an outcomes-based institution. After years of struggle, outcomes were embraced and used intentionally for teaching, curricular development, and assessment. That outcomes-based context framed documentation processes with a clarity and worked well with the need for evidence. Outcomes-based approaches were also a good fit with the campus culture of "student-centered learning." Most of the original faculty, many staff and administrators, and large numbers of students were attracted to the possibilities of such learning and brought with them intense commitment to making student-centeredness integral to the institution. Faculty and staff insisted on decisions based on student learning, and administrators attended to student-learning focus in their day-to-day operations. Students quickly learned to expect that their learning would be a top priority and often demanded such a focus in their courses and extracurricular activities. One can easily see why the campus culture felt like a good fit with WASC's priorities and new paradigm of educational effectiveness.

Summary

We must acknowledge that the newness of both campus activities and accreditation expectations contributed to the kinds of processes and strategies used at CSUMB to demonstrate Institutional Capacity and Educational Effectiveness. Those concepts are, however, easily generic for national thinking on assessment and accreditation. They are however, components of the unique context of the ideas and thinking in the chapters that follow. It is hoped that this attention to stage setting provides clarity and understanding of the cultures of innovation that were central to both the Western Association of Schools and Colleges and California State University Monterey Bay.

References

Banta, T., & Associates. (2002). *Building a scholarship of assessment.* San Francisco: Jossey-Bass.

California State University Monterey Bay. (2003a). *Essays: Educational Effectiveness Review 2003.* Monterey Bay: Author.

California State University Monterey Bay. (2003b). *Essays: Preparatory Review 2003.* Monterey Bay: Author.

Driscoll, A. (April 10, 2002). Paper presented at the annual conference of the Western Association of Schools and Colleges, San Diego, CA.

Ewell, P. T. (2002). A brief history of assessment. In T. Banta & Associates (Eds.), *Building a scholarship of assessment* (3–26). San Francisco: Jossey-Bass.

Mentkowski, M., & Associates. (2000). *Learning that lasts: Integrating learning, development, and performance in college and beyond.* San Francisco: Jossey-Bass.

National Survey of Student Engagement. (2003). *NSSE 2002 institutional report.* Bloomington, IN: Indiana University Center for Postsecondary Research.

National Survey of Student Engagement Institute for Effective Educational Practice. (2004). *Final Report: California State University Monterey Bay—Documenting effective educational practice.* Bloomington: Indiana University Center for Postsecondary Research.

Palomba, C. A., & Banta, T. (1999*). Assessment essentials: Planning, implementing, and improving assessment in higher education.* San Francisco: Jossey-Bass.

Ramaley, J., Desrochers, L., & Olsen, D. (2002). *Report of the site visit team: Extension of candidacy visit.* Seaside: California State University Monterey Bay.

Western Association of Schools and Colleges (2001). *WASC handbook of accreditation: User's guide.* Alameda, CA: Author.

Winn, R. (2004). *Preparation for WASC interactions: An overview.* Alameda, CA: Western Association of Schools and Colleges.

3

INSTITUTIONAL VISION, VALUES, AND MISSION

Foundational Filters for Inquiry

Diane Cordero de Noriega

C learly articulated campus vision, core value, and mission statements are the soul, heart and mind of the institution, and as such, they are vital attributes that provide a foundational filter for inquiry and a basis for long-term change. These statements of intention delineate the identity of an institution of higher education, and can be factors that persuade students and their families and faculty to consider a particular university. They are also the guiding principles that set a foundational or starting framework for both accountability and accreditation for an individual institution. Together, they are statements of intention that have the potential to serve as filters for the processes of inquiry, data collection, documentation, and reporting. They also have enormous potential for ongoing and long-term improvement insofar as they permeate the psyche of the institution at all levels, and guide campus decision-making processes.

This chapter describes each of those three statements of intention— vision, values, and mission—as important starting points for assessing the effectiveness of an institution. Each statement acts as a guide during initial and ongoing decision making and the development of programs, activities, and practices of all kinds. After such initial development, those statements remain as filters to assess the appropriateness of decisions, the effectiveness of programs and practices, and whether the institution is true to its intentions. Intentionality has become a significant consideration in whether a university or college is effective in its practices (J. Ramaley, personal communication, January 28, 2004). Thus, declarations of vision, values, and mission have become central to accreditation and assessment.

A Trio of Guides for Campus Practices and Assessment

Each of the three declarations of intentions provided guidance for the beginnings of California State University Monterey Bay and for the documentation of its effectiveness for accreditation. Those guides are close to being sacred to the campus and truly represent the way faculty and staff directed their early and ongoing efforts. The first to be created was the Vision Statement, and it was truly the foundation for what followed.

Vision—The Soul That Guides the Institution

Vision statements tend to describe what an institution aspires to be, and they define the institution's identity in a comprehensive and holistic format. They can vary in length from a single sentence, such as California State University San Marcos's vision to "become a distinctive university known for academic excellence, service to the community, and improving learning through creative uses of technology," or they may be lengthy, philosophical treatises, such as CSUMB's own Vision Statement. The campus vision is packed with descriptions of the student population to be served, the kind of curricula and pedagogy to be used, important issues to be addressed, a commitment to particular accountability, the kind of learning environment to be established, and how the university will serve the state and region.

Our Vision Statement is very much a proper noun, and may be unique in higher education in that it was the first guiding philosophical representation of what this new university would be. The Vision Statement was, and remains today after ten years, the soul of CSUMB's aspirations as a university. It describes CSUMB as a "model pluralistic academic community where all learn and teach one another in an atmosphere of mutual respect and pursuit of excellence." Through the Vision Statement, the campus makes a commitment to serving the historically underserved populations of California, particularly Latinos and the children of farm workers, thus targeting our student population. Indirectly identifying those targets has huge implications for many of our practices, such as curriculum, pedagogy, advising, budgets, and so on.

The vision further commits to a substantive focus on multilingual and multicultural learning, and envisions our graduates having "an understanding of interdependence and global competence, distinctive technical and educational skills, the experience and abilities to contribute to California's high quality work force, the critical thinking abilities to be productive citizens, and the social responsibility and skills to be community builders." Such intentions preview the curriculum of our institution and serve as filters for both planning and assessing the curriculum.

Further, the vision speaks to collaborative learning distinguished by partnerships with the community, both higher education institutions and community-based entities. The vision addresses the need to stay on the cutting edge in the creative and innovative use of technologies. It articulates the university's commitment to integrating learning with service and reflection, and also commits us to being accountable for student learning using an outcomes-based model and assessment of learning. Such prescriptions address the intended pedagogy, support for learning, and resources. From the very start of the institution, the components of the vision served as a blueprint for much of the academic planning. Later, the components directed an emerging alignment of faculty recruitment, faculty roles and rewards, and faculty development agendas. In preparing for accreditation, those same alignments served as foci for documentation. We were compelled to demonstrate that the vision was apparent when our courses, programs, resources, and faculty support were studied and assessed. The same filtering process was in place for the campus values, a set of intentions that emerged after the development of the vision.

Core Values—The Heart of the Institution

Much like a heart, the core values of CSUMB set a pulse for campus activity and clearly motivate and recharge the energy of its members. The core values are a critical guiding force for our university—a particular reflection of our approach to learning. The core values are a focused set of indicators of the university's intentions, and articulate what students can expect to experience. Sometimes core values are expressed as values, other times as purposes, principles, or goals. Whatever an institution chooses to call them, core values really get at the heart of what is important to the people who make up the institution. Core values are not always expressed formally, but they truly are at the heart of the institution's identity. If they exist, even informally, they will be reflected throughout curriculum, pedagogy, student services, administration, and indeed throughout the overall culture of the institution. If you listen, you will hear them. If you observe, you will see them. They are integrated in the day-to-day activities of a campus.

At CSUMB, a list of core values was distilled directly from the vision: interdisciplinarity, applied learning, multiculturalism and global perspectives, technological sophistication, collaboration, ethical reflection and practice, and service learning. These core values describe how we work—they characterize our pedagogy, coursework, curricular themes throughout each program, program assessment processes, and professional development. For example, course syllabi illustrate the value of applied learning with project-based pedagogy and assessment and with nontraditional assessment that requires students to display their learning with diverse forms of evidence.

For accreditation and for ongoing assessment, core values serve as criteria for assessing our intentionality. Are we operating as if those values were core to our work? If collaboration is one of our core values, will we find it in our classrooms, our meetings, our hiring, and our community interactions? For accreditation, our challenge was to document the integration of our values. What evidence can we provide to show that collaboration is integrated in our teaching, our work sessions, our hiring practices, and our engagement in community? At CSUMB, the core values are transparent in much of our curriculum. They are embedded in our general education curriculum in the form of requirements (called university learning requirements or ULRs). Those ULRs include democratic participation, ethical reflection, multicultural and global perspectives, information technology, and community participation. It's easy to see the core values in those requirements. Less transparent are the way the values connect to learning theory and best practices in higher education, while communicating and guiding the uniqueness of our campus.

The ULRs also appear as common themes throughout our major programs of study in each of our departments. They inform the specific requirements of each major, the major learning outcomes. When the major programs engage in assessment through the program review process, they must demonstrate how students are achieving those major learning outcomes, thus showing how the core values are threaded through student learning. One way of assessing curriculum in the majors is a review of the infusion of core values in those programs.

For both planning and accreditation, core values again serve as a filter for documentation and assessment of faculty development activities. At CSUMB, the Center for Teaching, Learning, and Assessment offers a variety of professional development workshops each year that are infused with the core values. The center has sponsored workshops dealing with topics like race in the classroom, collaborative learning, and practical reflection techniques. The center's "Teaching Co-op" brings faculty together to discuss reflective and multicultural pedagogy, and provides the opportunity for collaborative learning through peer observation. The center also produces a monthly newsletter, with each issue showcasing faculty work that aligns with the core values. Those newsletters served as compelling evidence of the campus being true to the core values in its activities as an institution and in its individual efforts.

Having clearly defined core values that are infused throughout the functions of the university serves accountability and improvement efforts. They provide programs, divisions, and units with focus. As a new campus we have been tempted to try to do everything, so the core values served as filtering priorities. For accreditation and for our ongoing work, we have been able to show that our work and our resources are aligned with our core values. We have also been successful in documenting our progress toward our intended outcomes with those values as criteria for how well we are doing.

Mission—The Mind of the Institution

After several years of becoming an institution of higher education with a vision and set of core values as our guides and motivations, it was time to distill those intentions into a succinct statement of our thinking. Our next step was a mission statement, and distilling our intentions into such a statement was a challenge. Mission statements are standard for institutions of higher education. Indeed, they are expected. A mission is really about what the university is thinking, reflecting the mind of the campus, the drive and the rationale behind all of the university's actions. Mission statements may be as short and concise as a tagline, such as Evergreen State College's "Make Learning Happen" or Portland State University's "Let Knowledge Serve the City." Or, they may be rather lengthy and philosophical, such as CSUMB's "To build a multicultural learning community founded on academic excellence from which all partners in the educational process emerge prepared to contribute productively, responsibly, and ethically to California and the global community."

Universities appear to be moving away from the broad, general, indistinct mission statements of the past, and are moving instead toward mission statements that set the university apart. In many ways, the university's mission helps the institution define its own understanding of itself, both to itself and to the external community (Holland, 1999). The "new" mission statement does not attempt to be all things to all people. Instead, it seeks to demonstrate the unique history and tradition of a particular institution. It has, however, become a focus of accreditation reviews and other forms of assessment. It is an important statement of overall intention and as such becomes a foundational filter for raising questions, seeking evidence, and documenting effectiveness.

A real mission statement is not a description of an ideal future or of institutional functions. Along with vision and values, it is a lens through which the campus community may assess its work, guiding decision making and setting priorities and goals. Many campuses have had missions for a long time—sometimes so long that they have been forgotten. Other campuses have used the revision or creation of a new mission as a restructuring or reenergizing process so there is a dynamic awareness of the intention. For CSUMB, writing a mission statement was an ideal process for its early years. It was probably best that the mission was not written at the start, but rather after the campus had begun with the vision and values as guides. A touch of reality and priorities guided the mission development, and its writing galvanized the campus in preparation for the strategic planning process that followed.

A Trifocal Lens: Filtering Our Intentions and Inquiry

The power of vision, core values, and mission comes when one can see evidence of these commitments throughout an institution. This is certainly the case at CSUMB. In its site visit report, our accreditation team noted that CSUMB is "as much vision-driven as it is outcomes based," and that we have made our vision "operational in very concrete terms in [our] standards, the principles upon which decisions are based, and in the everyday conversations on campus" (Ramaley et al., 2003, p. 22).

How have we been able to accomplish this? CSUMB has deliberately put our vision, mission, and core values at the center of our vital processes—from our academic programs, to recruitment and training of new staff and faculty, annual budgeting, and strategic planning. Some campus examples of processes will help answer the question of how we have accomplished this. Our trifocal lens has enabled us to filter, to reflect on, and to assess those vital processes for their success in achieving the vision, mission, and values, and to then guide improvements of them to achieve our intentions.

Academic Programs
The trifocal lens is prominent in the planning, design, review, and approval process for new programs. When a new program comes forward, one of the

primary criteria for evaluating the proposal is whether the program reflects the vision and mission of the university? For example, the Vision Statement speaks to academic programs that integrate the disciplines, and to the integration of technology to develop students' skills for the contemporary world.

For example, when faculty proposed a new master of science degree program in management and information technology, the Postgraduate Studies Committee of the Academic Senate reviewed the program in light of the criteria spelled out in the vision. Is the program interdisciplinary? Yes, it integrates business and information technology to focus on e-commerce. Does it integrate technology? Yes, it integrates technology in two ways: it incorporates the applications of technology in business environments, and it also takes advantage of technology by offering some of the coursework online. Every new program is evaluated for such alignment with the vision, whether it is a new major, minor, concentration, or certificate.

The lens is also evident in the review of existing programs. Our program review model requires that academic programs discuss their own mission and goals and how they align with the vision, mission, and core values of the institution. They must ask themselves: To what extent do the program's mission and goals contribute to the Vision Statement? And to what extent does the program holistically emphasize and integrate each of the seven core values? After the very first round of program review was completed for each of the academic programs, the campus found that core values were infused to varying degrees. Programs tended to emphasize those values that were closest to their focus. For example, communication science and technology emphasized technology, global studies emphasized multiculturalism and globalism, liberal studies emphasized interdisciplinarity, and so on. This finding was used to inform one of the outcomes and success indicators in our strategic plan. In our second round of program review, we will be assessing programs for improvement in this area. This progress will be reported to campus decision-making bodies through both the program review and strategic plan reporting processes.

Recruitment and Training

Our goal in recruitment is to find qualified, talented individuals who can contribute to making our vision a reality. It begins with our recruitment ads for faculty, staff, administrators, and students. We make sure that every ad begins with an overview of the vision and mission of CSUMB. All applicants must describe the contributions they feel they will make to the vision. In conversations with our visiting accreditation team, the team noted that many people said that the vision was central to their deciding to come to CSUMB (Ramaley et al., 2003, p. 16).

Once hired, new staff and faculty members are introduced at the fall convocation and presented with a copy of the Vision Statement to hang in their office. They are also invited to sign a communal copy of the Vision Statement as a symbol of their commitment to the vision of the university. New staff employees participate in an orientation to the vision and mission. Whether new staff members are working in accounting, information technology, or the residential life offices, the mission and vision of the institution are equally important. There is a clear message that all members of the campus community are here to support that vision.

New faculty orientation is an intense process, typically scheduled over several days, and it reflects the commitments of the vision, mission, and core values. The faculty orientation includes a field trip into the communities we serve. New faculty see firsthand what the vision means when we speak of "serving the historically underserved" or "reaching the children of farm workers." Significant faculty orientation is also directed to visualizing pedagogy and advising that are aligned with the vision. The orientation includes sessions on technology, multiculturalism, and collaboration, so that the core values are quite apparent.

Strategic Planning

The strategic planning process really began with the articulation of the Vision Statement. Our strategic plan represents the efforts of the campus to make the vision operational. Since collaboration and inclusion are central to our vision, it was important to engage members of the campus community in ongoing dialogue about vision, values, and mission as we developed our strategic plan. When issues were raised during early planning efforts, we modified our initial process to be even more inclusive. A series of vision dialogue sessions were held to give all university stakeholders an opportunity to express their views about the Vision Statement and to hear the views of others. In addition, participants provided thoughts on how the vision might be translated into a mission statement.

Following the vision dialogue sessions, a broad-based Strategic Planning Committee was formed and charged to work with the dialogue and to craft a draft mission statement for stakeholder review, develop a strategic planning process, and begin the work of thinking about themes for a strategic plan. Three draft mission statements were created and subsequently voted on by the campus community. In this way, our mission statement was not separate from our vision and core values, but, rather, it was a direct distillation of them. Broad-based involvement of the campus in its development and adoption helped to increase campus buy-in and ensure that the mission would have real meaning for people.

The strategic plan was developed over a two-year period by the Strategic Planning Committee, which consisted of faculty, staff, students, and community members. The committee synthesized four broad themes through which the core values from the Vision Statement could be threaded:

- A pluralistic academic community
- Student learning
- Support for learning
- An engaged campus

Outcomes and success indicators, which we could then use to measure our progress from year to year, were developed for each theme. An initial aspect of assessment was how well the themes of the strategic plan contribute to the achievement of mission, values, and vision.

In order for the vision, values, and mission to remain alive and vital to the institution, there must be ongoing reflection and study so that they maintain their importance as a filter for inquiry. Our strategic plan has become *the* lens through which we guide campus inquiry and decision making. Because of the way the plan was developed, the vision, core values, and mission are imbedded within the themes, outcomes, and indicators; and because of the way it has been implemented, it is a living document and not gathering dust on the shelf.

Budgeting and Resource Decisions

One of the ways the strategic plan guides priority setting for the campus is through our annual budget process. Each year, the Administrative Council proposes one of the four themes as the campuswide strategic theme that will be focused on that year. Every unit on campus has the opportunity to address that theme, as well as other themes that are relevant to its particular focus. Each unit begins its budget proposal with a report on progress made toward the previous year's strategic theme and outcomes. This process allows us to present clear evidence of progress and success in those areas we want to be held accountable for, specifically the vision, core values, and mission. Units and departments must also describe how new budget allocations and resources will achieve strategic themes, which is ultimately how they will achieve the mission, values, and vision. Even specific processes that involve budgets, such as hiring a staff person or sending faculty to a conference, must be filtered through the strategic themes. When anyone requests such specific funding, the person is asked to describe how the funds will support achievement of the strategic themes.

Those strategic themes were well crafted as a lens for our budgetary and resource decisions. They certainly minimize the kind of debate that usually accompanies such decisions especially in difficult budget times. Instead, the debate is focused on the intentions of the campus and, ultimately, student learning. Those become productive and collegial conversations rather than territorial arguments. At one time, everyone agreed on the intentions—mission, values, and vision—consequently they agree more easily on decisions that are directed to achieving those intentions. For accreditation, those discussions, and finally the decisions that emerged from them, were a compelling demonstration of our intentionality. Documentation such as meeting minutes, e-mail discussions, and the resulting decisions persuaded visiting teams that we were effectively achieving our intentions.

The importance of having clear vision, values, and mission, for an institution of higher learning, is that they set the framework for all accountability measures for the university, including accreditation. These statements of intention serve as touchstones for priority setting, resource allocation, and growth, development, or change within the institution. When all campus units align plans with the vision, values, and mission of the institution, planning can then be supported fully.

Bringing It All Into Focus

The vision, core value, and mission statements of a university describe what that university stands for, what sets it apart from others, and what it wants to be known for. They provide a lens the campus community can use to filter and focus questions for inquiry, which can subsequently help to guide planning. For example, does this new program proposal fit with our vision of who we are or who we want to be? Does this enrollment plan reflect our vision for a diverse learning community? Does this proposal serve our community the way we envision serving our community? The vision, core values, and mission are the source of significant questions to support valid decision making. Current accreditation processes insist that an institution begin with inquiry and further expect to witness a deep engagement in that inquiry. As presented in chapter 2, the Western Association of Schools and Colleges describes its expectation of "sustained engagement with issues of educational effectiveness selected by and of importance to the campus" (WASC, 2001, p. 45). Authors of the WASC guide were well aware of the importance of connection between the questions and issues to be addressed and the priorities of a campus. Thus, the questions addressed in accreditation must be ones campus members feel intensely interested in or passionate about. With those high levels of interest and passion, the institution and its members will dig deeply for answers, for reasons, for explanation, and for information to direct future work. For CSUMB, the mission, values, and vision held interest, sustained engagement, and led the campus in directions that mattered.

Accountability—Opportunities for Change

Clear statements of intention guide inquiry as it relates to accountability. They can become the basis for establishing appropriate outcomes and metrics designed to evaluate those outcomes. For example, if the vision states that the campus will reflect a diverse community, what metrics will measure progress toward that goal? How will we define diversity: student, faculty, ethnic, or other? Shall we include curricular diversity and if so, what does that look like? What benchmarks will we chose to compare ourselves with?

Sometimes an institution finds that it must redefine itself in order to maintain a competitive edge in the face of competition from private entrepreneurial universities or in the face of demands for accountability. This is extraordinarily difficult to do, akin to manually turning a large ship against a strong current. CSUMB had the unique privilege of starting from scratch ten years ago when this new university was founded. Many times it is easier to start with a fresh vision, values, and mission than to try to change these statements after a campus has matured. However, institutions of higher education may find opportunities to revisit their vision, values, and mission at various points in their ongoing development. For example, reaffirmation of accreditation, which can occur every ten years, presents one such opportunity. The development or renewal of a strategic plan can also provide an opportunity for reevaluation. A review of vision, values, and mission allows the campus to clarify its roles and purpose, to ensure that these statements of intention reflect what the campus really cares about, and, furthermore, to articulate what the campus wants its graduates to look like when they leave.

While the possibilities of revisiting or reaffirming or completely revising the intentions of a campus make sense, the task probably sounds overwhelming—much like turning that large ship. How could an institution even begin such a large and complex undertaking? Especially an institution with a large student body, with thousands of faculty and staff, and with years of tradition and a well-known image?

One way to get the conversation started is by engaging a representative group of people on campus in a dialogue about what really matters on campus. When a campus is preparing for reaffirmation of accreditation, this exercise can help the campus to focus on the issues or strategic goals the campus wants to reflect on as it prepares for its accreditation review. Individual participants can write down what they think really matters on campus. These issues may not be part of any strategic plan or mission/vision statement. Rather, these are the issues that are at the core of conversations at lunch, in the hallways, at faculty meetings. After writing as an individual, participants then discuss, share, and compare their ideas. What are the things that pop up as common issues? Are there significant differences, and what explains those differences? Finally, participants can challenge themselves to discuss how their colleagues can be engaged in these issues. Most important, how do these issues relate to the mission, vision, and core values of the institution? Recent WASC workshops have engaged participants in such conversations to model the process for them to take back to campuses.

Another stimulating way to use the opportunities for change is to address the task of describing the graduates of an institution. The discussion will be a challenging one—engaging all campus members, including students and alumni. Some of the processes suggested above could be used to achieve the descriptions of graduates. The vision, mission, and values, if current, will certainly begin to narrow these descriptions. Alternatively, the descriptions of graduates will influence the revision of those intentions. Once an institution has agreed upon and described the kind of graduates who will leave its programs, the campus will have another filter to assess its practices. A significant guide for such campus development is the report *Greater Expectations: A New Vision for Learning as a Nation Goes to College* (Association of American Colleges and Universities, 2002). Campuses have reported on the efficacy of the report for focusing their discussions.

A review of "Where have we been and where are we going?" is another path to reflecting on campus statements of intention. It is important to engage in an authentic, critical self-assessment as a first step to reaching a consensus on a vision for the future. It is also critical to assess the external forces that influence the future. What are the expectations of your constituencies? A critical factor in all of this work is achieving a common vision that everyone can embrace. While it can be time consuming, it is important to bring a broad representative group together that reflects all stakeholders and constituents. Faculty, staff, students, administrators, community members, and trustees, as appropriate, all need to be engaged in the process. In the case of CSUMB, the only thing that all stakeholders agreed upon was the Vision Statement, so that became the starting point. It is important for the constituent group to find common ground, whether it is a vision, or simply a shared history of the institution. The important thing is to find where there is agreement and to move ahead from there.

Environmental Scans—Internal and External

A starting point for developing or reviewing common vision is the use of an internal and/or external environmental scan. A campus can be well served by taking stock through an internal scan. Data can be gathered as a starting point for discussions about where the campus has been and where it is going. When reviewing enrollment trends, for example, a campus can begin to reflect on the sustainability of a steep growth curve, or in another case look at static enrollments and question whether it is timely to grow the enrollment to another phase. An external scan can sometimes be characterized as a marketing study. What is important to the community that your campus serves? Question the external community regarding the trends in employment, the critical needs of the community, and most important, the expectations with regard to its local higher education institutions.

Data from environmental scans can be useful documentation of the campus achievement of its intentions. As with so many campus practices, alignment of the data with vision, values, and mission, and with the campus practices will demonstrate the effectiveness targeted by accreditation reviews.

Conclusion

When the vision, core values, and mission of an institution are strong and deeply imbedded, all participants in the institution commit to them and articulate their importance. They are pervasive and cannot be ignored. These statements of intention also become the lens for a campus to use to assess its own continuous progress and determine areas for improvement. In order to become a "learning organization" as suggested by current practices in both assessment and accreditation, a campus needs to move forward in a process of inquiry with intentionality. Articulating a vision, values, and mission is the first step in that process. It is a significant step, one full of challenges and very hard work. It is not a fast process, and it deserves time for scholarly study, discussion, reflection, and consensus. Without clear delineation of the intentions contained in mission, values, and vision, an institution is lacking the foundation needed for a culture of inquiry. There is little to build on, to base decisions on, to question, and ultimately to determine effectiveness. Once developed, however, an endless array of uses can be found for those intention statements. They are indeed multipurpose filters and appropriate for assessing most campus practices.

Campuses that are able to demonstrate clear accountability to their vision, core values, and mission are able to make a compelling case for effectiveness. Those campuses have some common traits, one of which is that the campus has a "living" mission and a "lived" philosophy. CSUMB's vision, core values, and mission are present and evident throughout the institution on a daily basis. They inform conversations among faculty, staff, and students. They guide divisional functions and decision making, and provide for ongoing inquiry. A study of the campus by George Kuh and his colleagues from Project DEEP found that the campus truly has a "living mission and vision." As described in chapter 2, they reported that faculty, staff, and "more than a few students" could articulate the vision in their own words and with personal meaning (National Survey of Student Engagement Institute for Effective Educational Practice, 2004, p. 13). The strong cohesive sense of purpose intended by articulation of vision, mission, and values has been achieved and can be documented. The report also made connections between that sense of purpose and student engagement and, ultimately, student learning.

Mary Boyce in her article on sustaining organizational change (2003) states, "Inquiry and dialogue enable organizational members to examine assumptions and strategies, and to plan, implement and sustain change" (p. 123). This chapter contends that such examination is best supported by a clear statement of purpose, and with detailed statements of intention. When institutions go to great lengths to make their missions, values, and aspirations transparent, public, and understandable to their constituencies, internally and externally, those statements of intention serve them well as filters for inquiry from within and from those outside the campus. They provide a strong foundation for self-assessment, for accreditation processes, and for significant improvement and change.

References

Association of American Colleges and Universities. (2002). *Greater expectations: A new vision for learning as a nation goes to college.* Washington, DC: Author.

Boyce, M. E. (2003). Organizational learning is essential to achieving and sustaining change in higher education. *Innovative Higher Education, 28,* 119–136.

Holland, B. (1999). From murky to meaningful: The role of mission in institutional change. In R. G. Bringle, R. Games, & Rev. E. A. Malloy (Eds.), *Colleges and universities as citizens*. Boston: MA: Allyn & Bacon.

National Survey of Student Engagement Institute for Effective Educational Practice. (2004). *Final report: California State University Monterey Bay—Documenting effective educational practice*. Bloomington: Indiana University Center for Postsecondary Research.

Ramaley, J., Bringle, R. G., Freund, S. A., Harding, E., Hengstler, D., Hutchings, P., & O'Brien, K. (2003). *Report of the educational effectiveness site visit team: California State University Monterey Bay*. Monterey, CA: Authors.

Western Association of Schools and Colleges. (2001). *WASC handbook of accreditation: User's guide*. Alameda, CA: WASC.

4

PREPARING FOR ACCREDITATION

Sowing the Seeds of Long-Term Change

Salina Diiorio

L iterature has identified an explicit link between organizational learning and sustained organizational change (Boyce, 2003). Our accreditation experience provided a unique opportunity for the campus to
learn about itself and its processes. As discussed in the following chapters,
accreditation was also an opportunity to take the results of that learning and
institutionalize processes for change and improvement. Like gardeners preparing the soil for a cycle of change and growth, the Western Association of
Schools and Colleges Accreditation Project Team, of which I was a part,
helped to prepare the way for CSUMB to deepen its commitment to institutional learning and inquiry-based improvement. Of course, at the time we
were engaged in this work, we hardly thought of ourselves in that light. The
groups and individuals on campus that were involved in the work probably
thought of us more as demanding taskmasters bearing the "accreditation
club" and frequently shrieking, "We need evidence! No data dumping allowed! Continuous improvement!" However, that's hardly a pleasant image
to work with, so just go with me on the gardening metaphor, all right?

Directions for Preparation

The three primary objectives of the work I was involved in were (1) preparing
the soil by communicating and working with the various campus constituen-

cies to familiarize them with the new accreditation model that had been adopted by our accrediting body; (2) weeding through the vast amounts of documentation and evidence available, leaving only the best representative samples to be grown and developed; and (3) picking, arranging, and presenting those samples in a harvest that ensured that the accreditation body and the visiting review team would acknowledge their quality and worth. For each of these three objectives, I will discuss the strategies CSUMB used, how these strategies contributed to long-term change and a sustained focus on educational effectiveness, and how similar strategies could be used on other campuses.

Preparing the Soil: Communicating and Working with Campus Constituencies

As stated in previous chapters, our accrediting body is WASC. Like most of the regional associations, WASC adopted a new model of accreditation in 2001. Rather than relying on a vast checklist of data and documents for institutions to provide, the new model sought to engage institutions in deeper inquiry around educational effectiveness while also reviewing their resources to fulfill their stated mission. The new model split the review into two phases: a preparatory review to look at institutional capacity (resources, processes, and infrastructure) and an Educational Effectiveness Review to look at teaching and learning, as well as institutional learning and improvement. The campus had to select evidence to support its bid for initial accreditation, and present that evidence in a portfolio. The portfolio included reflective essays that synthesized the evidence, required data elements stipulated by WASC, and evidentiary documents included in appendices.

Our campus was the first public four-year comprehensive university to become accredited under the new WASC model. As described in chapter 2, the approach, language, and standards of accreditation had all changed: the entire process was new to everyone. In order for our two primary work groups and the Steering Committee to work effectively, the members had to become well versed in the new model in a relatively short time. "Reprogramming" people familiar with the old model from an audit mentality to an assessment and educational effectiveness mentality was no small feat. This effort was worth it, as the new mentality had greater relevance for the work of the campus and greater potential for improvement beyond the accreditation process.

CSUMB's Strategies for Working and Communicating with Groups

To begin, our provost constituted two primary work groups that were charged with doing the bulk of the hard, manual labor: the Preparatory Review Team for the first phase and the Educational Effectiveness Team for the second phase. As illustrated in chapter 2, the Preparatory Review Team was staffed primarily by top-level administrators and unit leaders, and a few faculty and students. They were responsible for assessing and gathering evidence for review and analysis, determining gaps in evidence that would need to be filled prior to the accreditation review, and designing action plans to close those gaps. They also participated in drafting and providing feedback on the essays that were written for the campus's portfolio presentation to WASC (see figure 4-1).

The Educational Effectiveness Team was made up of faculty, as well as the directors of institutional effectiveness and research and the Center of Teaching, Learning, and Assessment. Faculty members were selected primarily based on their scholarly work, which could be used for the portfolio presentation to WASC.

The provost chaired a Steering Committee that oversaw the two work groups. This committee consisted of the vice presidents of each division, as well as top administrators in key units (such as institutional assessment and research; teaching, learning, and assessment; the library; and information technology) and faculty representation from the Academic Senate. This group was kept apprised of the accreditation work, and was responsible for the final approval of selected evidence. Members also helped with the drafting and review of the portfolio essays.

More than sixty-five people contributed to CSUMB's accreditation effort, either as a member of a work group or the Steering Committee, or in other capacities. Because we had involved a broad selection of campus community members, most of whom were leaders of key units, we had built in a structural link to those units that would eventually be tasked with providing evidence and closing evidentiary gaps. This intentionality in staffing and structuring the committees served us well. It created a more diffuse and decentralized structure through which we were able to increase campus buy-in. Individuals across campus felt a sense of involvement in and ownership of the process and the work.

The accreditation project team (i.e., myself and my supervisor, then senior associate for accreditation and policy development) was responsible for

FIGURE 4-1
Organization of Accreditation Leadership:
Responsibilities and Contributions

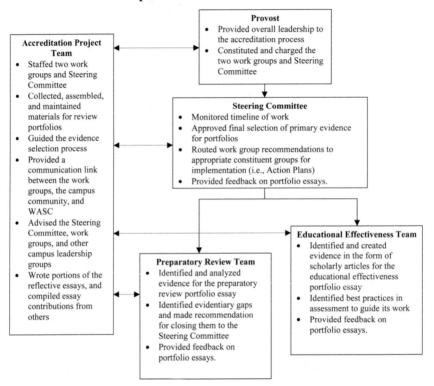

guiding all of the work done by the work groups, Steering Committee, and others. My supervisor and I were members of both work groups and the Steering Committee. We developed strategies for communicating and presenting information to the work groups and to the larger campus community. We also developed specific exercises to help the groups' transition to the new accreditation model, and to focus on quality evidence selection.

The Accreditation Project Team was very determined about trying not to overload people with too much information at one time. Rather than just handing work group members a copy of the 137-page WASC accreditation handbook, we made copies of only the relevant sections and included them, along with supplemental information, in a reference binder for everyone.

From then on, whenever we introduced new information we tried to pare it down to no more than a page.

We also tried to keep presentations of information to a minimum, and used the bulk of our meeting times for more interactive, collaborative group work. We split the Preparatory Review Team into four subgroups, one for each of the accreditation standards. They were encouraged to really dig into their assigned standard and get their hands dirty—deciphering what the standard meant and selecting relevant evidence to support CSUMB's case for accreditation.

The Educational Effectiveness Team was also engaged in interactive, collaborative exercises. For example, early in its work the group was split into smaller groups and asked to discuss "best practices" in assessment taken from current scholarly literature. They then came together and selected a list of these best practices to guide their subsequent work. This list was later developed into a survey that was administered to each of the university's colleges and that ultimately became a primary piece of evidence for that review. Betty McEady describes the group's processes in more detail in chapter 8.

Communicating Through a Variety of Venues

We used a variety of methods to update the broader campus community on the work that was being done. It was important that the accreditation process be as transparent and as open as possible. We wanted broad-based involvement and interest in our process, rather than a Dr. Strangelove-type scenario of a handful of people holed up in an undisclosed location plotting behind closed doors (and possibly with a finger poised on the button of a doomsday device). This transparency and resulting buy-in increased the potential for us to create the culture and institutional environment that could sustain long-term change and improvement.

Our communication plan used well-established communication venues on campus. We wrote and submitted articles to the staff and faculty campus newsletter, as well as to the student newspaper. Also, a folder of frequently updated accreditation information was sent to everyone's e-mail account—staff, faculty, and students. We also had a Web site that housed some of the portfolio evidence we presented. Once accreditation was granted, this became a primary depository of the campus's accreditation history (http://csumb.edu/academic/accreditation/). And finally, the accreditation project team would frequently go "on the road" with humorous PowerPoint presentations to various groups to entertain and inform.

Now, when you think of accreditation work, what are some of the words that come to mind? Chances are, "dry," "boring," and "shoot me now" made your top ten list. So, how can you overcome this hurdle of negative associations in the mind of your audience? Make 'em laugh! I consider it quite an achievement that members of the campus community eagerly anticipated our WASC presentations. Yes, I am serious. No, I don't have sworn affidavits to that effect. You'll just have to trust me—it's not impossible to make these things entertaining.

We chose themes for our presentations—from the game show *Who Wants to Be Accredited?* to our critically acclaimed spoof of the movie *Star Wars.* For the latter, the chair of the Educational Effectiveness Team gave a stellar performance as Uncle Owen (even though she hadn't a clue who he was), while our provost did a very convincing impression of Darth Vader, complete with heavy breathing into a microphone. Graphics included an image of the Death Star with "WASC" written across it, and Yoda sitting on top of a classroom desk. The climax: an image of the head of the review team chair digitally placed on Darth Vader's body, accompanied by the *Imperial March* playing in the background. The effect was perfect, hilarious, and engaging for the audience. We had their full attention, and so we were able to slip them substantive information without them falling asleep or tuning out. The point is to have fun and be informative at the same time.

How These Communication Strategies Led to Long-Term Change

Our focused exercises with the two work groups and our presentations and other modes of communication with the campus community helped to create broad-based campus buy-in and participation. Most people on campus knew what accreditation was, and also knew at least something about the work we were doing. In this way, the accreditation process offered a tremendous opportunity for the campus to engage in a process of long-term change by positioning the university to become more of a "learning organization."

The American Council on Education's Project for Leadership and Institutional Transformation has indicated the following strategies for substantial institutional change: using "change teams" charged with strategic purposes; engaging the campus community in the process; and aligning the necessary time, resources, and attention to the process (Boyce, 2003). Our "change teams" were the Preparatory Review and Educational Effectiveness Teams, the Steering Committee, and the Accreditation Project Team. We made every effort to engage the campus community through a variety of venues, and largely succeeded. And the tremendous importance of obtaining initial accreditation ensured that people's attention was focused on it, and that time and resources were devoted to it. This has created some fertile soil for the seeds of change to continue to grow.

The most satisfying moment of this work came during our final Steering Committee meeting. Our vice president for university advancement made a (spontaneous and unsolicited) observation about his work and the work of his department, and what they could do to link assessment results into their five-year planning. This, of course, is in stark contrast to the fairly common "we've completed our plan now let's put it on the shelf to collect dust for the next five years" planning strategy. I stood up next to my supervisor and solemnly declared, "Our work here is done." Finally, finally, it felt as though people who did not live and breathe accreditation every day were really getting it. The need for deep inquiry and evidence-based decision making, the idea of continuous renewal and of feeding assessment results back into the planning process in order to "close the loop"—those things that would make CSUMB a learning organization—were slowly seeping into the consciousness of the institution. Barr and Tagg (1995) suggest that even small changes, such as speaking within the new paradigm you want to establish, can prepare the way for deeper change. Once people begin to speak the new, common language, they begin to think and act from it as well. One year later, with no pending accreditation work hanging over our heads, the continued awareness initiated by the process can still be found at major planning tables across campus. At Administrative Council meetings, for example, language that was first introduced as part of accreditation has become common parlance. Words and phrases such as "evidence," "closing the loop," and "continuous renewal and improvement" have become ingrained in the dialogue and behavior of individuals across campus as they continue to integrate these concepts into the work they are doing within their departments and divisions.

Advice for Other Campuses: Communicating Effectively and Promoting Change

Based on what was learned from our processes and strategies to communicate with and engage our campus, I have five general recommendations for you to try at your own institution:

1. Don't dump massive amounts of information on people. If you just copy the accreditation handbook and hand it out, what do you *really* expect people will do?

    a. Actually read the thing

    b. Toss it on a shelf to gather dust and never give it another thought?

If you chose *b*—you understand human nature very well. Take the time to break information down and introduce it incrementally—preferably in one-page summary documents. Not only will this allow people the time and space they need to absorb everything they need to know, without overloading them, it will also strengthen your own understanding.

2. Develop interactive exercises in order to engage people, and encourage them to work with the information collaboratively. This allows them the opportunity to really internalize the information so that they can engage in dialogue around it and use it in meaningful ways. These interactions truly increase the potential for the work to have a long-term impact.

3. Be open and transparent in your process. This can encourage campus buy-in and interest, while helping to defuse the tensions that tend to develop when people feel shut out of a process.

4. Make a communication plan, employing the outlets already established for information dissemination. This will allow you to be intentional in your communications, while following the path of least resistance. No need to reinvent the wheel. If you have a campus newsletter that goes out to all staff and faculty, use it. Ditto for Web sites, student newspapers, and e-mail or electronic message boards.

5. Yuk it up, but be mindful of your audience. In order to keep from sounding like the *bwah bwah bwah* of Charlie Brown's teacher in the minds of your audience, try infusing humor into your informational presentations. Not only does it help to keep interest up, it can also be a survival mechanism for those closest to the work.

Weeding and Pruning: Selecting the Best Evidence to Grow

The primary task of the work groups was to select the evidence that would support CSUMB's accreditation and that the portfolio essays would be written around. This was a lengthy, iterative process, which focused on selecting evidence that was both high quality and authentic. By "authentic" I mean evidence that truly captured work that was already being done on campus—things that were important to the institution independent of the accreditation process. This helped to minimize the amount of work that needed to be done solely to meet accreditation criteria, thereby increasing the likelihood of long-term change. Most of the chapters of this book describe such processes and inquiries.

We tried to make the process of evidence selection an organic one. We engaged the work groups in exercises that systematically built upon each other, and that allowed people the opportunity to synthesize and use the information presented to them. For example, both work groups began with brainstorming exercises, to simply list every possible piece of evidence they could think of that would align with the accreditation requirements and standards. For the Preparatory Review Team, each subsequent exercise called on them to winnow and refine those initial lists, while introducing them to more and more detailed information regarding WASC's expectations. The Educational Effectiveness Team engaged in an organic process to identify best practices in educational effectiveness, which they then used to guide their work. These were time-consuming processes, but essential in building both understanding and buy-in of the accreditation process.

CSUMB's Strategies for Selecting Evidence

We employed some different strategies with the two work groups, reflecting the different natures of the two phases of the accreditation process. We also used a common strategy of using "evidence layers" for presenting the evidence in both reviews.

For the preparatory review phase, the Preparatory Review Team broke into subgroups and participated in a brainstorming exercise, listing potential evidence under each standard. From there, the subgroups began a process of identifying primary evidence—the key pieces of evidence that were analyzed in the preparatory portfolio essay to make the case for CSUMB's initial accreditation. Their work was guided by the criteria for evaluating evidence provided to us by WASC:

- Is it *relevant* to the accreditation standard being addressed?
- Is it *verifiable* through documentation and replication?
- Is it *representative* of the institution's processes, rather than being an isolated example?
- Is it *cumulative*, in that there are multiple other sources that will corroborate it?
- Is it *actionable*, so that the institution can use it to make decisions and changes for improvements? (WASC, 2002, p. 10)

We also asked, "How is it important to the institution?" It was helpful to use these criteria as a guide because it gave us an idea of how our accrediting commission and reviewers would be thinking about and evaluating the evidence we presented. From this initial selection work we produced a gap analysis report, which laid out what evidence we had on hand and what we would need to do in order to fully address each of the standards. The report became affectionately known as the "shock doc," named for the stunned-deer-in-the-headlights look on the faces of those who read it as they realized the seemingly gargantuan extent of the work that needed to be done. It was useful as a wake-up call in that respect, but it also helped to focus and prioritize the work of the institution.

The gap analysis was used to produce "action plans" for the work each department needed to do. This is where the unit leaders sitting on the Preparatory Review Team and Steering Committee became the essential links between those groups and the work of their units. They took responsibility for developing the action plans with their staff, and were responsible for reporting on progress to the provost. These action plans themselves became key pieces of evidence, particularly for work that was still in progress by the time of the review visits. They showed the reviewers that the institution had plans and timelines to guide critical work that would continue well past the time of the review. The action plans also continue to prompt ongoing improvement efforts.

For the Educational Effectiveness review phase, our process also involved an initial guided brainstorming exercise. However, rather than organizing around the accreditation standards, we organized it around five specific questions posed by the visiting review team. These were

1. Does the institution have effective means to review and evaluate the outcomes of its educational model?
2. Is there a continuous process of inquiry and engagement by the institution to enhance educational effectiveness?
3. Does the institution utilize good practices to assess student learning?
4. Are institutional resources aligned with activities designed to achieve educational effectiveness?
5. Does CSUMB's educational model yield our unique intended outcomes for students?

Primary evidence pieces for the portfolio were then chosen based on their relevance to one or more of the five questions, their importance to the university based in part on their alignment with campus and system priorities, and the expertise and interests of the work group members. Examples of the faculty's work can be seen throughout this book.

Three Levels of Evidence

In addition to the primary evidence selections for the preparatory and the educational effectiveness portfolios, we also identified secondary and tertiary levels of evidence to allow reviewers to "dig down" further into the evidence. Primary evidence directly supported whatever claims were made within the essays. Secondary evidence supported the primary evidence, and tertiary evidence most often referred to the raw data upon which the primary or secondary evidence was based. For example, the campus program review process (see chapter 5) was cited as primary evidence for both reviews and was supported by three levels of evidence (figure 4-2).

Presenting the evidence in this way allowed us to demonstrate that our data met the accreditation criteria for evidence (verifiable, cumulative, representative, etc.). It showed that our evidence was not only broad but also deep—each standard was addressed by evidence that was supported at multiple levels.

How Our Evidence Selection Processes Led to Long-Term Change

The gap analysis and action plans that came out of the Preparatory Review Team's work brought to light critical work the institution needed to do— work that continues even today. For example, our Administrative Council

FIGURE 4-2
Levels of Evidence

Primary	Program review process	Scholarly articles written by faculty and incorporated into the accreditation essay
Secondary	Program review discussion document	A report by the campus Program Review Committee that aggregated the findings of the review of all of the degree programs
Tertiary	Program review portfolios	The actual and complete program review portfolio for each of our degree programs

became the primary group responsible for assessing effectiveness at the institutional level. Three subgroups were created within the Administrative Council: planning alignment, costing the model, and institutional effectiveness. The planning alignment group has identified common planning assumptions for the campus, and is using those assumptions to align and integrate all of the major campus plans with the strategic plan. The costing the model group is identifying the core components of CSUMB's unique educational model and analyzing the costs associated with delivering it, so that the campus can better prioritize the allocation of dwindling resources to preserve the core elements of the model. The institutional effectiveness group is currently working on a preliminary assessment of progress that has been made toward the campus's achievement of its strategic plan goals.

Evidence identified for the educational effectiveness review also led to long-term change for the institution. An example of this would be the study that Dan Shapiro describes in chapter 7, which looked at the senior capstone process and how it was administered by different degree programs across campus. The results of this study have been presented to the Administrative Council, and have helped to inform the work of the costing the model group. Another example is program review. During the course of developing the program review process evidence, we found that there was a lack of alignment between program review results and program initiatives and planning processes. This alignment issue is being further addressed as the program review policy is assessed and revised as part of the campus's established continuous renewal process.

Advice for Other Campuses: Selecting Your Evidence

Based on our evidence development, selection, and organization strategies, I have three recommendations to offer:

1. Devote the time to develop an organic process. Who doesn't prefer organic produce to the pesticide-laden variety? Sure organic foods cost more, but they taste better and they're better for you! In the same way, developing an organic process in which people are allowed the time to really learn and internalize the information takes a greater commitment of time, but the quality of the evidence developed and the probability for the resulting long-term change can also be much greater.

2. Give priority to evidence that is important to the institution. If it is important and integral to the institution, it is much easier to talk

about. And, chances are good that those items will align quite well with what the accrediting body will want to see, whether you are developing a "theme-based" portfolio or one based around specific standards and criteria.

3. Identify and build on the work the institution is already doing so that you have "added value" instead of just added work. This is related to the previous point. If the evidence is important to the institution, and is work that the institution is engaged in independent of the accreditation review, there is a greater likelihood that the work will continue into the future.

Harvesting and Arranging: Presenting the Evidence

Getting back to the garden metaphor—we've prepared the soil and done some weeding and pruning to leave us with our best evidence, so now it's time to harvest. Your garden might produce the most beautiful flowers or the most succulent fruit, but if they are just picked and jumbled together any which way, it would be easy for people to overlook them or miss their quality. In the same way, your evidence can be the most brilliant in the world, but if you don't present it in ways that communicate its significance to the accrediting body and the review team, it may not be convincing. The diligence of development and selection would be virtually wasted. In contrast, the materials we presented made explicit the relevance of each piece of evidence, both to the accreditation standards and to the institution's own mission and goals. We took great care to create portfolio documents and on-campus document rooms that were well organized and user friendly.

CSUMB's Strategies for Evidence Presentation

The Accreditation Project Team developed two strategies for presenting our evidence: "evidence maps" and document room archives that organized CSUMB's evidence in a useful manner. They also helped us translate that evidence and its relevance to the accrediting commission and visiting reviewers. This work was commended by the review team in its *Report of the Educational Effectiveness Site Visit Team* (Ramaley et al., 2003):

> The team was impressed with the quality of the institutional educational effectiveness report and the evidence presented there, the use of a map to guide the team in finding and understanding the evidence presented and the care that was evidenced in the way the document room was organized.

It was extremely easy to find and study the evidence compiled by CSUMB in support of its case. (p. 13)

Evidence Maps

The "evidence maps" were color-coded matrices that (1) coordinated with the essays written for each of the review phases, (2) listed and briefly described each of our evidence selections, and (3) described where to find them. They provided the review teams with a handy way to locate all of the exhibits and data displays CSUMB was presenting in support of its bid for initial accreditation. The evidence maps for the preparatory and the educational effectiveness reviews (see figures 4-3 and 4-4) were quite different, and reflected the way each of the portfolio essays were written. The concept is flexible enough to adapt to any number of ways you may want to organize your evidence.

Document Room Archives

The user-friendly setup of the portfolios also extended into the document rooms we created for the review teams during their two visits to campus. The color-coding of the essay and evidence map sections translated to the same color-coding of the files in the file cabinets. Also, the filing system tracked the flow of the evidence map precisely. For example, if a piece of evidence was referenced under more than one standard, that piece of evidence was copied and placed in a folder for *each and every* standard it was referenced under. This may seem like a lot of unnecessary duplication, but it makes the review team's job a lot easier. I was on call as the "document librarian" during the team's visits, and I did not have to field a single call from them asking for additional documentation, or where to find any document that was there in the room.

How Our Presentation Strategies Led to Long-Term Change

Our systematic selection and presentation of evidence contributed to the success of CSUMB's bid for initial accreditation. However, the process of being intentional about supporting claims with several levels of evidence also helped to plant the idea with members of the campus community of what it means to be a learning organization based on a culture of inquiry and evidence. The president's cabinet and others across the institution have expressed continuing commitment to these ideas, and we are confident that the notion of CSUMB as a learning organization will take root even more strongly as the campus grows.

FIGURE 4-3
Sample Evidence Map from Preparatory Review

Criteria for Review	Guidelines If Applicable	Evidence	How Evidence Meets Criteria	Access Portfolio	Access Web Page	Access Document Room
		PRIMARY				
2.7. In order to improve program currency and effectiveness, all programs offered by the institution are subject to review, including analysis of the achievement of the program's learning objectives and outcomes. Where appropriate, evidence from external constituencies, such as employers and professional societies, is included in such reviews.	The institution incorporates in its assessment of educational objectives results with respect to student achievement, including program completion, license examination, and placement rates results.	Program Review Model	Each of the academic programs, including the ULR program, is subject to Program Review. This includes a peer review element.	Appendix H-7; Essay, p. 71	X	X
		SECONDARY				
		Sample Program Review Improvement Plan	As part of the review process, programs submit Improvement Plans based on their Program Review findings.	Appendix H-8		X
		Tertiary Program Improvement Plans (Academic Plan, App. 21)	As part of the review process, programs submit Improvement Plans based on their Program Review findings.			X
		Tertiary Program Review Portfolios	Specific examples of portfolios, including External Review reports.			X
		Tertiary Chancellor's Office Memo #71-32	Program Review is mandated by the CSU every 5 years.			X

FIGURE 4-4
Sample Evidence Map from Educational Effectiveness Review

Evidence Samples and Supporting Documentation	How Evidence Sample Responds to Questions	Criteria for Review (WASC Standards)	Access		
			Portfolio	Web Page	Document Room
PRIMARY	**Question 1: Effective means to review and evaluate outcomes**				
Evidence Sample 4: Program Review Process	As a result of the Program Review Process, the Academic Program Review Committee identified a series of common themes and issues, which included the need to finish the development of the MLOs and assessment protocols, as well as develop the capacity to collect and analyze data on student learning. The completion of MLO development has received focused attention, and the collection and analysis of student learning data has been initiated in at least half the institutes through Capstone analysis and portfolio review.	2.7, 4.4, 4.6, 4.7	Appendix G; Essay, p. 18	X	X
	Question 2: Continuous process of inquiry/engagement				
	The Program Review process is a continuous process of inquiry and engagement. Institute Directors provide Program Improvement Update Reports to reflect and assess with their faculty those goals and objectives previously proposed for their institutes.		Essay, p. 19		
	Question 3: Good practices to assess student learning				
	One of AAHE's Principles of Good Practice in Assessing Student Learning is that the importance of institutional values is affirmed in the process. CSUMB's Program Review process is strongly grounded in the principles of the Vision and core values, with each program being asked to explicitly address "how CSUMB core values are infused" in the program.		Essay, p. 19		

Question 4: Resources aligned to achieve ed. effectiveness			
There is a significant investment of resources and faculty and administrative time and expertise in the Program Review process. Evidence of improvements resulting from the process are an indicator that this is an activity designed to contribute to CSUMB's educational effectiveness.	Essay, p. 20		
Question 5: Educational model yields intended outcomes			
The Program Review Model includes guiding review questions for programs regarding the development of expected knowledge and skills in the program and the collection of summative evidence of student learning. The Campus Grid of Best Practices begins to show evidence of progress in answering these questions. 9 institutes report that student work is collected systematically for review of program effectiveness (this would include attainment of outcomes by students), and that faculty collaborate to review/analyze student work for feedback to program effectiveness. See also Evidence Samples of Individual Programs' Educational Effectiveness.	Appendix J; Essay, p. 26		
SECONDARY			
Program Review Discussion Document	Essay, p. 19		X
Tertiary			
Program Review Portfolios			X

Even the way we chose to present our evidence has added support for long-term improvement. The evidence maps and document room archives have provided the campus with a quick and easy reference of evidentiary materials. Because the evidence selected for inclusion in the maps was predominantly current and ongoing, these maps will remain relevant for years after accreditation. They are now being used to identify evidence for a preliminary assessment of progress that has been made toward the achievement of the campus's strategic plan goals.

Advice for Other Campuses: Presenting Evidence Effectively

Based on the strategies for evidence presentation we developed, I have two recommendations to offer:

1. Tell the accreditation body and review team what it is you want them to know. You are extremely familiar with the information you are presenting, while your reviewers are not. Tell them what it is you are showing them, why you are showing it to them, how it is important to the institution, and how it relates to the accreditation standards. This may seem as if you are stating the obvious or being redundant, but keep in mind that your reviewers are not experts on your institution. They have a lot of information to assimilate in a very short amount of time, and everything you can do to provide them with greater clarity will be appreciated.

2. Presentation is everything, or very close to everything. Let's say 80% of everything. Strive to make the documents you present as user friendly as possible. Put yourself in the position of somebody who doesn't know the institution and is unfamiliar with the evidence you are presenting. What would be the easiest way for someone to navigate through the tremendous amount of material needed for an accreditation review? Be creative—use color coding, cross-referencing to appendices, evidence maps tailored to the structure of your particular review—anything that will guide your readers seamlessly from point A to point B. Your review team will thank you for it, and you will gain useful insights from the process.

Moving On to Other Pastures?

Of course, the work of organizational learning and long-term change is never truly done. Would that it were! The point of sowing the seeds is to begin a dynamic and cyclical process—a process in which the university can be seen as a living organism itself, one that is never finished growing and changing. An accreditation process that intentionally provides the right environment to nourish real opportunities for learning and change can be a valuable initiator of such a process.

The time that we took to engage with people across campus ensured that this process would become deeply rooted throughout the institution, and would not be dependent on the individual people involved. Accrediting committees and work groups may move on to other pastures, but the process will go on because of the nature of the work that we did. When that work is eventually passed along to others who will continue to tend and sow, weed and harvest, we will know that we laid the fertile groundwork for CSUMB to thrive.

References

Barr, R. B., & Tagg, J. (1995, November/December). From teaching to learning: A new paradigm for undergraduate education. *Change, 27,* 12–25.

Boyce, M. E. (2003). Organizational learning is essential to achieving and sustaining change in higher education. *Innovative Higher Education, 28,* 119–136.

Ramaley, J. A., Bringle, R. G., Freund, S. A., Harding, E., Hengstler, D. D., Hutchings, P. A., & O'Brien, K. (2003, May 5–7). *Report of the educational effectiveness site visit team: California State University, Monterey Bay.* Seaside, CA: Authors.

Ramaley, J. A., Desrochers, L., & Olsen, D. (2002). *Report of the site visit team: Extension of candidacy visit.* Seaside, CA: California State University Monterey Bay.

Western Association of Schools and Colleges. (2002, January). *A guide to using evidence in the accreditation process: A resource to support institutions and evaluation teams* (working draft). Retrieved September 27, 2004, from http://www.wasc senior.org/senior/inst_resource.htm

5

PROGRAM REVIEW AS A MODEL OF VISION-BASED CONTINUOUS RENEWAL

Seth Pollack

Typically, the prospect of conducting a program review is met with less than enthusiastic response from faculty and administrators alike in higher education. All too often, the program review process is seen as a perfunctory exercise to be performed at specific predetermined intervals to meet the requirements of an external authority or institution. The process generates reams of paper, which while satisfying the needs of the external authority, have little or no impact on the day-to-day life of the academic unit. The process, like other aspects of accreditation, is often seen by faculty as busy work, and has very little to do with the units' academic goals or processes of continuous renewal.

CSUMB committed to making the program review process meaningful, and intimately connected to the overall process of continuous renewal and growth toward initial accreditation. Campus leaders determined that the program review process would (1) use CSUMB's vision, mission, and core values as the framework for evaluation of individual programs and (2) be conducted in an open and visible manner, so that the findings could directly contribute to individual program improvement as well as to the overall growth of our young campus. In a sense, the program review process was a

Special thanks to Joe Larkin for his insights on the process of developing the program review framework, and for sharing the formative documents for the process.

73

way for each of our academic units (and our young university as a whole) to look themselves in the mirror, and evaluate their reality in comparison to the goals and ideals elaborated at the campus's founding five years earlier. It also served as a kind of prescriptive assessment process, to help us direct our efforts and resources for the future.

This chapter will describe both the process and the results of CSUMB's program review process. It will then reflect on these processes from a "best practices" perspective, and summarize the impact that program review has had on the growth of our campus culture. Although it was our first program review process, our experiences provide significant insights for our ongoing reviews, as well as for review processes on other campuses. The guiding theme is to help ensure that the resources your campus invests in program review will contribute to the growth and fulfillment of your own academic program vision.

Overview: CSUMB's Academic Program Review Process

When time came for the initial program review process to be developed and implemented, the campus had only been in operation for three short years. While the teaching and learning process was quite functional (courses were being taught and the first two graduating classes had even been awarded degrees), many of the administrative and governance functions of the university were still in an emergent phase. At the time, the faculty senate committee, which would normally have been charged with the development of the program review plan, did not possess the knowledge base or have sufficient time to devote to the task of developing the initial program review framework. The process began with a wide-ranging discussion at the Dean's Council, clarifying the context and purpose of the program review. Their inquiry raised questions such as

- What programs are to be reviewed?
- Which program functions are to be reviewed?
- What are the purposes for program review?
- For whom is program review being conducted (and what do they want to know)?
- What level of resources can and should be invested in program review?
- What are the time parameters within which program review will be conducted?

Joe Larkin, assistant vice president for academic development, facilitated this discussion. Larkin would ultimately serve as the supervising administrator for the program review process. The result of this initial discussion was the identification of a set of principles to guide the development of the program review. These guiding principles included

1. All units in academic affairs should undertake a "program review," and not just the degree-granting programs.
2. The process should be portfolio based, with each group preparing a portfolio to be reviewed by a committee, rather than a "show-and-tell" presentation.
3. There should be one single committee to review all programs.
4. All programs should respond to a standardized analytical framework.
5. The committee should be big enough to represent all constituencies, but small enough to be affordable and manageable.

While there was strenuous debate in the development of the final product, these initial principles remained strongly present in the various iterations of the model.

Recognizing that the final product would need significant faculty buy-in, Larkin assembled, in the fall of 1998, the Joint Faculty/Administration Committee on Program Review. The committee consisted of five faculty members and four academic administrators chosen from across the campus. Using the guiding principles, the Joint Faculty/Administration Committee developed a plan that was ultimately approved by both the Administrative Council and the Academic Senate.

This would be the first time since the campus opened its doors in fall 1995, that the academic programs would be reviewed as part of the regular five-year program review cycle. As the inaugural program review process, and the only formal review that would occur during the initial accreditation period, this first review was seen to be an important landmark in the development of the campus' academic programs. In addition, the review had to walk a fine line between its dual purposes of accountability on the one hand, and program development on the other. Given the developmental phase of our young campus, the process ultimately came to focus on its contribution as a tool for program development. The inaugural academic program review would give the campus the opportunity to get a "snapshot" of each of its academic programs, and review the progress that each program had made from a common framework and with clear criteria.

The creation of the Program Review Model was important, as it not only set the agenda for the review, but also specified a unique, centralized, standardized, and inclusive approach to the process. The model identified these three primary purposes for undertaking this review of the university's academic programs:

1. Quality assurance: program review is one way for CSUMB to fulfill its responsibility to assure the public, the board of trustees, WASC, and its students and parents that it is providing quality academic programs.

2. Program improvement: program review should provide individual program faculty and staff, as well as university administrators, with information and feedback that will assist in their responsibility to continuously improve program quality and cost effectiveness.

3. Program and resource alignment: program review should help university faculty and administrators ensure that CSUMB is offering an appropriate array of academic programs and that resources are effectively aligned with those programs (see appendix 5.A, Program Review Model, January 1999).

Identification of purposes is a critical starting point in the program review process. Though the purposes might differ from institution to institution, starting with clear goals allows the campus to publicly acknowledge that the program review process is more than a formality. It states clearly that the process has relevance and meaning for the campus's own growth and development. Establishing clear priorities is the first step in the institution taking ownership for the program review process.

Academic Program Review: Formal Process and Timeline

The Joint Faculty/Administration Committee developed the timeline, prescribed the contents of the portfolios, and articulated the program review criteria that would be used for this initial review. The criteria included three major areas: (1) quality of the program, (2) need for the program, and (3) cost of the program. The Program Review Model outlined specific "guiding review questions" that would be used by the reviewers of the portfolios (see appendix 5.A, Program Review Model). The questions were designed to have the programs base their self-analysis in the context of the educational needs of the local community (an important aspect of the CSUMB academic program), and with regard to CSUMB's Vision Statement and core values. For example, questions included

- To what extent does the program clearly articulate how it intends to serve the needs of students, the community, and the broader society?
- To what extent do the program's mission and goals contribute to the CSUMB Vision Statement?
- How clearly does the program identify the personal development, employment, and graduate school opportunities that students can expect to gain from the program?
- To what extent does the program holistically emphasize and integrate the CSUMB academic core values of interdisciplinarity, applied learning, multiculturalism and globalism, technological sophistication, collaboration, ethical reflection and practice, and service learning?

These questions exemplify how the program review incorporated CSUMB's core values and vision as the primary framework for analysis. This provides important coherence to the departmental self-reflection process, and creates a common framework and language for departments to engage in campuswide dialogue.

The committee also developed a list of materials for each program to submit, a list of supporting material to be gathered by academic affairs, and a list of questions forming the basis of the review. The fact that some materials were gathered centrally was an important element in the analysis, as it gave a baseline set of data that was common for all programs. This included

- Data on enrollment, student-instructor ratios, graduation rates, faculty composition, and so forth
- Focus group interviews with graduating students from each department
- Focus group interviews with recent graduates from each department

In addition to these materials, an external review team reviewed each program. Each academic program had the opportunity to identify two experts to serve as its external reviewers. Departments were encouraged to include one external reviewer from a sister California State University campus, as it was thought that faculty working in another CSU campus would have an appreciation for the particular constraints experienced in the CSU system. As it turned out, many of the programs identified one CSU reviewer and a reviewer from outside the system whose particular expertise was relevant to the program's goals. The external reviewers received the prepared portfolio and had the benefit of two working days on campus to review additional documents and meet with faculty, staff, and students before submitting their report. In most cases, the external reviewers brought a fresh perspective to the review process, and as outsiders, were able to ask the hard questions that can often go unasked, even in the context of a program review. The external reviewers also played an important role as a reality check, ensuring that the culture and work of the department was being communicated clearly to outside entities.

The Program Review Model was presented to the campus in January 1999, at which time the degree programs and the central administration began the yearlong process of data gathering culminating in the preparation of individual portfolios by each of the academic units. The portfolio compiled for each academic unit consisted of three distinctive parts: (1) the department's own internal portfolio based on the Academic Program Review Model, (2) the data compiled by the office of academic affairs, and (3) the report written by the external reviewers.

In the spring 2000 semester, the Academic Program Review Committee was assembled, with faculty, staff, and student representatives. The committee consisted of ten people: five faculty, two academic administrators, two students, and one staff person. The faculty represented each of the university's four colleges and the universitywide programs area. The two administrators came from the president's office and the library. Thus, the various academic affairs units were all represented on this important committee. Committee members were chosen explicitly for their demonstrated skills in collaboration, the high esteem in which they were held by their colleagues, and their capacity to be "critical listeners." The entire campus community was invited to self-nominate to be considered for the process. Ultimately about 20 nominations were received, and the final decision on the composition of the committee was made jointly by the deans, the provost, and the Academic Senate Executive Committee.

Each faculty member of the committee was given release time to compensate for the significant time conducting the program review would require. This is an important consideration for campuses. Having a centralized committee responsible for the entire review requires a greater commitment of resources. But, this approach also generates a significant body of knowledge, and a group of individuals with a deep and broad understanding of the campus's academic programs. This proved to be a powerful investment. The

Program Review Committee met weekly during the spring 2000 semester, systematically reviewing each of the twelve degree-program portfolios that had been submitted. The committee members wrote individual reports, summarizing the data that had been collected for each degree program, and providing an overview of the degree program's progress with regard to each of the three areas of concern (quality, need, and cost). Each academic program was then asked to write a response to the program review report during the fall 2000 semester.

The process of self-reflection, external review, and dialogue, followed by further self-reflection, is a powerful model. It ensures that self-reflection does not take place in isolation, and that external examiners (in this instance, the Program Review Committee) do not have the final say in the process. Rather, it embodies a process of continuous renewal and improvement, which is the overall goal of the program review process.

Revision of the Initial Committee Mandate

It is important to note that the "cost" section of the program review criteria included a final category called "viability," with these two guiding questions:

- What types of resource adjustments would enable this program to meet the needs that it serves with greater quality, effectiveness, and efficiency?
- To what extent would such resource adjustments be warranted relative to other priorities and needs at CSUMB?

When the committee was seated, it was decided that the viability section would not be part of the committee's mandate. While the committee was given authority to review and comment on program quality and the need for the program, it was only requested to summarize information with regard to cost and efficiency. The committee was not to make recommendations to the university concerning the viability of programs, nor was the committee to decide whether university investment in programs was warranted by program efficiency or quality. The sole responsibility of the committee was to synthesize the material provided for review without making recommendations related to resource allocation. This kind of decision can have a huge impact on the process and deserves careful consideration. It is important to distinguish between a reflective process that gathers information to facilitate ongoing improvement and growth, and an evaluative process that has specific consequences related to resource allocation. Later in the chapter we describe our reasons and how the decision affected our process.

The overall timeline of the formal academic program review process is summarized in figure 5-1. As you can see, the process took two years to complete. A full year was devoted to the data-gathering process, and a full semester devoted to portfolio review by the Program Review Committee. This was followed by an additional semester devoted to the integration and the writing of a formal response by the individual departments.

Additional Processes: Facilitating Campuswide Discussion

In addition to analyzing the twelve individual degree programs and writing the individual reports summarizing the accomplishments and challenges faced by each program, the Program Review Committee felt that it had gained an extremely important (and unusual) perspective on the campuses' overall growth and evolution. During the process of reviewing the individual programs, common themes and issues emerged that had relevance beyond the scope of a specific degree program. The emergence of these issues was an unexpected outcome of the review process, a result of the emerging collective wisdom and deepening insights of the Program Review Committee. These issues were termed "parking lot issues," and were gathered for further discus-

FIGURE 5-1
Academic Program Review, Formal Process Timeline

Academic Program Review Formal Process Timeline	
Fall 1998	Design of program review process
Jan 1999	Program Review Model presented
Jan 1999–Dec 2000	Data gathering, portfolios assembled, external review visits
Jan 2000–May 2000	Program Review Committee reviews portfolios and collected data
July 2000	Program Review Committee writes reports on individual degree program
Fall 2000	Academic programs write responses

sion and analysis by the Program Review Committee. Ultimately, a list of twenty-one parking lot issues was assembled (see appendix 5.B, Parking Lot Issues).

The committee decided that it was important to capitalize on this unusual insight and share its perspective and the questions that had been raised with the campus community. During the fall 2000 semester, the committee drafted a discussion document that was then circulated throughout campus. "Academic Degree Program Review Discussion Document" contained three sections. First, in the spirit of continuous renewal, it reflected on the scope, opportunities, and challenges of the academic program review process itself. Second, it provided an overview of the ten areas highlighted in the "Program Quality" section of the program review criteria, while drawing attention to the parking lot issues that emerged over the course of the committee's work. Finally, it highlighted three critical areas that the committee felt were especially in need of attention by the campus community:

1. Finishing the development of learning outcomes and assessment protocols
2. Addressing interdisciplinarity and cross-institute collaboration
3. Developing the capacity to collect and analyze data on student learning

The discussion document was a way for the Program Review Committee to spark continuous renewal not only at the level of individual programs, but for the university as a whole. After spending an entire semester with significant documentation on academic program quality, need, and cost, the committee was able to summarize its insights and share them with the university community as a whole. The "Academic Program Review Discussion Document" was presented to the campus community at a meeting of the Academic Leadership Team (ALT) on December 6, 2000. The Academic Leadership Team was the only forum on campus where deans, program directors, and department chairs would meet to discuss academic affairs policy. The ALT was the ideal venue for the Program Review Committee to facilitate a campuswide dialogue on its overall findings. The conversation was so rich, that a follow-up discussion was then held at a second ALT meeting on January 23, 2001, focusing on the three critical areas identified in the document.

The process of summarizing and disseminating the campuswide insights is one of the most powerful contributions of the centralized approach to analysis and review that was taken. Had the campus chosen a more decentralized approach, with individual committees reviewing individual programs, then this collective wisdom and the dialogue that it generated would not have emerged. It is a significantly rewarding aspect of the program review process.

Reflections on This Process Through a Best Practices Lens

What does the best practices literature in assessment tell us about the process that CSUMB employed to review its academic degree programs? Underlying much of the literature on assessment is the idea that assessment works best (1) when there are clear outcomes, (2) when those outcomes represent issues that faculty care about and had a stake in developing, and (3) when the assessment processes themselves are developed and carried out by faculty. In other words, successful assessment is a community endeavor, developed and carried out by those most intimately involved. These three guiding principles offer an important starting point for most campuses. But, they require a significant investment of faculty time and program resources.

Wergin and Swingen (1998) identify three key factors for effective academic department assessment:

1. The degree to which the *organizational and cultural setting* promotes a conducive atmosphere for evaluation
2. The credibility and fairness of *evaluation policies and practices*
3. The validity and reliability of *evaluation standards, criteria, and measures* (p. 12)

Underlying each of these factors is the issue of faculty engagement in and support of the assessment process. In addition the authors urge campuses to take ownership of the criteria underlying and definitions being used regarding the concept of "quality" (Wergin & Swingen, 1998, p. 22), admonishing universities not to just reach for the most convenient or the most socially acceptable definition of quality. Involving faculty in discussions of quality at the program and campus levels prior to the development of program review processes can be very educative, and greatly contribute to creating an atmosphere conducive to assessment.

In their work on the faculty role in assessment, Maitland Schilling and Schilling (2000) also emphasize the importance of faculty involvement in the assessment process. They emphasize the importance of assessment being seen as a "stimulus to reflective practice by faculty":

> Assessment can be presented as an effort essential to scholarly reflection on a campus's collective educational endeavors, providing information that will allow the quality of educational offerings to be improved, or it can be presented as a burden that the campus must endure to satisfy others. (p. 72)

As it did with the overall accreditation procedure, CSUMB approached the program review as a scholarly endeavor focused on the process of reflection. The portfolios developed by the departments were more than compilations of data, but clearly reflections of their achievements and struggles related to the overarching campus vision and core values. The Program Review Committee's work was more than just a summative evaluation and certification, but contributed to the generation of new insights about teaching and learning, and most important, about structural impediments to the successful achievement of program goals. For example, the discussion document generated by the Program Review Committee asked important questions about the feasibility of ongoing programwide assessment, and identified ways for programs to learn from each other.

Finally, the American Association for Higher Education's (AAHE) *Principles of Good Practice for Assessing Student Learning* (AAHE, 1992) offers a relevant perspective on departmental assessment as well. Among the ten principles are the following statements that are especially relevant for departmental and programmatic assessment:

- Assessment of student learning begins with educational values. (number 1)
- Assessment works best when the programs it seeks to improve have clear, explicitly stated purposes. (number 3)
- Assessment makes a difference when it begins with issues of use and illuminates questions that people really care about. (number 7)
- Assessment is most effective when undertaken in an environment that is receptive, supportive, and enabling. (number 10)

As you will see in a number of the chapters by my colleagues, the AAHE principles served as guideposts for a number of campus inquiries and assessment processes. Again, the importance of faculty involvement, specific and relevant goals, and a focus on learning emerge as fundamental principles for successful assessment. Campuses should not hesitate from grounding their own program review criteria in the overarching values of their institution. In fact, this is precisely the place to ensure that the words used in lofty mission statements have a connection to the nuts and bolts of the work of an institution's academic departments. Taking time to develop criteria that are meaningful to the campus, and that resonate with the faculty, is critical to the development of a successful program review process.

Reflection on CSUMB's Process

CSUMB's approach to the academic program review process incorporates to a great extent many of these best practices concepts. First, there was significant faculty participation in each stage of the process. Faculty were majority members of the Joint Faculty/Administration Committee on Program Review, which established the review process and criteria, and of the Program Review Committee, which carried out the review. Thus, there was significant participation by faculty in the creation and implementation of the review process. The CSUMB program review process was not imposed from the outside, but rather was a community product.

More important, the review itself was strongly grounded in the principles of the CSUMB Vision Statement, and its core values. The Vision Statement was the yardstick by which the mission and goals of the degree programs were measured. The Program Review Committee was asked to consider "to what extent do the program's mission and goals contribute to the CSUMB Vision Statement" (see appendix 5.A, Program Review Model). As described in chapter 3, each degree program had to explicitly address "how CSUMB core values are infused" in the degree program. The Program Review Committee was then asked to consider "to what extent does the program holistically emphasize and integrate the CSUMB academic core values." This clearly demonstrates that the intentions communicated by the CSUMB Vision Statement, a strong reason why many faculty chose to come to CSUMB, are a foundational component of the program review process. To a significant extent, CSUMB created its own definition of quality, based on the values and principles embedded in its Vision Statement.

The discussion document created by the Program Review Committee is further evidence that the process was seen as an opportunity for the university to ask fundamental questions about what we were doing, and to determine if we were still on the right track. The process was seen by the committee as a rich learning experience, as is evidenced by the following excerpt from the document:

The purpose of this document is to stimulate discussion and exchange campus-wide about many of the positive programmatic features that the degree programs have developed, as well as about the critical issues that remain to be tackled. After reflecting on our work of reviewing dozens of syllabi, mission statements, and MLOs, the committee felt that it had received an extremely valuable education about where CSUMB has come in its first five years. We would like to share this with our colleagues campus-wide. (Program Review Committee, 2001, p. 1)

This sentiment is clearly in line with the perspective provided by Wergin and Swingen (1998):

Faculty members who accept responsibility and ownership for program review and view it as the impetus for dialogue, a chance to reflect upon the work of the department, and a vehicle for possible changes are crucial to meaningful reviews centered on quality improvement. (p. 13)

The fact that the committee went beyond its charge to review individual program portfolios and put together a document synthesizing its learning is a significant statement. It shows that the process was valued and was viewed as a learning process, and not merely a required exercise.

On the other hand, there are ways in which CSUMB's process did not meet some of the best practices expectations. The Program Review Committee was frustrated by the frequent use of the word "appropriate" in the criteria, without a specific, tangible definition of what is seen to be "appropriate." This is reflective of a general lack of explicit standards and measures by which to compare many of the questions related to "program need" and "program cost."

One can also raise the question of whether the CSUMB academic program review process had significant "consequences," or "high stakes" attached to it. Wergin and Swingen acknowledge the important fine line between high stakes that might feel coercive, and the importance of real consequences to generate sincere interest and commitment to the process. The fact that the original Program Review Model contained a section on viability is an indication that the original model had significant consequences attached. But, the Program Review Committee was not given the authority to comment on this dimension, so, it could be argued that there was little at stake in the process. On the other hand, given the importance of this review—the first snapshot after the initial five years of development—it can be argued that the consequences were clearly evident to the entire community.

Overall, it is clear that CSUMB's process was fully grounded in the spirit of continuous renewal. This was the first chance for the community to look back on the progress that had been made during the university's first five years, and collectively reflect on what had and had not been accomplished. The Program Review Committee went out of its way to share its learning, and the Academic Leadership Team and the campus community responded enthusiastically. Some of the impacts of this collective reflection are addressed below.

Conclusion: Enhancing Educational Effectiveness Through Academic Degree Program Review

Overall, the academic degree program review process has made a significant contribution to the campus's ability to evaluate the outcomes of its educational model, and to the development of a continuous process of inquiry and engagement to enhance educational effectiveness. To accomplish this task, significant resources were invested to first gather data, and then to have this data reviewed systematically by a committed group of faculty, administrators, and students. The committee saw this process not as an isolated set of academic reviews, but as an opportunity to engage the campus in significant reflection on the state of development of our academic programs, five years after their inception. The committee identified a series of issues that were brought to the attention of the university community, and that served as the source of future program improvement initiatives.

For example, in the discussion document, the committee acknowledged that many of the learning outcomes and assessment procedures were not fully developed (Program Review Committee, p. 18). The development and assessment of learning outcomes then became the focus of a full-day professional development session offered by the Center for Teaching, Learning, and Assessment in December of 2001. This workshop was attended by teams from nearly all academic degree programs. Many departments have done significant work restructuring their major learning outcomes in response to the input received from the program review process, and many have sought support from the center to do so.

In addition, the issue of developing the capacity to collect and analyze evidence of student learning is being discussed at both the department and college level. While universitywide policies and practices have yet to develop, individual departments have begun to address this important issue, as faculty and staff resources are being devoted to the collection and analysis of student learning evidence.

By choosing to create one team to systematically review all twelve degree programs, the campus made the decision to invest resources in the academic program review process. In effect the Program Review Committee became the embodiment of the conscience of the campus, having devoted a significant amount of time to understanding the status of each program, and determining the extent to which each program meets the ideals established in the campus vision, mission, and core values. The investment in this level of review was significant, but resulted in a significant contribution to the overall growth of the campus.

Program review is the ideal time for an institution to connect the dots between the lofty words of its mission statement and the day-to-day operations of its academic departments. To be successful, it must be seen to be fundamentally about learning and growth, and not about external validation and justification. Significant time must be invested in clarifying the goals of the review, and in developing questions and criteria that are pertinent and meaningful to the academic departments. Faculty must not be seen as objects of the review, but as authors of the review, and play key roles in all phases of the process. Faculty must be intimately involved in the establishment of the review criteria, and in the assessment process itself. The decision to invest resources in the program review process will enhance the likelihood that the review becomes a central component of the institution's own process of growth and renewal.

References

American Association for Higher Education. (1992). *Principles of good practice for assessing student learning.* Washington, DC: Author.

Maitland Schilling, K., & Schilling, K. (2000). *Proclaiming and sustaining excellence: Assessment as a faculty role* (ASHE-ERIC Higher Education Report Vol. 26, No. 3). Washington, DC: George Washington University.

Program Review Committee (2001). *CSUMB degree program review discussion document.* Monterey, CA: California State University Monterey Bay.

Wergin, J., & Swingen, J. (January, 1998). *Departmental assessment: How some campuses are effectively evaluating the collective work of faculty.* Paper presented at the American Association for Higher Education Forum on Faculty Roles and Rewards, Washington, DC: AAHE.

PROGRAM REVIEW MODEL, JANUARY 1999

California State University Monterey Bay
Spring, 2000

Degree Program Review

Degree Program: _____

A. Program Quality

1. Program Mission and Goals
   - To what extent does the program clearly articulate how it intends to serve the needs of students, the community, and the broader society?
   - To what extent do the program's mission and goals contribute to the CSUMB Vision Statement?
   - How clearly does the program identify the personal development, employment, and graduate school opportunities that students can expect to gain from the program?
   - Are the mission and goals appropriate, realistic, and achievable?

2. Infusion of CSUMB Core Values
   - To what extent does the program holistically emphasize and integrate the CSUMB academic core values of interdisciplinarity, applied learning, multiculturalism and globalism, technological sophistication, collaboration, ethical reflection and practice, and service learning?

3. Major Learning Outcomes: MLOs
   - Do the MLOs describe learning outcomes in terms of observable and assessable student behaviors?
   - Are the MLOs clear, concise, and unambiguous?
   - Do the MLOs describe complex, higher-order knowledge and skills?

- To what extent does the set of MLOs represent a scope and depth of student learning that are appropriate for a baccalaureate degree?
- To what extent will achievement of the MLOs prepare students for the societal service, employment, and graduate school opportunities articulated by the program?

4. Assessment Protocol for the MLOs
   - How clearly does the assessment protocol stipulate the types of documentation students should or may submit as evidence of learning for each MLO?
   - How clearly does the protocol identify the criteria that will be used to review student work or documentation for each MLO?
   - How clearly does the assessment protocol explain the standards that will be used to rate student work?
   - Overall, to what extent does the protocol represent a valid assessment of student learning related to the MLOs?
   - Does the protocol emphasize consistency between assessors and between assessment venues?

5. Academic Curriculum
   - To what extent does the program's formal curriculum exhibit the breadth and depth commensurate with the expectations for student learning contained in the MLOs?
   - How clearly does the program identify the curricular pathways available to students to fulfill each MLO?
   - Conversely, how clearly does the program identify the roles or functions that each formal course performs related to the MLOs?
   - To what extent does the program provide or allow for students to engage in alternative means for gaining and demonstrating the knowledge and skills contained in the MLOs?

6. Student Learning
   - To what extent are students developing the expected knowledge and skills in the program?
   - To what extent does the program collect and maintain summative evidence of student learning?
   - To what extent does the program collect the type of information to enable it to gauge student growth during the program?
   - Does the program have a plan for using evidence of student learn-

ing as a means of assessing its program effectiveness and improvement?

7. Faculty Composition
   - Does the program's faculty have an appropriate distribution of academic expertise and professional experience to deliver this degree program?
   - Does the program have an appropriate mix of senior and junior faculty?
   - Does the program have an appropriate balance of full-time and part-time faculty?
   - To what extent does the program effectively integrate nonfaculty specialists (e.g., technologists, advisors, field coordinators, assessors, etc.) into the professional team?
   - In what ways does the program faculty reflect CSUMB's commitment to diversity?

8. Current Student Satisfaction
   - What do students view as the strengths of this degree program?
   - What do students view as components of the program that could be improved?

9. Graduates' Success and Satisfaction
   - How much do graduates of the program feel that the program has helped them to achieve their personal and professional goals?
   - To what extent are graduates engaged in relevant and appropriate jobs and/or graduate programs?

10. Quality Improvement Plan
    - To what extent does the program's plan for improvement establish appropriate priorities?
    - To what extent is the quality improvement plan supported by the self-review and other available evidence?

B. Need for Program

   1. Student Need
      - What are the number and proportion of students enrolled in this program?
      - Are student enrollment indicators stable, increasing, or decreasing?

2. University Need
   - To what extent does the program contribute to the university's unique Vision Statement?
   - To what extent does the university depend on the program to carry out its function as a comprehensive state university?
   - How important is the academic substance of this program to the operation of the ULR general education program?
   - To what extent do other degree programs depend on the academic services of this program?

3. Societal Need
   - How well does this program provide a persuasive rationale for society's need for persons with the knowledge, skills, and dispositions developed in this program?
   - Does the program provide credible evidence of a labor market need (job opportunities) for graduates of this type of program?
   - Does the program provide good evidence that the program prepares students to meet admissions standards for particular types of graduate programs?

C. Cost of the Program

1. Program Operating Costs
   - What is the annual cost of operating this program?
   - What is the cost per credit or cost per FTES of operating this program?
   - How do the operating costs of this program compare to other programs?

2. Operational Efficiency
   - Can students complete this degree in an appropriate amount of time?
   - Are full-time and part-time faculty engaged in levels of direct instruction that meet the expectations adopted in the planning and budgeting process?
   - Do course enrollments in this program meet the expectations adopted in the planning process?

D. Summary Observations

PARKING LOT ISSUES

1. Degree programs tend not to frame their goals and missions in terms of the particular student populations that are served by CSUMB.
2. There is not a consistent definition and use of the concept of "institute" across campus.
3. Degree programs typically do not document or support their claims of the employment and graduate school opportunities following from their programs.
4. How much consistency (format, substance, style) should be expected in how programs articulate their MLOs?
5. Should all programs be expected to develop the capacity to provide the option of independent assessment for all MLOs?
6. Most programs do not yet make an effort to systematically assess aggregate student learning apart from the assessment that is conducted by instructors within courses.
7. Is it problematic that some topics (history, statistics, culture, writing) appear to be taught in a number of different degree programs?
8. For one program to have its majors take coursework in another program is an exceptional rather than a common practice.
9. Our degree programs tend to be built on academic foci and values that are strong, sharp, and nontraditional. How can or should our degree programs accommodate students whose needs and interests are outside these foci?
10. It appears that most programs have part-time faculty teaching critical courses within the major.
11. Is it problematic that HCOM and Liberal Studies appear to offer two "liberal arts" degree options on this small campus?
12. Who on campus should track degree program graduates, and how?
13. In the future, how should external reviewers be selected? Does this constitute a potential conflict of interest? What to do about the fact that some reviewers had trouble understanding our values, language, and OBE model?
14. For Service Learning, we should cost out the "decentralized" model be-

cause this seems to have been central to successful and applied SL in the majors.

15. There appears to be lack of consistent understanding between Interdisciplinary and Multidisciplinary.

16. How can we capture (document and analyze) the richness of Capstone projects as one dimension of program evaluation?

17. How can the programs learn from each other, building on the strengths of each and identifying crosscutting functions that would help us be more efficient?

18. Do we expect that each "core value" will be evident to the same extent in each degree program? Do we "do it all," or is it okay to just do some of the core values?

19. How can we build the "distributed learning" capacity in our own degree programs before we launch into "distance learning?"

20. Is the expectation that programs collect data on "summative" and "in-process" student learning a realistic goal? What resources are required to achieve it?

21. Some programs link individual courses to MLOs, while others evaluate MLOs together in a portfolio at the end of the program. It is okay to have these two approaches? What are the advantages and disadvantages of each?

6

MULTILAYERED INQUIRY FOR PROGRAM REVIEWS
Methods and Analysis for Campuswide Implications

Annette March

If assessment is a means to an end, the values that define that end must be in harmony with the highest values of higher education. Assessment must call us to the best in ourselves, just as we call for the best in each of our students.

—Marcia Mentkowski, *Learning That Lasts*

I undertook a comprehensive assessment of the writing support program at California State University Monterey Bay because I care deeply about student learning. Because there is now widespread agreement among those who study and practice assessment that "improving student learning is the primary goal of assessment" (Angelo, 2002, p. 188), I considered the assessment as a means to that end. My approach follows in spirit a nationally accepted definition of assessment as "the process of collecting, reviewing, and *using* information about academic programs in order to *improve student learning* [italics added]" (Palomba & Banta, 1999, p. 297).

Rationale for Inquiry

A strong institutional mission statement can help focus an assessment more clearly on institutional values as well on as student learning (Banta, Lund, Black, & Oblander, 1996). As our readers are well aware, CSUMB's Vision Statement is a guiding principle for our campus. The vision pointedly states that we will serve "the diverse people of California, especially the working class and historically undereducated and low-income populations." At the time I undertook the project in 1999, widespread agreement within the institution had marked the writing support program as an especially critical component for student success for most of the student populations we serve. Nationwide, solid writing support programs are essential to strengthening students' ability to undertake and perform academic writing, a skill underlying students' success in all classes across the curriculum. In CSUMB's 1999 student population, over 50% of entering freshmen and transfers scored below college level in writing and only 40% of Hispanic students were retained through the third year. Although these testing and retention figures are typical of many institutions, I recognized the need to determine whether the strength of the writing support program aligned with the strength of the university's Vision to effectively serve our underrepresented student population.

The program had grown substantially during its first three years of operation, indicating that it was providing increasing writing support for some students. But, the anecdotal evidence was ambiguous; I had tacit knowledge that the program was serving some parts of our student population less well than others. I knew that some students, faculty, staff, and administrators across campus perceived the program as ineffective writing support for some students. Typically, institutions are willing to rely upon this kind of anecdotal data, but I wanted to provide more substantial evidence about the program's effectiveness. Because the program had been necessarily engaged in intensive "start up" during the first three years, the staff, resources, expertise, and interest had not been available for an effectiveness assessment of the program. Although the program had been collecting some data, it had done so only sporadically. I hoped that my comprehensive assessment could highlight the program's strengths and weaknesses, as well as lay the groundwork for ongoing assessment practices for this program critical for student achievement.

Because the writing support program was so central to student success on our campus, as it is at most others, it seemed important to conduct a comprehensive inquiry-based assessment that deeply probed the multiple layers that composed programmatic support, not just within the program itself, but also the multiple levels of decision makers involved in the program and who ultimately contribute to its effectiveness.

This project was conceived by the director of the Center for Teaching, Learning, and Assessment (TLA), who asked me to undertake it. In my own dual role as faculty associate in the center and as a faculty member with extensive experience in teaching writing-intensive courses linked to the writing support program, I had some previous experience conducting assessment as well as participant experience and some knowledge of the writing support program before I began this project. My fifteen years of experience and scholarship in composition and rhetoric provided me with the disciplinary base to approach the program review of the writing support program. And, my own commitment to our Vision to serve underrepresented, diverse, working-class, historically undereducated, and low-income students was a strong impetus for me during this assessment process.

However, I had never undertaken individually an assessment project of this scope or depth. At some stages, I was daunted by the enormity of the project I had undertaken. The assessment progressed over the course of an academic year and through the summer. It was a highly rewarding project, but also a very labor-intensive one. To have followed best practices in assessment, I know in hindsight, this project should have been carried out collaboratively in order to take advantage of the benefits that collaborative work in program assessment has to offer; national assessment leaders agree that collaboration in program assessment by a variety of decision-making stakeholders results in the most effective assessments (Allen, 2004; Banta et al., 1996; Banta et al., 2002; Maki, 2004; Mentkowski & Loacker, 2002). However, at this time, when the university was still undergoing "start up" and accreditation was imminent, faculty, staff, and administrators were already heavily engaged in other projects and none were free to undertake new ones. Therefore, I agreed to conduct the assessment by myself. Although the work was invigorating and absorbing, both the process and the product would have benefited from some of the kinds of collaboration I will suggest here.

Resources for Inquiry

Assessment is always time consuming and costly, even in limited approaches. Eventually, the writing support program would undergo a traditional program review as described in chapter 5. However, in 1999, with accreditation in view, a comprehensive review was needed. Resources earmarked specifically for assessment accelerated and expanded the possibilities of a comprehensive assessment of the writing support program, a critically important element in our mission and Vision.

Because the project's workload was indeed a heavy one, I was fortunate that the resources supporting me were considerable. To offset the labor-intensive nature of the project, the Center for Teaching, Learning, and

Assessment provided me with indirect teaching units for two semesters and with a student research assistant. And, importantly, the director of TLA provided rich support and encouragement from the project's inception through every stage of the process. Although specific budgetary amounts may not be useful, it is important to note that work on this assessment, if done by one individual, requires the equivalent of a half-time faculty appointment for one academic year. A qualified assessor will require expertise in application of research methodologies, interviewing, focus group facilitation, and literature review in the appropriate discipline(s), all of which have budgetary implications. As Allen reminds us, "Assessment takes time and support. It does not come for free, and administrators may have to provide start-up funds or incentives to move forward, as well as support for ongoing assessment activities" (2004, p. 17).

Decisions for Inquiry

In order to make full use of the investments in the assessment, I intended for the project to produce as much evidence as possible about support for student learning in writing. I wanted to find concrete evidence about what was working in the writing support program and what was not. My overarching question, therefore, was a broad one: I wanted to know how the program was providing effective support for *all* students' academic success, a goal implied by our institutional Vision. I wanted to identify direct student learning, identify the program's good practices and areas in need of strengthening, describe campuswide perceptions about the program, and present relevant findings and recommendations to multiple stakeholders throughout the campus.

To answer these questions, I decided on an approach not usually used in reviews of writing support programs. Typically, quantitative, not qualitative, data about writing support programs are gathered, and the program is reviewed summarily by an internal committee or by external reviewers during a brief site visit. But very little is usually done to assess all the components that affect student learning, including the program and its curriculum, and the perspectives of students, faculty, staff, administrators, and the program's campus context. The largely qualitative assessment I designed was multilayered, using multiple methods and integrating multiple perspectives of various stakeholders. This approach blended a variety of assessment techniques gathered from best practices in qualitative program review with ethnographic methodology and several quantitative methods.

Various models for effective program review that improve student learning have been proposed by the leaders in the assessment field (Allen, 2004; Astin, 1991; Conrad & Wilson, 1985; Ewell, 1994; Huba & Freed, 2000; Maki, 2004; Mentkowski, 2000; Palomba & Banta, 1999). My assessment contained features of the models outlined by these assessment scholars (most of them not found in traditional program review). These included the following:

- Assessing for student learning
- Linking data collection efforts to campus-shared goals and issues
- Assessing with the goal of affecting campus decision making about the program
- Assessing the program in the campuswide context

Unique to my assessment were some additional features:

- It probed deeply using ethnographic methodology, a strategy that influenced all facets of the assessment and produced especially rich results.
- It also took a multilayered approach in data collection and analysis, considering all campus constituencies connected with the program so that meaningful recommendations could be addressed to each constituency.

Using multilayered strategies allowed me to construct a full picture of the program and its context, an outcome not often achieved in traditional program review.

In order to produce this evidence, I designed the methodology carefully so that the report could provide recommendations closely linked to decision making about the program at all levels—students served by the program, student tutors within the program, program administrators, faculty, and other stakeholding administrators. If the report was to be effective to "impact courses, curriculum, and the institution" (Allen, 2004, p. 55), then I wanted to be able to specifically address recommendations to all the stakeholders involved in decision making at all these levels. Although most program reviews occur in isolation, focusing only on the program itself, current assessment scholars agree (Allen, 2004; Mentkowski, 1991, 2000; Serow, 1998) that improved student learning should be the ultimate goal of program review. And, improved student learning can only result from assessments that influence decision making campuswide. I wanted the writing support program assessment to have the potential for strengthening the program and realigning it more solidly with CSUMB's institutional Vision.

Implementing a Multilayered Inquiry: Planning and Design

A comprehensive assessment such as this one is called for when it becomes evident that a critical program needs immediate attention to increase effectiveness or to prepare for accreditation. Comprehensive assessment may also be used when a traditional program review of a critical program, like a writing support program or other crucial student programs, cannot sufficiently investigate the multiple levels of decision makers involved in the program who ultimately contribute to the program's effectiveness. Streamlining the process for specific programmatic needs is addressed later in this chapter. Such an assessment process can originate within the program itself or from an executive council.

My experience conducting this assessment through all of its stages has led me, with some hindsight, to be able to offer steps for implementing a multilayered assessment that can have campuswide implications.

Design of methods is ultimately influenced by the scope, focus, and purpose of each assessment project. And, of course, assessors will select strategies they find most compatible for themselves. However, thinking through a detailed plan and design before data collection begins is essential. Fundamentally, any assessment plan should explain "who is going to do what, when they will do it, and how they will use the information that is generated" (Palomba & Banta, 1999, p. 46). However, before these can be determined, some preliminary research needs to be conducted.

Collecting Preliminary Research Data to Inform Assessment Design

Although not often used in traditional program review, preliminary research, including a review of relevant literature, is crucial information gathering in order to establish the most precise overarching questions and subquestions. Before I designed my assessment, I needed to further familiarize myself with the program, so I conducted a preliminary inquiry, asking questions of the program director, the writing director, writing faculty, and the director of teaching, learning, and assessment. I read program curricula and other materials and observed the program's setting. I also conducted a review of current literature in several related areas in order to further clarify for myself the significant issues that have emerged in the fields of remediation in higher education, writing center history, theory, and practice; literacy theories; mainstreaming in higher education; and diversity theories in composition and rhetoric. Once I was more familiar with the program itself, the concerns and perspectives of some of the major stakeholders, and the context of the scholarship about writing programs, I was ready to design the assessment questions.

Constructing an Inquiry Focused on Institutional Goals and Outcomes

"Good research includes asking good questions, and good research questions are both interesting and important; important questions are those linked to the institution's missions, goals, and objectives" (Pike, 2002, p. 132). In the writing program assessment, the most important question was clear: how effectively was the Vision Statement being implemented in the program? This inquiry was embedded in the assessment's overarching questions, which were kept intentionally simple and direct: In what ways is the program effective? In what ways can it become more effective? These questions assessed congruency between the program's intentions and its actual practices as well as probed the contingency factors affecting the program's ability to achieve its outcomes. The preliminary research provided information from which to construct specific subquestions, and in these were embedded inquiries about the program's fulfillment of the university Vision, such as: How accessible is the program to diverse campus populations? Does the program provide a sequential and developmental program that meets the students at their skill levels? What kinds of interactions occur between faculty and program staff? What role does the program play in the writing culture across the campus? With clearly designed questions, I was then able to begin to select the methodology and to identify the stakeholders.

Designing the Inquiry to Systematically Examine Multiple Forms of Data from Multiple Stakeholders

In order for the assessment to have an impact on multilevels in institutional decision making, the assessment design should have a campuswide scope, unlike most approaches that focus only on the program under inquiry. Whatever the size or focus of the plan, careful design for multiple methods to include multiple audiences should not be compromised. As Palomba and Banta (1999) remind us, "there are multiple views of reality requiring educators to examine diverse opinions and perspectives" (p. 338). It is this characteristic of the assessment that can assure the sharpest reliability and validity and can give the instrument its widest campuswide impact.

In the writing program assessment, it was already evident that the program was deeply interconnected with campuswide policies and other programs, so I focused not only on the program itself, but also on the spectrum of stakeholders campuswide who had interests in the program and its outcomes, including students, tutors, staff, faculty, and administrators. This strategy allowed me to capture institution-wide perceptions about the way the program's goals and objectives were operative in the university Vision. It also prompted me to expand my initial notion of the program's stakeholders.

Selecting Stakeholders for Interviews Who Represent All Campus Constituencies Connected to the Program

Stakeholders should be strategically identified and selected, and, of course, campus politics within the institution often influences the identification and selection of subjects from the various campus communities. So, choices of respondents to interview and settings and events to observe should be selected carefully in consultation with colleagues from varying perspectives in order to verify the most appropriate selections.

During the process of selecting the stakeholders for interviews in my assessment, I continued to expand my list of stakeholders during data collection, especially staff, administrators, and cross-campus faculty, when it became apparent that additional stakeholders were essential links in the writing support program.

Using Varied Empirical Data Methods to Provide Triangulation

An assessment design that intentionally focuses on institutional goals and objectives and asks the right, specific questions of multiple stakeholders needs careful planning for triangulation of methodology. Triangulation, a method that brings more than one source of data to bear on a single point, can verify, expand, or illuminate the research question in important ways not otherwise obtained (Marshall & Rossman, 1995, p. 144). I knew that in this multilevel assessment, relationships among all the stakeholders would result in a wide variety of complex responses to the program. So, use of triangulation of multiple measures was key in capturing the various perspectives within and across these communities. Therefore, I designed a variety of empirical data collection methods, both direct and indirect, which would allow me to use triangulation during analysis. These included interview protocols, focus groups, questionnaires, surveys, and a review of the literature, a review of relevant documents and of selected relevant quantitative data from other research and assessment projects within the university. Many of these data collection methods were labor intensive and contributed significantly to the time commitment required by the assessment. However, these multiple methods of data collecting ensure better veracity and completeness in the findings and avoid subjectivity. For instance, to answer a question about program and faculty interaction, faculty were asked in interviews, "What kinds of contacts have you had with the program?" while program staff and tutors were asked, "What kinds of contacts have you had with faculty and their courses?" and administrators were asked, "What are your perceptions about the links between the program, the faculty, and the curriculum?" To provide further triangulation within these findings, statistical data about faculty and program contacts were obtained from the program while a review of the literature supplied me with best practices in faculty/program interaction.

Using Ethnographic Techniques to Contextualize the Assessment Data

Ethnography is particularly appealing for its ability to illuminate a holistic picture of a culture—or of a campus program. Gardner found that when used in assessment, ethnography can increase the instrument's ability to describe "a forest, rather than [just] trees" (as cited in Allen, 2004, p. 52). Ethnographic "thick description" generated from ethnographic data can produce "snapshots" of the program and its surrounding stakeholder communities. These descriptions can richly contextualize other found data to construct a full picture of the program being assessed.

As Palomba and Banta point out, ethnographic techniques can build in flexibility so that "the unintended and accidental effects of a program, as well as the intended effects" can be discovered (1999, p. 338). While collecting data in interviews, I encountered a number of "accidental" effects of the writing support program. For instance, although the program's goals and intentions were to support student writing in a holistic way, widespread campus perception about the program was that its goal was to improve students' grammar. This finding later proved very significant when I composed the recommendations.

In order to apply ethnographic methodology more precisely in assessing a learning environment, I found that Alexander Astin's I-E-O (input, environment, output) model (1991) gave me a useful framework. Astin suggests that the goals, objectives, or outcomes (or "outputs") being assessed for effectiveness should be evaluated in terms of both "input" and "environment." In my project, for instance, I envisioned the students' environment as widening concentric circles. At the center was the student working with a tutor in a writing tutorial at the center, surrounded by gradually larger circles including the tutorial physical classroom; the program office as a whole; the student's classroom learning environment in the course linked to the tutorial program; the departments, committees, and administrative policies that oversaw the learning; and the wider, and more elusive, culture of writing on the campus as a whole. In order to gather data about all aspects of this institutional environment, I needed to understand students' actual experience with these various environments. Gathering the data requires focus not only on the student herself, but also on each of the "circles" that compose the entire campus learning environment.

Implementing a Multilayered Inquiry: Collecting the Data

Data collection is one of the most labor-intensive aspects of qualitative assessment, but it also can be one of the most invigorating. As a picture begins to emerge from the rich data, the complex interrelation of the constituencies begins to point to clear findings. During this process in my assessment, for instance, I was surprised to discover unforeseen faculty attitudes and perceptions about the program. Seeing this data emerge next to the interview data gathered from administrators and students presented an especially sharp snapshot of the complexity with which the program was viewed across campus.

Using Interviews to Probe Deeply

Interviewing is the most time-consuming kind of data to collect and to analyze, but it is also the most direct and reliable way to assess perceptions about effectiveness. However, it is important to ensure that the "right questions [are asked] of the right individuals" (Palomba & Banta, 1999, p. 185). To accomplish this alignment of questions and stakeholders, designing interview protocols for each group is key. These specific protocols will allow for refined data that distinguish all the perspectives among the various stakeholders (see figures 6-1 and 6-2).

Using both structured and open-ended sets of interview questions will build in flexibility so that ideas emerging during interviews can be pursued further. To collect a representative sample in my assessment, I conducted 47 one-hour, in-depth interviews with writing tutors (both peer tutors and

FIGURE 6-1
Interview Protocol—Students

Students who have participated in ASAP services

1. How did you first hear of ASAP?
2. Why did you first decide to go to ASAP?
3. What had you heard about ASAP before you went?
4. What did you expect to get from ASAP before you went?
5. Did your feelings about ASAP change after you went the first time, the second, and so on?
6. Did your overall experience meet your expectations?
7. Tell me about your level of satisfaction with your experience at ASAP.
8. If you had your own ideal tutor, what characteristics would she/he have?
9. How did you feel about your writing before you went to ASAP?
10. How did you feel about the outcome(s) of your paper(s) after working with a tutor at ASAP?
11. Has working with a tutor at ASAP changed your writing in any way? Has it changed your thinking about writing in any way?
12. Do you ever ask your professor questions about writing papers?
13. Are you involved in any other support services on campus?

Students who have not participated in ASAP services

1. Where did you first hear of ASAP?
2. Have you ever been required to go to ASAP?
3. Has anyone ever recommended that you go?
4. Have you ever thought about going?
5. Do you think there is room for improvement in your writing skills?
6. Do you think that ASAP would benefit or not benefit your writing ability?
7. What is your impression of the ASAP program?
8. What, if anything, prevents you from using ASAP?

professional tutors) in the program, with writing faculty and nonwriting faculty, and with program directors and other administrators. A tailored set of questions was designed for each group, but consistently aligned by theme across the stakeholders. During these interviews, I also collected data from each subject in a short questionnaire. E-mails proved to be an important method for further observation and data collection, as staff and administrators answered numerous questions in countless e-mails during the research process.

FIGURE 6-2
Interview Protocol—Cross-Campus Faculty

---

1. What do you understand to be the purpose of ASAP? Where did you get this information?
2. Do you understand the way the writing support program is structured at CSUMB?
3. Do students in your classes use ASAP?
4. How do they get there? Do you refer them?
5. If you refer students, what factors help you decide whether or not to refer a student to ASAP?
6. What do you tell your students about ASAP, if anything?
7. What percent of the students whom you think probably need ASAP actually go for tutoring? How do you know this?
8. What have you heard from students about how they feel about their ASAP groups? About the one-to-one tutoring sessions they have had?
9. What kind of communication do you have with ASAP (tutors, program director, the front desk) during the time you are teaching your course?
10. What kinds of contact does/has ASAP made with you?
11. What do you think of the tutors who run the groups?
12. What is your understanding of the approach to tutoring taken by the ASAP writing tutors?
13. What's your understanding of what goes on in the groups?
14. Are ASAP groups effective for your students? How do you tell?
15. Do you think that CSUMB has a "writing culture"?
16. What do you see as the role of ASAP in the writing culture across the university, as ASAP now exists?
17. Do you think ASAP is successful? How would you define "successful" here?
18. What do you think about remediation?

Focus groups can address a number of topics among a variety of stakeholders and can offer insights to the researcher that other methods may not reveal (Palomba & Banta, 1999). In the focus groups I conducted, I prepared questions, with predetermined objectives, and kept these in mind while allowing for free-flowing discussion among the participants. Data gathered here provided me with new and unexpected insights, which led to the construction of additional or more specific questions. For instance, I discovered in the focus groups that there were differing perceptions about the quality and extent of tutor training in the program. So, a new question probing this perception was added to the faculty interview protocols. Although traditional focus groups require a skillful facilitator (Allen, 2004, p. 119), they can also reveal the unusual or serendipitous—the unlooked for but often useful data that can enrich the fund of data being collected. These insights can then be refined by further inquiry.

Using Ethnographic Methodology to Probe Deeply for Program Effectiveness

In order to capture both the learning environment and the campuswide setting, I used ethnographic methodology to conduct a variety of strategically selected observations. I collected "thick description" in my role as observer and sometimes as observer-participant, staying open to the unexpected insights this method often uncovers. I observed the program's setting in a variety of ways, such as the tutoring in the building on various days of the week and at different times of day and evenings. The program's larger campus context was observed in several carefully chosen administrative/staff meetings, faculty department meetings, and university program meetings. These observations provided ample data to capture snapshots of the learning environment and the program's campuswide context.

Using this methodology allowed me to experience the program as much as possible from the inside, in its daily workings, rather than just as a distant bystander looking at recorded data. Only by knowing the program as intimately as possible was I able to understand and analyze stakeholders' perceptions and to accrue a fuller picture of the program and its effectiveness.

Using Direct and Quantitative Methods to Triangulate Indirect Qualitative Methods

To gain depth and breadth in the assessment, combine the indirect qualitative methods like those described above with direct and qualitative methods. In my assessment, entrance and exit surveys of students served by the program's group and individual tutorials were used to assess students' learning, satisfaction, and persistence to completion. Written documents and Web sites held important background history and information about the program and its curriculum, reviews of related programs, and evidence of campus policies. I also made use of quantitative data that already existed, for example, retention analysis data (provided by the director of institutional assessment and research); statistical data collected by the program; student scores for entrance and exit standardized writing examinations (obtained from the writing director); and government guidelines and mandates from Web sites.

Practicing a Recursive Collection Process

Assessment is a dynamic and recursive process. Anticipating recursive measures when new or refined data appear requires thinking about the design as flexible at both the planning and data collection stages. I used a recursive practice often during design, data collecting, and analysis. The flexibility built into the multiple qualitative and ethnographic methodologies allowed me to revisit the original assessment questions and interview protocols for refinement or revision. Subquestions sometimes became more specific as the assessment progressed. For example, in the interview protocol for cross-campus faculty whose courses do not require writing tutorials, I originally asked these faculty where they first learned about the writing support program. When I discovered that none of them had ever been contacted and given direct information about the program, I added the more specific questions, "What do you understand to be the purpose of the program?" "Where did you get this information?" and "What kinds of contact has the program made with you?"

I was also able to use the recursive process to add further focus or pursue a new line of inquiry when I noted a gap in the data. Using this inquiry loop, I was able to frequently check whether the data were illuminating the overarching questions to ensure the most reliable empirical evidence. For instance, three months into the research, it became clear that to ensure completeness of the data on effectiveness, I needed to assess not only students' learning in the tutorials, but also their persistence and satisfaction with the tutorials. So, student participant entrance and exit surveys were added the next semester in order to fill this data gap. Since I had conducted preliminary analysis during the last stages of research and throughout the data collection, I could begin to identify themes and still modify the design where needed. The categories that had suggested themselves during the preliminary research and design stages were subsequently all useful ones.

Practicing a recursive process means that when a measure is unworkable, it can be omitted and a new one put into place. Or, when unforeseen data emerge, a new strategy can be constructed to explore the new avenue. It is a good idea to do occasional preliminary analysis during data collection to check that the measures are uncovering all the information needed to answer the research question. During preliminary analysis in my data collection process, I discovered that I needed several more quantitative measures than I had originally planned for. So, I gathered further retention analysis data from our institutional research director and also added more quantitative measures to the student questionnaire.

Although traditional program review does not often use these recursive methods borrowed from ethnographic methodology, this practice sharply refines the assessment instruments to produce the most unambiguous results.

Implementing a Multilayered Inquiry: Analyzing Data

The various methodologies selected in an assessment will often suggest the techniques most effective for data analysis. The process of analysis is a process of "making sense of the data" (Allen, 2004, p. 131), and important insights that lead to crucial results and recommendations are formed during this process. The guidelines suggested here are ones that allowed me during analysis to keep improvement of student learning as the focus of my assessment.

Applying Simple and Direct Techniques

Effective data analysis techniques need to be "simple, direct, and effective" (Allen, 2004, p. 131). An initial summary can reduce the masses of data considerably. My first attempts at data analysis revealed a great deal of ambiguity within the complex information. Yet, careful application of the data analysis techniques led to quickly emerging patterns, bringing order and structure, as well as meaning, to the raw data. While analyzing the interviews, I searched for patterns, both overt and subtle, began to make lists, formulated categories, and noted relationships within or among categories. I constantly evaluated the data, continuing to use a recursive process, to make sure it contained adequate information, that it was credible and useful, and that it was central to the questions I was asking (Marshall & Rossman, 1995, p. 116). A graphic recording scheme was key in managing the complex and rich, raw data from the many perspectives and stakeholders, to see the emerging patterns, and to check for internal consistency and gaps in the data.

Two strategies to simplify complex data that proved useful to me were to employ coding methods and to establish categories of data early on in the analysis. As I began to analyze the raw data from the interviews, for instance, I numbered responses within each interview to match the questions in my research design. In a second level of analysis, I sorted and coded responses to each of the questions by stakeholder and then by perspectives within stakeholder positions. Both these strategies were essential steps for reducing ambiguity and making precise meaning of the data. Categories could also be sorted by theme or issue or by other organizational strategies suggested by initial readings of the raw data.

Applying Triangulation to Cross-Check Reliability of Emerging Findings

Analysis will quickly begin to reveal relationships among sets of data when triangulation is employed. In this way, findings from each data set can be verified. In my process, for instance, observer/participant ethnographic data from tutorials, meetings, and setting observations was cross-checked against student interview data and quantitative data about student persistence and completion rates in the program. Then these were set alongside administrator, faculty, and program staff interview data. When multiple data forms began to lead to matching conclusions, I could verify the reliability of the data. A picture finally emerged of the multiple perspectives among the multiple stakeholders, which was then triangulated with surveys, questionnaires, and quantitative data to verify the findings.

Triangulation can also uncover further patterns and can be used to cross-check facts and "hunches." By no means a linear process, triangulation applied stringently will soon begin to build a grounded analysis.

Returning to the Literature During the Research Stage to Pursue New Lines of Inquiry

If a review of the literature is carried out at all in most program reviews, it is conducted during the preliminary planning stage only. However, returning to the literature to pursue new questions or to refine previous findings is in part what assessment leaders mean when they refer to "scholarly assessment," which leads to scholarly products (Mentkowski & Loacker, 2002, p. 87).

Although I had made a preliminary review of the literature before designing the assessment, I continued this review for the duration of the research. Often, newly discovered data led me to pursue new lines of inquiry in the literature. For instance, early in the research, it became clear that writing remediation, in both the campus and national contexts, was a necessary theme to revisit in the literature to better understand in context some of the barriers faced by the program. I knew I would be able to fold this new information into the report when contextualizing the program's approaches and effectiveness.

Implementing a Multilayered Inquiry: Writing the Report

When it is effectively communicated to audiences, a good assessment report can answer key questions about a program, suggest changes or improvement, and lead to increased student learning. In order for a written report to have the impact to "prove and improve" (Mentkowski, 2000, p. 353), it must (1) be accessible to the various audiences, (2) speak to the interests of the various audiences, and (3) be specific in recommendations to specific stakeholders.

Like any effective communication, it must attend first to purpose and to audience to ensure accessibility. Decisions about the format of the written report need to be made in combination with the decisions about dissemination methods, so that specific audiences can be explicitly identified and the report tailored for each audience.

Recording the Comprehensive Assessment in a Comprehensive Report

A comprehensive written report can capture a complete picture of a program to share with key stakeholders, while other concerned audiences receive variations excerpted from the whole report. A comprehensive report might prove to be a useful future written record for the program or the campus in a number of expected or unexpected ways. The one I wrote, which included the history and context of the program, as well as a snapshot of the program at a specific point in time, may prove useful on my campus as a detailed written record for future accreditation or other reviews.

My comprehensive report contextualized the subject of the assessment and reported findings, results, and recommendations/action steps. Because the comprehensive report would address various campus audiences of various campus communities and individuals, it was important to provide a way for audiences who were unfamiliar with the discipline and its practices to contextualize the assessment information. I included a description and history of the program and its curriculum, a summary of national writing center theory and praxis and the issues commonly faced nationally by writing programs, and an overview of remediation and open admission in the national context.

Reporting the Results in a Consistent and Clear Manner

Results of a multilayered assessment need to be reported concisely for easy audience access. It is important not to overwhelm audiences with too much information in the comprehensive report. At the same time, "if we build meaning into [reports] . . . the results matter to educators and administrators who are in a position to use the information to improve teaching and learning" (Mentkowski, 1991, p. 256). Building meaning by providing description, context, and selected quotations or composite voices of respondents can powerfully illuminate the findings and help audiences make important connections between the assessment information and their own interests.

I used ethnographic reporting techniques so that participants' own voices could be heard. I synthesized these voices into composite speakers; subjects were never directly quoted and privacy and confidentiality of respondents was preserved. Each finding presented a synthesis of student, faculty, program, and administrator perspectives about the question. Synthesizing the responses in composite speakers allowed for accurately reporting the perspective of that particular group about that particular theme. At the end of each of these sections, I included a percentage response and a summary of the characteristics of the sample for each group of stakeholders.

Emphasizing Alignment of the Data, Results, and Recommendations

Audiences should be able to see the way that each recommendation is clearly an outcome of the results of the assessment—based on the data. If the data is carefully sorted by stakeholders during analysis, it is a relatively simple process to create alignment among the data, results, and recommendations, thereby illustrating the internal consistency in the data analysis categories. In my report, each recommendation was explained in a paragraph or so to link the results to that particular recommendation. Each recommendation suggested a way for the campus to reach our goals for our Vision students—the working class, historically undereducated, and low-income students to which our campus is especially committed—and to institutionalize best practices in the teaching and learning of writing.

Linking Recommendations to Each Decision-Making Stakeholder

When using multilayered assessment of multiple stakeholders, it follows that the recommendations themselves should be addressed to specific groups of stakeholders who hold decision-making power to implement the recommendations. Information about findings should very clearly delineate between and among stakeholders, as well as the various perspectives within stakeholder positions. Careful attention should be given to linking the recommendations to the findings and results. Recommendations written as realistic action steps, divided into short and long term, with timelines provided, are an effective encouragement to stakeholders to take up action.

In my report, there were a number of recommendations for each group. So, I further organized each set into short-term and long-term action steps.

Each set of action steps was tailored specifically for each audience at the program, curricular, and policy levels and pointed to direct actions each group could take to address that particular recommendation. For instance, general recommendation: institute a four-unit tutor training course. Program level: strengthen tutor training by requiring tutors to take a four-unit tutoring course. Curriculum level (external programs linked to writing): work with the program on curricular issues involved in establishing a four-unit tutor-training course. Policy level (administrative committees): identify departments to offer a four-unit writing tutor course that emphasizes an assets-based and multicultural tutorial model.

Tailoring a Report Format That Fits the Assessments' Intentions and Audiences

The report format I used worked well for my purposes, but other approaches to the written report can also be employed (Palomba & Banta, 1999, pp. 318–322):

- Theme reports (about a particular issue in the assessment)
- Institutional report cards or other summaries (e.g., combining assessment results with other campus-gathered data)
- Overview reports of results about selected goals or outcomes
- Reports tailored for specific audiences, excerpts for colleges or departments with relevant findings
- Oral reports (informal sessions like brown bag lunches, or poster sessions or open forums), faculty and staff newsletters, student newspapers
- Flyers and brochures
- Formal presentations
- The Web

Implementing a Multilayered Inquiry: Dissemination

Disseminating Widely and Strategically Across Campus

Assessment experts emphasize the need for wide and strategic dissemination of the information gained, viewing this stage as the final step in the assessment process. This step is one that is often neglected during the process. Typically, program assessment is not much valued or of much interest to either faculty or other stakeholders who are not directly addressed in the assessment. Reports are often read only by a few administrators. As Wergin (2003) observes about a typical program review, "When it's over, the final report disappears into the bowels of the administration and nothing much changes" (p. 27).

Yet, as Palomba and Banta note, "much of the value of assessment comes from the systematic way it makes educators question, discuss, share, and observe" (1999, p. 298). If assessment is seen as an integral part of a learner-centered university, then the findings have strong potential to affect changes in pedagogies, curriculum, and policy (Allen, 2004, p. 14). Lopez found that "failure to integrate assessment into campus-wide decision-making" is one of the main reasons why assessments often do not stimulate action and change (as cited in Allen, 2004, p. 161).

"Assessment information is of little use if it is not shared with *appropriate audiences* and used in *meaningful ways* [italics added]" (Palomba & Banta, 1999, p. 297). Because my assessment was a large undertaking with a considerable expenditure of time and resources, I wanted to ensure campus-wide attention to the findings and recommendations. A variety of strategies were used to disseminate the information to the relevant stakeholders to ensure the widest circulation of the report. Dissemination of the report was done incrementally. The program received the report first, and the report and its recommendations were discussed individually with the program director, who, as the key stakeholder, had the first opportunity to examine them. Then the program's staff received the report. A summary of the findings, their implications, and the action steps were next presented to the governing campus administrative body and to relevant program and policy committees over the course of a month. Written copies were also provided to interested faculty at this point. Discussion of the results and recommended action steps gave each group of stakeholders the opportunity to determine the implications for change and to consider the recommended strategies for implementing them. In this way, the assessment inquiry had the potential to become institutionalized through the campuswide relevant channels of support.

Tailoring Various Venues for Opportunities to Interact About the Information

Since the goal of program assessment is ultimately to improve student learning, finding ways for the stakeholders to engage with the information of the report should be carefully considered. Mentkowski (1991) advocates strategies that allow interaction and reflection among the stakeholders: "Interactive processes create a context where people can respond to each other, connect with each other's interests, work out emerging concerns, and begin to construct meaningful action. . . . They thus begin to collaboratively take responsibility for the assessment information and recommendations" (p. 262).

To build meaning into both written and oral reports, findings and results can be illustrated through some visual means, such as graphs, grids, pie charts, spreadsheets, diagrams, tables, or maps. Audio aids can be combined with means for visualization with effective results. Mentkowski (1991) describes a presentation using "slide-tapes"—audio student voices and student photographs—in order to create interest and impact for a faculty audience she wanted to motivate to apply assessment results on a particular aspect of student learning (p. 272). She suggests that "aggregate data can be valuable if we make the link between it and the individual data" and that audiences "are motivated to help students improve by listening to them, one at a time" (p. 272).

Implementing a Multilayered Inquiry: Closing the Loop

Aiming for Appropriate Changes from Assessment Results

Assessment results from program reviews are often ignored, shelved, or acted upon minimally by the program and the institution. For the results to have impact, to "close the loop" between assessment and student learning, the assessment needs to result in "appropriate changes to what is being assessed" (Allen, 2004, p. 169).

An assessment is optimally effective when it is part of a program's long-term assessment plan. Writing specific recommendations into the report for follow-up or next-step assessments can encourage programs to begin to view and use assessment as an ongoing cycle rather than a one-time (often mandated) effort.

Our campus has responded at multiple levels to the specific recommendations in the report in a twofold, ongoing process. In general, closing the loop in the program assessment cycle has benefited students through improved writing support. In the writing support program, seven of the eight major recommendations and many of the action steps have been implemented. For instance, responding to a recommendation in the report to "establish and maintain a sustained method for assessment of student learning," the program coordinator implemented annual data collection and assessment of student progress in writing as a result of students' involvement in the program and conducted a series of other qualitative assessments. In addition, curricular and pedagogical improvements still continue to be made within the program, including revision of the tutorial curriculum, another recommendation made by the report.

Outside the program, faculty capacity to support writing literacy has been somewhat strengthened, although the absence of a writing director for three years has deterred faculty development. However, following the year of the report's publication, broad campus awareness was directed at writing literacy through a two-day campuswide literacy focus funded by the provost, among others. During the same year, the Center for Teaching, Learning, and Assessment focused faculty development efforts on the teaching and learning of student literacy. The urgency of student needs for writing support prompted the provost to form a writing program task force composed of campuswide stakeholders who produced a collaborative report for the provost, leading ultimately to the hiring of a new writing director.

Considering Assessment a Transformative Cycle

This step will raise more questions than the answers offered in the assessment (Mentkowski, 2000, p. 343). New questions can be a beneficial outcome of the assessment, highlighting areas for future change and suggesting future directions for program and campuswide attention. On our campus, one way the process is being kept alive is by the ongoing work of the English Communication University Learning Requirement Committee, where the coordinator of the writing support program continues to offer input and receive suggestions for the continuing implementation of the recommendations and where new questions arising from these implementations are raised by the committee. On campuses where learning communities are not in place, the transformative cycle might be implemented by intentionally scheduling institution and program-level times to interpret and act upon the results. For instance, interdisciplinary teams can be formed to interpret the result from their perspectives; a team of students, librarians, student affairs staff, and faculty might suggest ways to interpret and act upon the results, thereby contributing to "collective institutional learning" (Maki, 2004, p. 161). In this way, the program assessment can be seen as the same kind of cycle—a transformative cycle—that students experience as learners: inquiry, experiential, reflection, and return to inquiry (Mentkowski, 2000, p. 352).

Adapting the Writing Program Inquiry Process for Your Campus

A comprehensive approach to program assessment, like the one described here, is appropriate for all programs that are intensely critical to student learning. Such an assessment can attend to the large issues like institutional policy as well as smaller procedural issues to offer a widespread and strategic plan for change and development of a program. Nevertheless, it is unusual, particularly in current budgetary climates and scale backs, for an assessment of this scope to be feasible. If done by one individual, or in such depth, the model offered here is probably an unrealistic undertaking in most assessment situations. However, the techniques I used can easily be adapted to conduct "meaningful, manageable, and sustainable" assessments to assist programs in improving immediate and long-term services with wide campus implications and impact (Allen, 2004, p. 157). I offer here two general ways to adapt the writing program model: (1) conduct the assessment collaboratively, and (2) streamline the model to individual programmatic needs by determining a less comprehensive but more manageable scope.

Conduct the Assessment Collaboratively

Assessment scholars agree that taking joint responsibility for assessment of programs is not only laborsaving, but it also produces the best scholarship of assessment (Allen, 2004; Banta et al., 1996; Maki, 2004; Mentkowski & Loacker, 2002). Sharing the assessment among faculty or faculty and staff can not only spread the workload among a number of stakeholders, but it can provide the project with a variety of valuable perspectives and can increase the assessment group's breadth of the skills, knowledge, and experience. It can also help to ensure assessors' commitment and cross-stakeholder collaboration in the project. Lopez found that one of the reasons assessments are ineffective can be attributed to "failure to establish appropriate collaboration among all campus professionals" (as cited in Allen, 2004, 157–158). So, collaboration from the start of the project is a desirable practice for effective assessment and also has the most promise for ensuring expanded impact for student learning as a result of the assessment.

Sharing the project among a number of members can also reduce individual workloads. After initial meetings, participants might work in pairs as they collect data and conduct recursive preliminary analysis and formal analysis. Two or more programs sharing some common goals or outcomes could collaborate on a project, or two key committees within or across programs that have overlapping concerns could share an assessment. In order to include representation of all stakeholders, participants in the assessment group can also be selected to represent various stakeholders, or these stakeholders can be included among the respondents during data collection. Since assessment experts emphasize the need for wide and strategic dissemination of the information gained, a wide spectrum of cross-campus stakeholders collaborating closely in the assessment can later serve as a core group to bring central attention of all stakeholder groups to the assessment.

Staff resources within the program or in other settings in the university may provide additional clerical, collating, or collection support, as may teaching and learning centers and educational research offices. Student assistants can also be included in the project to help with data collection, audio transcription, and perhaps some qualitative analysis. As Maki notes, "involving student representatives in institution-and-program-level assessment brings learners' perspectives into this collective effort and encourages students to take responsibility for their learning" (2004, p. 7). Student participants can also help to verify the accuracy of the assessment procedures.

Joint responsibility for assessment can result in "a means of communication across campus, a credibility and trust-building exercise that creates public dialogue with outside audiences asking for accountability and a scholarly activity that leads to new discourses, connections, applications and improved teaching and learning" (Mentkowski & Loacker, 2002, p. 84).

Streamline the Process for Individual Programmatic Needs

All campuses need strong writing support programs, and the process described here can easily be used for reviewing these crucial programs. This process can also be adapted for a variety of programs whose assessment goal is to create change and for those critical programs that warrant close study. These might include support programs such as health services and counseling; academic support programs such as tutoring centers, technical help centers, and libraries; student leadership programs or student learning communities; laboratory services; student organizations; residential life programs; new student orientation programs; curricular programs such as first-year experience programs and writing programs; student services such as admissions, registration, financial aid, mentoring and advising programs; service-learning or community participation programs; and co-curricular athletic or recreational programs. It could also be adapted for review of departmental curricular programs.

A streamlined project could focus on one or two key program issues or problems, such as characteristics of students, meeting of students' learning needs, or student success in meeting the program's goals, objectives, or outcomes. Although addressed to specific programs, Upcraft and Schuh's *Assessment in Student Affairs: A Guide for Practitioners* (1996) offers many easily adaptable ideas for ways to focus program reviews on student learning.

Several other ways to create a manageable scope, other than narrowing the focus of the assessment, include the collection of a smaller representative sample, or collection of data from only the most crucial stakeholders. Alternatively, a project could be planned consecutively so that the assessment would occur over a period of three or more years, investigating a different aspect of the program each year. Or, a "tiered" assessment could be employed, one that builds annually upon a small initial-year project.

Thomas Angelo (2002) found that faculty members will engage in the scholarship of assessment "only if they find it intellectually compelling, professionally rewarding, and relatively unburdensome" (p. 186). The first two criteria were easily fulfilled for me by the project, and the benefits to me were abundant. I was able to integrate my commitment to our university's vision, my own inherent intellectual curiosity, and my academic skills. I gained further assessment expertise and, just as significantly, I came to value assessment highly. I became absorbed not only by the process of assessment itself, but also by the scholarship about assessment. Assessment as a scholarly activity is becoming more widespread and is innovative in the way it can integrate "discipline-related expertise" with the scholarship of assessment (Mentkowski & Loacker, 2002, p. 85). During my project, I was able to apply many of the best practices in assessment I had been reading about and discussing with colleagues and to integrate these with application of my own discipline-based expertise. One of the greatest rewards was my strengthened working relationships with faculty and other campus constituencies who participated in the assessment and its public dissemination. And, because faculty often do not view assessment highly, it was gratifying when some participants became interested in what they saw as a unique assessment project and when they recognized in the project the value of the scholarship of assessment itself. Participating in this transformative assessment process opened my eyes to the potential for institutional assessment to place student learning, about which I care deeply, at the center of the assessment process.

Assessment is part of the larger project of providing the best teaching and learning for students. When we consider assessment as central to the learning process, rather than as a means in itself, it can align with the institution's highest goals and values. Assessment can truly "call us to the best in ourselves, just as we call for the best in each of our students" (Mentkowski, 2000, p. 279).

References

Allen, M. J. (2004). *Assessing academic programs in higher education*. Boston, MA: Anker Publishing.

Angelo, T. A. (2002). Engaging and supporting faculty in the scholarship of assessment: Guidelines from research and best practice. In T. W. Banta & Associates (Eds.), *Building a scholarship of assessment* (pp. 185–200). San Francisco: Jossey-Bass.

Astin, A. W. (1991). *Assessment for excellence: The philosophy and practice of assessment and evaluation in higher education.* New York: Macmillan.

Banta, T. W., & Associates. (2002). *Building a scholarship of assessment.* San Francisco: Jossey-Bass.

Banta, T. W., Lund, J. P., Black, K. E., & Oblander, F. W. (1996) *Assessment in practice: Putting principles to work on college campuses.* San Francisco: Jossey-Bass.

Conrad, C. F., & Wilson, R. F. (1985). Academic program reviews: Institutional approaches, expectations, and controversies. Washington, DC: Association for the Study of Higher Education. (ASHE-ERIC Higher Education Report 0084-0040, No. 5)

Ewell, P. T. (1994). Information for decisions: What's the use? In J. S. Stark & A. Thomas (Eds.), *Assessment and program evaluation* (pp. 733–742). Needham Heights, MA: Simon & Schuster.

Huba, M. E., & Freed, J. E. (2000). *Learner-centered assessment of college campuses: Shifting the focus from teaching to learning.* Boston: Allyn & Bacon.

Maki, P. L. (2004). *Assessing for learning: Building a sustainable commitment across the institution.* Sterling, VA: American Association for Higher Education, Stylus.

Marshall, C., & Rossman, G. B. (1995). *Designing qualitative research* (2nd ed.). Thousand Oaks, CA: Sage.

Mentkowski, M. (1991). Creating a context where institutional assessment yields educational improvement. *Journal of General Education, 40,* 255–282.

Mentkowski, M. (2000). *Learning that lasts: Integrating learning, development, and performance in college and beyond.* San Francisco: Jossey-Bass.

Mentkowski, M., & Loacker, G. (2002). Enacting a collaborative scholarship of assessment. In T. W. Banta & Associates. *Building a scholarship of assessment* (pp. 2–12). San Francisco: Jossey-Bass.

Palomba, C. A., & Banta, T. W. (1999). *Assessment essentials: Planning, implementing, and improving assessment in higher education.* San Francisco: Jossey-Bass.

Pike, G. R. (2002) Measurement issues in outcomes assessment. In T. W. Banta & Associates (Eds.), *Building a scholarship of assessment* (pp. 131–147). San Francisco: Jossey-Bass.

Serow, R. C. (1998). *Program evaluation handbook.* National Society for Experiential Education. Needham Heights, MA: Simon & Schuster.

Upcraft, M. L., & Schuh, J. H. (1996*). Assessment in student affairs: A guide for practitioners.* San Francisco: Jossey-Bass.

Wergin, J. F. (2003). *Departments that work: Building and sustaining cultures of excellence in academic programs.* Bolton, MA: Anker Publishing.

7

EXAMINING CAPSTONE PRACTICES

A Model of Assets-Based Self-Study

Dan Shapiro

One of the characteristics of any effective institution is the ability to engage members at all levels in productive, supportive, and cooperative self-examination and dialogue that leads to meaningful change. Achieving this requires concrete, deliberate processes that prompt us to collectively ask and struggle to answer difficult questions. The campus self-study I describe in this chapter is one such process that we have implemented at California State University Monterey Bay for the purpose of collectively and cooperatively examining and enhancing the educational effectiveness of our unique approach to higher education. This self-study was initiated by our Center for Teaching, Learning, and Assessment and was led by myself, a faculty associate of the center. We have dedicated a chapter of this book to describing the model of self-study we used to examine our senior capstone programs because we believe this model can be generalized to effectively examine a wide diversity of campus programs and processes for the purpose of institutional development, accreditation, and improvement. This chapter has two goals: (1) to explain why and how we designed and implemented our campus self-study, and (2) to highlight the ways a campus self-study and accreditation collectively can facilitate institutional improvement.

We did not implement this self-study in anticipation of our upcoming accreditation agency's site visit. Rather, we implemented the self-study for the purpose of better understanding and improving a crucial component of our educational model, our senior capstone programs. We acted in the spirit of Palomba and Banta (1999), who claim that "[a]mong the most valuable aspects of assessment are the clarity it brings to goals and objectives for learning, the systematic look it encourages educators to take at issues of student learning and development, and the emphasis it places on improvement" (pp. 298–299). However, during the early stages of developing the self-study, it became clear to us that our capstone self-study could also aid our accreditation agency in assessing the educational effectiveness of our educational model. Furthermore, as I will explain later, it soon became clear to us that guidelines developed by our accreditation agency could be useful to us in interpreting and applying our campus self-study. Ultimately, then, this self-study was not done for accreditation, but for our campus, thus making it an effective and authentic illustration of our commitment to improving our institution as opposed to extra work for our accreditation agency that had little or no internal use. We had a win-win situation: we learned more about our educational model and how to improve what we do, and our accreditation agency learned about our educational model and the processes we use to assess, maintain, and enhance the educational effectiveness of our approach to higher education.

Our model of self-study is low budget, but not low impact. Our short-term goal was to gain useful information efficiently and economically, without having to engage complex and expensive processes and consultants. This is not to imply that more elaborate processes and outside consults are not useful. They are. But an effective and inexpensive self-study is an excellent starting point that, when complete, promotes productive campuswide dialogue and helps determine where and how to allocate scarce time and resources. By fostering internal dialogue, problem identification, and collaborative problem solving, we believe that the self-study model I present here supports long-term institutional change and improvement. Campuses can use the recommendations and descriptions of this chapter to both study and improve their own programs.

The Self-Study Model

Our generalized model of campus self-study can be broken down into five steps:

1. Identify student learning and assessment programs or processes on campus common to multiple departments.

2. Of these programs or processes, select one that should be given high priority for a campus self-study.
3. Identify and prioritize goals for the self-study of this program or process.
4. Determine the methods and audience(s) for the self-study.
5. Determine how the results of the self-study will be used to achieve the intended goals.

Asset Versus Deficit Model of Self-Study

Before illustrating our self-study model, I want to emphasize the benefits of adopting an assets-based approach. An assets-based approach is one that assumes every department or program has strengths, as well as weaknesses, and that all departments have something to collaboratively learn from each other. The assets-based self-study has two intentions: (1) to identify strengths and make them public so that all departments benefit, and (2) to make common challenges visible to collaborative problem solvers. This contrasts to a deficits-based approach that assumes a priori that some departments or programs have significant problems that require top-down—perhaps drastic—measures to improve the situation. The importance of *explicitly* adopting an assets-based approach is crucial for implementing an authentic and effective self-study. If participants in the self-study believe—rightly or wrongly—that the purpose of the self-study is to find problems, they will be less likely to present authentic descriptions of their program: strengths will be overemphasized at least and fabricated at worst, and weaknesses will be minimized at least and ignored at worst. Even if an assets-based approached is used, departments will likely emphasize strengths over weaknesses. Nevertheless, if participants understand that the purpose of the self-study is to both share best practices among departments as well as identify common challenges for the campus to address collaboratively, it is more likely that discussions will be authentic and meaningful. So, in developing and implementing our capstone self-study, we made a conscious effort to maintain an assets-based mind-set throughout the entire process.

The assets-based mind-set of our self-study was articulated in the introduction to the final capstone self-study report:

this report is not meant to be used as a means for ranking or comparing the effectiveness of different capstone programs; this is *not* an evaluation. Each and every department has worked very hard over the past six years to create a capstone experience they are proud of. In the spirit of the assets-based model of education CSUMB strives to actualize, this report is meant to help name what individual departments are doing well so that all departments can benefit (Shapiro, 2002, p. 3).

We strongly recommend this approach as a context for most any self-study processes, not only for obtaining quality findings but also for maximum impact.

Implementing the Self-Study

In this section, I illustrate the five steps listed above using our self-study of our senior capstone program as an example. Again, the primary purpose here is not to present CSUMB's capstone model, but rather to illustrate how you may apply our study model to your own campus.

Step 1. Identify student learning and assessment programs or processes on campus common to multiple departments

When looking to make assessments and improvements across an entire campus, identifying programs or processes with campuswide influence is an effective place to begin. This helps to promote "collective responsibility for learning" in which "individuals and departments see themselves as responsible for learning across the institution, not just for their individual course, disciplines, or specific areas of expertise" (Doherty, Riordan, & Roth, 2002, p. 24). Identifying such programs or processes has many benefits. First, it is a chance to revisit and refine those qualities that unite a campus and make it unique. Second, it provides and helps maintain a common language and understanding that facilitates effective cross-campus dialogues that have the maximum potential for influencing lasting and meaningful change on an institutional level. The most visible such program on our campus is the senior capstone. All CSUMB students are required to complete a capstone experience that typically consists of two components: (1) a portfolio, assembled by the graduating student, that demonstrates how she has met each of the major learning outcomes for her degree program, and (2) an independent individual or group project that demonstrates the student's ability to apply the knowledge and skills she developed in her degree program.

Step 2. Of these programs or processes, select one that should be given high priority for a campus self-study

Prioritizing campuswide programs can be difficult because, by their very nature, any campuswide programs will likely be central to an institution's mission and core values. Factors to consider when prioritizing can include perceived importance, visibility, connections to other campus programs, and a priori interests or concerns regarding the relative costs and benefits of different campuswide programs. That we should give capstone high priority was self-evident. First, as Gardener and Van der Veer claim, "the senior year presents an unparalleled opportunity to collect meaningful outcome data for purposes of accountability and to provide meaningful insight regarding the full spectrum of the undergraduate experience" (1998, p. 10). Second, capstone provides a means for defining and assessing our educational model on multiple levels. Capstone is central to individual students' chosen field of study: everything students learn in their major should prepare them to complete their capstone, and capstone creates an opportunity for students to synthesize and demonstrate competency in the skills they developed in their major. Because of this, faculty can use capstones to assess cumulative student knowledge and skills developed in the major.

Capstones are a form of pedagogy as well as a form of assessment; they facilitate an ongoing learning process that extends and enriches the previous processes. Capstone can also be important to students in gaining employment after graduation, for example, by improving students' ability to articulate and demonstrate their skills. On a departmental level, collective student performance on capstones can provide degree-offering programs with a means for assessing their educational effectiveness. Additionally, departments often define what they teach students to do by listing completed capstone projects. On a campus level, capstones provide us with a means of defining the unique nature of our education model and a means to display that model during the capstone festival: an end-of-the-year forum where students from all majors publicly present the capstone work to their families, the campus community, local community members, and other interested parties. A third reason we gave capstone high priority for self-study was that capstone requires significant human and fiscal resources. Capstone advising, capstone seminar courses, staff support for capstone projects, physical space and equipment, archiving of capstone projects, the capstone festival, and other capstone-related activities all require significant faculty, staff, administrative, and monetary support. Capstone represents a significant institutional commitment to engaged, innovative learning and assessment.

Step 3. Identify and prioritize goals for the self-study of this program or process

Before embarking on a campuswide self-study, identifying and prioritizing the potential goals for the study is essential for maintaining focus and keeping the project manageable. Otherwise, the project might quickly become unwieldy and overwhelming, or might provide data of little use. At this stage, we recommend first brainstorming a list of the possible self-study goals without evaluating the merits of those goals. Then, once a list has been determined, begin to assess the merit of each goal and begin the process of determining which goals should be given highest priority. There are various questions you can consider when prioritizing goals. For example, what are the costs and benefits of meeting each goal? This means determining how much time and effort you will need to effectively meet that goal. Another question useful for prioritizing goals is, at what stage of development is the topic of self-study? The most useful goals for a new program still in the process of growing and maturing might be very different from the most useful self-study goals for a well-established, mature program.

In developing our capstone self-study, we identified eight potential goals: (1) provide the campus with a better understanding of how the capstone requirement has been implemented across campus, (2) identify strategies for improving the educational effectiveness of individual capstone programs, (3) provide information about our capstone programs to those outside the university (e.g., our accreditation agency, community partners, other campuses, etc.), (4) evaluate the effectiveness of capstone programs individually and collectively, (5) determine whether the capstone requirement improves student learning in the majors, (6) evaluate whether the educational benefits of having a capstone requirement justifies the financial costs, (7) determine the extent to which completing a capstone project helps students get jobs and improves their job performance, and (8) identify student, faculty, and administrator perspectives on the capstone requirement. For our own self-study, we decided to focus on the first three goals. Program stage of development, necessity, and efficiency determined the particular set of goals we selected. To best continue the development of CSUMB's capstone programs, we felt we needed to better understand how different departments implemented the capstone requirement. This was particularly true because of the bottom-up approach CSUMB took to implementing the capstone requirement. During the initial stages of CSUMB's development in the mid-1990s, founding faculty, administrators, and staff decided that all majors would require students to complete a culminating senior capstone project as part of their degree program, but left the details to individual departments. Subsequently, each major developed a capstone program to fit its own needs. For the most part, except for impromptu discussions among faculty within departments, each major developed their capstone process independently of other capstone programs. The benefit of this independence has been the freedom each academic department has had to develop unique programs and innovations that might not have materialized had greater coordination been attempted. However, after six years of development, it seemed time for departments at CSUMB to share their capstone programs and experiences for the purpose of highlighting strengths, identifying common challenges, and beginning a campuswide dialogue about evaluating and enhancing the educational effectiveness of the CSUMB capstone.

Efficiency also played a role in determining the goals for our self-study. The next two goals—identify strategies for improving the educational effectiveness of individual capstone programs and provide information about the capstone process to those outside the university—we believed would emerge from the first. In describing and exploring capstone programs across campus, we knew we would discover a suite of best practices that could be shared among departments as well as identifying common challenges we could collectively overcome, thus improving the educational effectiveness of capstone programs individually and collectively. Concomitantly, we could share these same descriptions and explorations with others outside the university.

Only after we gained a shared understanding of how capstone had been implemented across campus and only after further development of capstone programs across campus did we feel we would be in a position to address some of the other goals, which while of utmost importance, were also more challenging and costly to address. In terms of educational effectiveness, what could be more important than determining the effect of senior capstone on student career development since the ultimate goals of capstone is to prepare students to be successful in their chosen careers? From a pedagogical standpoint, what can be more important than determining whether capstone increases learning in the major? Acknowledging their importance is an easy process, but addressing such questions is challenging and required—we believed—a better understanding of how individual departments conceived of and implemented capstone. Thus, we decided that we would be best served by starting with an initial survey of all campus capstone programs.

Step 4. Determine the audience(s) and methods for the self-study

Determining the audience and methods for a self-study are crucial components for obtaining and disseminating results that maximize potential for gaining useful information that leads to meaningful dialogue and change. The more collaborative and inclusive this step the better, both for generating ideas and for increasing investment in and support for the process. In our self-study process, capstone instructors and interested administrators from across campus determined the audience and methods for the self-study. To begin, we organized an initial meeting among capstone seminar instructors and department directors from each major. This was the first-ever meeting among all capstone seminar instructors. In addition to identifying several areas of common concern, the group solicited volunteers to help design and implement the self-study. At a subsequent meeting, after acknowledging how little each department (as well as the entire campus) knew or understood about how other departments implemented their capstone requirement, the subgroup felt that instructors, administrators, as well as outsiders, such as our accreditation agency—our intended audiences—would benefit from a survey of all capstone seminar programs in order to consolidate in one place information about each department's program. To achieve this, the subgroup decided that the self-study should consist of two components: interviews of all capstone seminar instructors, and collection and consolidation of all capstone materials (e.g., capstone outcome, capstone seminar syllabi, etc.). All of this information would then be synthesized and presented in a single, capstone self-study report.

The subgroup then came up with a list of interview questions for capstone seminar instructors that covered the range of information necessary for gaining a better understanding of how the capstone requirement had been implemented across campus. Interview questions addressed basic departmental characteristics (e.g., how many faculty? how may students?), specific details such as how capstone seminars are run and how capstone projects are assessed, and more general, open-ended topics such as self-perceived strengths and weaknesses of current capstone programs. Additionally, the group identified capstone materials to be collected, consolidated, and reviewed. These materials included capstone seminar syllabi; capstone proposal, report, and portfolio guidelines for students; and capstone assessment outcomes, criteria, and standards.

Step 5. Determine how the results of the self-study will be used to achieve the intended goals

During the design of the self-study, and before the self-study is initiated, we recommend spending time thinking about how the results will be used to meet the intended goals. Trying to make these connections before starting the study can be incredibly valuable. In doing so, you may realize that your results may not actually address some of the intended goals, prompting you to either modify the goals and/or change the methods of the self-study early in the process. For our self-study, we saw the following connections between our results and our three major goals. To make progress on the first goal—to provide the campus with a better understanding of how the campus requirement has been implemented across campus—we determined that we would present the final report to all capstone instructors, department chairs, program directors, and upper-level administrators. To make progress on the second goal—identify strategies for improving the educational effectiveness of individual capstone programs—we decided that the report would include a set of recommendations for improving capstone programs across campus. To make progress on the third goal—provide information about the capstone process to those outside the university—we decided that we would provide our accreditation agency with a copy of the capstone self-study report.

Brief Summary of Self-Study Results

When analyzed, the results yielded two categories for consideration. Those categories were shared perceptions and concerns. From those categories of data, a set of recommendations was generated.

Self-Study Perceptions

In addition to the important work of describing and consolidating detailed information about each department's capstone program, the self-study revealed several shared perceptions among capstone faculty: (1) having students do a culminating project is much more effective than an exam; (2) the capstone experience helped reinforce major learning outcomes; (3) completing a capstone project left students with a sense of pride and accomplishment, particularly after presenting their work at the capstone festival; (4) the capstone seminar was very helpful to students (although most faculty also saw room for improvement); (5) faculty were generally impressed by student capstone work, and faculty felt many projects approached graduate-level work; and (6) anecdotal evidence suggested that capstone projects helped students get jobs. Furthermore, on a department level, faculty also found that informal discussion about capstone had lead to positive curricular changes in the major. Each of these perceptions provides an excellent starting point for further study, perhaps with or by outside consultants.

Self-Study Concerns

There were also several widely shared concerns. Capstone instructors also felt that (1) the capstone requirement, while worthwhile, is too time- and resource-intensive for students, faculty, and departments, particularly in the face of projected student population increases; (2) current capstone programs are unsustainable, and will become more so as the campus continues to grow; (3) maintaining current capstone programs will require additional resources; (4) guidelines for capstone projects need to be more detailed and specific; and (5) faculty need to develop more specific capstone assessment outcomes, criteria, and standards. Furthermore, the self-study made it clear that because of time and resource constraints, no departments were systematically reviewing capstone projects to assess the educational effectiveness of their programs, despite a strong desire to do so. As with the positive perceptions, each of these issues calls for more detailed examination and study.

Self-Study Recommendations

The self-study report also generated a list of recommendations based on the data gathered by the self-study. For example, the report identified a need and desire for forums that allowed departments to share best practices (e.g., teaching cooperatives, capstone faculty workshops on facilitating effective peer review in the classroom, and a Web site where capstone materials can be made public and easily accessible to other departments). Additionally, the report identified a need and desire for more explicit and deliberate use of a capstone report for self-assessment of CSUMB majors. The report also identified a need and desire for greater involvement of community partners and future student employers in capstone outcome development and assessment. Perhaps most significantly, the report also identified a need and desire to develop strategies for maintaining and improving the quality of current capstone programs in the face of increasing fiscal and logistical constraints. Recommendations for improvement included the provision of adequate resources for maintaining and improving capstone programs and the development of strategies for working with greater numbers of capstone students (e.g., develop strategies for working with greater numbers of capstone students by relying more on internship-based capstones, group capstones, and alternative, less resource intensive, capstone pathways). Once again, each of these recommendations could be the focus of additional, more detailed study and examination.

The CSUMB Capstone Self-Study and Accreditation: Emerging Institutional Improvement

After the capstone self-study report was completed and as we prepared evidence for our upcoming accreditation agency's site visit, we realized that our capstone self-study embodied two distinct "layers" of evidence of educational effectiveness we could and would present to our accreditation agency. The first layer consisted of the descriptions of individual capstone programs across campus. Had we stopped there, however, we would have only created a disembodied encyclopedic archive of little use to us; the potential for institutional improvement would have been minimal. By embedding the consolidation of capstone materials in the self-study process, we created the second layer of evidence: the capstone self-study itself. In collecting capstone materials as part of an organized and deliberate effort to explore the effectiveness of the ultimate component of our education model, we created a catalyst for lasting and meaningful institution change and improvement.

Direction From Accreditation

We were aided in this effort by a set of five questions our accreditation agency asked us to address in preparing and presenting evidence for the upcoming educational effectiveness accreditation team visit. Although these questions were developed specifically for our accreditation team's upcoming site visit, we found them to be incredibly helpful and recommend that any campus serious about improving its educational effectiveness continuously ask itself the following:

1. Does the institution have effective means to review and evaluate the outcomes of its educational model?
2. Is there a continuous process of inquiry and engagement by the institution to enhance educational effectiveness?
3. Does the institution utilize good practices to assess student learning?
4. Are institutional resources aligned with activities designed to achieve educational effectiveness?
5. Does the institution's educational model yield better outcomes for students and their employers than more traditional models, and is there convincing proof of the value of this approach for student learning and talent development?

In developing these five questions, our accreditation agency intended to create questions that would help them understand our campus and help us identify our strengths and areas needing improvement. These questions met both objectives. To illustrate the mutually supporting roles of our campus self-study and accreditation in facilitating institutional self-reflection and improvement, I present below our responses to these five questions in the context of capstone and the capstone self-study.

1. Does the institution have effective means to review and evaluate the outcomes of its educational model?

At the departmental level, senior capstone projects are perhaps one of the best pieces of evidence CSUMB has for evaluating the effectiveness of its educational model. The capstone experience at CSUMB represents the culmination of students' work in their major and an opportunity for students to demonstrate that they can use their education to *do* something. What better way to document and demonstrate the effectiveness of the CSUMB model than through careful review and evaluation of capstone work?

At the institutional level, CSUMB has gathered copious evidence we can use to review and evaluate the outcomes of our educational model: all departments have most of their past capstone projects, some have all of them, and all are now beginning the process of routinely archiving all current and future capstone projects in the CSUMB library. Capstone projects are direct evidence of student learning. However, the crux of this question is whether CSUMB has an *effective means* to evaluate this evidence. The answer to this question is yes and no. One of the results of the capstone self-study is that nearly all programs have made curricular changes in direct response to the review and assessment of student capstone work, thus providing evidence that one benefit of the capstone model is that it makes visible strengths and weaknesses of individual programs, and that programs have made changes in light of student capstone work. However, these changes were generally not the result of a deliberate and systematic process of reviewing capstones for the purpose of program assessment, independent of individual student assessment, but rather as a result of obvious deficiencies faculty noticed during routine assessment of individual capstone projects.

The insights from faculty observations have clearly been valuable, but there is more that can be done to establish systematic procedures for using student capstone work to assess the effectiveness of CSUMB's unique educational model. Furthermore, the capstone self-study generated suggestions individual departments might implement to further evaluate their capstone programs, for example, by surveying CSUMB graduates to find out whether they feel their capstone experiences helped them develop useful skills they later used in their job or at graduate school. And perhaps most significantly, the report provides evidence that the majority of current capstone programs are not sustainable, and thus important decisions need to be made regarding allocation of resources at departmental and institutional levels.

2. Is there a continuous process of inquiry and engagement by the institution to enhance educational effectiveness?

At the departmental level, the evolution of the capstone process clearly demonstrates a continuous process of inquiry and engagement to enhance educational effectiveness. The capstone processes in place now are the result of six years of experimentation and reform based on input from capstone seminar instructors, faculty and staff, and students. For example, several departments changed their capstone from a one-semester to a two-semester model when they realized the one-semester model was inadequate. Other departments completely restructured their capstone program to enhance the effectiveness of the capstone experience and better prepare students for their future career. Many departments changed their curriculum and/or courses in response to faculty assessment of individual student capstone work. Thus, not only is the senior capstone a powerful educational tool for students, giving them the opportunity to synthesize what they have learned in their major, but the capstone is also actively used by departments to enhance student learning.

At the institutional level, while the capstone self-study report was still in draft form, it was already being used by CSUMB in its continuous process of inquiry and engagement to enhance educational effectiveness. For example, a draft of the report was presented to CSUMB's deans and department directors. One of the major issues that emerged directly from this report and a topic of sustained conversation at this meeting was the sustainability of the capstone programs. The report helped make clear to campus leaders that capstone programs were very effective—both with respect to student learning and program development—and very costly, at least in their current forms. It raised important questions in advance of the changes expected on campus. As the student population increases, what will happen to the capstone programs? Will they each be scaled up in their current form, and if so, what are the costs? Do the benefits of capstone justify the costs? Should capstone programs be modified so that they serve more students at a reduced cost? If so, what would be lost?

We also presented a draft of the capstone self-study report at a meeting of all campus department chairs and program directors. In addition to fostering active and engaged discussions about capstone, several additional issues were raised at this meeting. For example, one issue was the relationship between capstone and CSUMB's Service Learning Program. At that time there were few explicit connections between these two programs, but it became clear that making such connections could benefit both of them. Another issue that was raised at the same meeting was the demands capstone programs place on university staff and support services other than faculty. For example, each degree-offering program organizes a Capstone Festival where students present their capstone work. These events are very powerful learning experiences for students, and they provide a forum where people from within and outside the university can learn more about what CSUMB teaches students to do. But these events require resources: space, equipment, technology and technical support, scheduling, and coordination. This point raises crucial questions: as CSUMB grows, will it continue to support the Capstone Festival, and if so, to what extent, and where will the resources to support the Capstone Festival come from?

In addition, an important action that resulted from the same presentation to the Academic Leadership Team was the addition of capstone-related questions to a survey of CSUMB alumni that was in development at the time. Questions added to the survey were designed to gain information on student perceptions of the capstone experience. In particular, students were asked to what extent they felt the capstone experience was helpful to them in their post-CSUMB careers. Such information leads not only to improvement, but also identifies questions for further study.

Thus, the capstone self-study was undertaken as part of a continuous process of campus inquiry and engagement for the explicit purpose of improving CSUMB's educational model. Never did anybody assume that the capstone programs were static entities at or near completion. Rather, this work was initiated for the explicit purpose of discovering what was working well and what needed improvement so that capstone programs can remain an effective component of the dynamic CSUMB educational model.

3. Does the institution utilize good practices to assess student learning?

In assessing capstones, all departments at CSUMB strive to implement sound assessment practices. First, departments strive to make as seamless as possible the relationship between learning and assessment. For example, one department uses a detailed set of capstone outcomes, criteria, and standards not only to assess completed student work, but also to teach students. In this department's capstone seminar, students work through all of the capstone outcomes, criteria, and standards during the semester, applying them to their work in progress. Second, although not all departments have developed detailed criteria and standards for assessment of student capstones, all departments are aware of what work still needs to be done, and there is a general appreciation for the ways clear assessment outcomes, criteria, and standards enhance student learning. Third, many departments have multiple readers assess capstones. Several departments have two faculty members read each capstone, other (smaller) departments have all faculty assess all capstones, and some departments have community partners participate in capstone assessment. While having multiple people assess student work is more intensive in time and resources, the payoffs are substantial: having multiple readers results in a more thorough assessment of student work, and it promotes discussions among faculty about what they want their students to learn and how they can tell whether students have learned it. Even among those departments that have one person assess capstone work, typically assessment is done in consultation with other capstone advisors. Finally, several departments require that student capstone work directly demonstrates learning outcomes covered elsewhere in the curriculum, ensuring that learning and assessment in capstone builds on and is supported by learning and assessment elsewhere in the curriculum.

4. Are institutional resources aligned with activities designed to achieve educational effectiveness?

This is a crucial question for capstone. There is some alignment. For example, all departments fund sections of the capstone seminar, and are given resources for teaching these sections. However, almost all majors indicated that institutional resources are not aligned with the capstone activities. Supporting one student in a CSUMB capstone course requires far more time and resources than supporting one student in a noncapstone course. Most capstone seminar instructors indicated that current capstones practices were barely sustainable or already unsustainable for them and other capstone advisors. Given that over the coming years our student body will be growing in size at a greater rate than faculty, many capstone seminar instructors are concerned about the future of capstone in their department. A crucial question CSUMB needs to answer is, what kind of capstone process are we willing to support? The existing models are powerful, but also time and resource intensive.

5. Does CSUMB's educational model yield better outcomes for students and their employers than more traditional models, and is there convincing proof of the value of this approach for student learning and talent development?

This is another crucial question for capstone, at the departmental and institutional levels, particularly in light of the previous question about resources. Strong capstone programs required resources, not only to pay faculty to mentor students, but also to pay for the staff and facilities that allow capstone students to do meaningful work. Unless capstone is reduced to a term paper or multiple-choice exam, as occurs at some other institutions, it will require significant resources. It will be much easier to justify and obtain those resources if the value faculty see in capstone can be demonstrated. If CSUMB wants to demonstrate that its educational model is effective there is no better way to do this than through capstone. If careful studies can demonstrate that the CSUMB capstone experience enhances educational effectiveness and produces more effective individuals—however that is defined by individual departments and majors—there will be more support for maintaining and enhancing current capstone practices, as well as other components of the CSUMB educational model. Determining the educational effectiveness of the capstone process will become particularly important as increasingly scarce resources force departments to justify the significant time and energy capstone requires.

At the institutional level, it is too early to evaluate the extent to which a campuswide capstone requirement influences student learning and talent development. But just asking this question prompts further questions, the exploration of which can surely help CSUMB better understand the effectiveness of its educational model. For example, if we can demonstrate that the CSUMB capstone requirement yields better outcomes for students and their employers than more traditional models and there is convincing proof of the value of this approach to student learning and talent development, one could ask the follow-up question: has the process of producing and presenting this report influenced individual capstone programs for the better? If it can be shown that the answer to this question is yes, then that would support the claim that this campus self-study—through its influence on campus capstone practices—yielded better outcomes for students and their employers.

In summary, while our capstone self-study was not initiated for our upcoming accreditation visit, the self-study both influenced and was influenced by the visit in important and positive ways. First, the capstone self-study report provided our accreditation agency with background information on our capstone model and its relationship to our campus curriculum in advance of their capstone-related meetings with students, faculty, and administrators. The capstone self-study provided documentation that allowed our accreditation agency to understand our capstone requirement, how we have implemented it, its importance to our educational model, and the challenges that our capstone model poses. This is captured accurately by our accreditation agency's site visit report that states:

The [CSUMB] capstone experience offers students a powerful opportunity to integrate their learning across courses and disciplines and, especially, between the classroom and the world of work and civic engagement. We observed that the capstone takes quite different forms from field to field and that there is some concern among faculty in some areas, expressed for instance in the study of capstones but also in our interviews during the visit, about maintaining the special capstone experience in the face of increasing enrollments and declining budgets. That is always a challenge and we take these concerns seriously. On the other hand, it was clear in our focus group with capstone students that the experience is a defining feature of a CSUMB education, and it behooves the institution to find ways to continue the capstone in less labor-intensive formats where necessary. For instance, we noted that some fields have students work on projects in collaborative groups; doing so is completely consistent with campus values and vision. Further, students might themselves be able to shoulder more of the responsibility for their learning in the capstone; placing greater emphasis on peer and self-assessment might allow faculty to work with larger numbers of students while maintaining the quality of the experience. Whatever the approach, the capstone is a crucial vehicle for learning and must be preserved. (Ramaley et al., 2003, pp. 23–24)

Our accreditation agency's assessment of our capstone model felt accurate to us. Its recommendations were both similar to and went beyond our own. We felt that the agency understood the spirit of our capstone model and its strengths and its weaknesses. Consequently, not only were we better able to hear our accreditation agency's recommendations for improvement, but those recommendations were more valuable as a result of its clear understanding of our capstone program. The same report goes on to identify "the needs of the campus community as a whole for clarity and coherence in the interpretations of those functions that are widely shared, such as approaches to the capstone" and recommends "the use of data to guide effective decision-making, and program review"(Ramaley et al., 2003, p. 25). The CSUMB capstone self-study combined with our accreditation agency's recommendations puts us in an excellent position to continue to study and use the CSUMB capstone experience to improve the efficiency and effectiveness of our educational model.

Conclusion

Many of the potential benefits of CSUMB's capstone self-study have yet to be realized while others have already served the campus well. Institutional change, even in a young university, is often a slow, resource-intensive process. As a result, acting on self-study recommendations requiring even minimal time and resource investment is proceeding slowly. The proposed teaching cooperative has yet to materialize, as faculty, already stretched, were unable to find the time to devote to a teaching cooperative. A central Web site containing updated capstone materials and requirements from across campus has yet to be created; such a Web site would need resources for its creation as well as continued resources to keep it current and up-to-date. The department on campus that made the most extensive use of community partner consultants to build and assess its capstone program did so only because of a significant outside grant. Now that that grant is no longer in effect, the department has been forced to scale back on that community involvement.

Overall, though, we believe the CSUMB capstone self-study was clearly a success with respect to engaging individuals at all levels in productive, supportive, and cooperative self-examination and dialogue that is leading to meaningful change. The self-study consolidated extensive materials on capstone programs across campus; it generated discussions among faculty and administrators on the both the strengths of CSUMB's capstone programs and serious challenges to those programs; it provided documentation that allowed our accreditation agency to understand our capstone requirement, how we have implemented it, its importance to our educational model, and the challenges that our capstone model poses. Furthermore, examining capstone at the departmental and institutional levels though the five educational effectiveness questions proposed by our accreditation agency provided us with the opportunity to reflect upon our practices, identify what we are doing well, and identify what we can do better. That we are now raising questions at all campus levels—from faculty to deans to the provost—about the strengths and weaknesses of a central and shared component of our educational model greatly increases our long-term potential for effective institutional change and improvement.

References

Doherty, A., Riordan, T., & Roth, J. (2002). The learning-centered institution: A framework. In A. Doherty, T. Riordan, & J. Roth (Eds.), *Student learning: A central focus for institutions of higher education: A report and collection of institutional practices of the student learning initiative* (pp. 1–26). Milwaukee, WI: Alverno College Institute.

Gardner, J. N., & Van der Veer, G. (1998). The emerging movement to strengthen the senior experience. In J. N. Gardner, G. Van der Veer, & Associates (Eds.), *The senior year experience: Facilitating integration, reflection, closure, and transition* (pp. 3-20). San Francisco: Jossey-Bass.

Palomba, C. A., & Banta, T. W. (1999). *Assessment essentials: Planning, implementing, and improving assessment in higher education.* San Francisco: Jossey-Bass.

Ramaley, J., Bringle, R., Freund, S., Harding, E., Hengstler, D., Hutchings, P., & O'Brien, K. (2003). *Report of the educational effectiveness site visit team: California State University Monterey Bay.* Monterey, CA: California State University Monterey Bay.

Shapiro, D. (2002). CSUMB Capstone Survey Report. Monterey, CA: California State University Monterey Bay.

8

A STUDY OF "BEST PRACTICES" IN ASSESSMENT

A Visible and Public Learning Process

Betty McEady

Public stakeholders have a right to know about the performance and quality of institutions of higher education. As described in chapter 1, public demands for educational effectiveness and accountability in higher education have emerged from multiple forces. They challenge us to articulate and make public our intentional learning outcomes, measures of student success, and assessment results—all as evidence of institutional quality and integrity to purpose. CSUMB has been—and continues to be—responsive to these public demands, contending that assessment and accountability expectations of stakeholders meld very well with our culture of inquiry and continuous improvement model.

Our highly successful seven-year accreditation process is an example of congruence between external demands and our intrinsic culture of inquiry and improvement. The new accreditation model of WASC fostered integration of our outcomes-based assessment model with documentation for accreditation. The focus on student learning for accreditation supported our efforts well and promoted long-term improvement practices.

Linking accreditation and assessment is a concept supported by Gelmon (1997), who posits that continual or "intentional improvement" results from the "deliberate linkage of assessment and accreditation" (p. 51). While "assessment offers internal systematic analysis of activities [based on standards], accreditation validates the standards of performance and assures a baseline level of uniform quality across comparable programs or institutions" (p. 53).

Evidence of best practices in assessment in academic programs at CSUMB is the focus of this chapter. Our practices are grounded in Pascarella's thesis that when effective educational practices are the criteria by which institutional quality is measured, "the assumption . . . is that an excellent undergraduate education is most likely to occur at those colleges and universities that maximize good practices and enhance students' academic and social engagement or effort" (2001, p. 22). Thus, Pascarella's thesis of "maximizing good practices" and Gelmon's assessment-accreditation-improvement model frame the goals of this chapter, which are

1. To describe the process we used to translate "best practices in assessment" into a survey. This survey yielded a campus profile that documented the presence or absence of best practices on our campus. The campus profile also became the basis for accreditation documentation and long-term improvement for educational effectiveness.
2. To make our processes visible and public in order to facilitate transferability of our best practices survey approach to other campuses

The campus profile and description of processes that produced the profile will be useful in helping other campuses assess best practices that could lead to long-term improvement.

The Research Processes

Following approval of our extension of candidacy in 2000, the campus prepared to present evidence of our educational effectiveness in response to five questions posed by previous accreditation team evaluators in 2000. CSUMB's responses to the five questions are addressed in several of the chapters in this text. However, one question—the focus of this chapter—provided an especially significant opportunity for campus learning, reflection, and self-assessment at the programmatic level: "Does the institution utilize good practices to assess student learning?" To address this question, our Educational Effectiveness Committee engaged in a scholarly process designed to unveil data that would result in learning and improvement for committee members as well as academic programs on our campus. The concurrent purpose was to meet accreditation expectations.

This chapter specifically (1) describes research processes that we used to develop and administer a survey of best practices on our campus, (2) discusses our campus assessment profile, including an analysis of the profile based on evidence of best practices as represented by faculty in academic programs on our campus, and (3) provides a set of assessment guidelines to facilitate replication of our assessment processes and survey on other campuses.

By linking accreditation and assessment-for-improvement, this research and survey process grew into a dynamic learning experience for us. Other campuses that are preparing for accreditation, with the intention of improving teaching and learning practices, could have similar benefits by translating our best practices survey into language appropriate to the mission and core values of their respective campuses. The next section of this chapter describes the four research and development processes that resulted in the survey of best practices and our campus profile.

Research Process 1: Search for Best Practices

Learning should be the primary aim of integrating assessment, evaluation, and improvement (Gelmon, 1997). In this accord, the Educational Effectiveness Committee held to the conviction that the research and accreditation preparation would be a learning experience for committee members as well as the campus. As previously described, the process was "public and visible" and was conducted through scholarly means. Realizing the value of current research in assessment to support our response to the question "Does the institution utilize good practices to assess student learning?" the committee searched the literature for best practices in assessment over the last ten years.

An endless array of studies, reports, and articles explicating various principles of effective assessment of student learning and collegiate quality emerged. (See Resource List Number 1, appendix 8.A, and the reference lists of my colleagues' chapters in this book.) However, it is the seminal publication by the American Association for Higher Education, *Principles of Good Practice for Assessing Student Learning* (Astin et al., 1992), that structures the wealth of research into a set of generalizations about effective assessment practices for collegiate effectiveness, accountability, and continuous improvement. The nine principles in this AAHE publication lay the theoretical foundation for this chapter (see appendix 8.B).

From this rich array of research and principles of assessment, we developed a set of campus guidelines about assessment-for-learning that steered the development of our survey questions and analysis of responses. These guidelines will be discussed in detail in the second section of this chapter.

For campuses beginning either assessment development or accreditation, or both, the assessment literature, along with AAHE's principles, offer excellent introductory guidance.

While our search yielded an extensive, but rich, list of best practices, we decided to reduce the list to a set of 19 practices that were manageable for a survey that had value for our campus. It must be acknowledged that 19 items may be more than desirable for practical interview protocols, but all 19 were particularly relevant, and thus critical for our campus. The process of determining a fit between particular best practices and our campus culture and intentions was a valuable learning process. It is the context of specific fit to campus culture that other campuses also must consider as they adopt these processes. That fit makes possible the ongoing and long-term improvement that adds value to the assessment process.

Research Process 2: Develop Survey Questions

The committee then translated the 19 practices into an interview protocol of questions designed to solicit information about the presence or absence of best practices in assessment in academic programs on our campus. These questions are discussed in the next section of this chapter, "Evidence of Best Practices in Campus Assessment Profile."

Other campuses may find that some of the questions address their priorities, and that some might be confusing to their faculty. One of the most critical recommendations this chapter makes is that the language and content of the survey questions should be tailored to the culture of each campus.

Research Process 3: Develop Faculty Response Tables

The committee wanted a survey protocol that would identify where best practices were being used, but also on what issues the campus and specific programs would need to focus their strategies for improvement and institutional change. Given this strategy, the survey first asks faculty a dichotomous question requiring a yes or no response. Should the faculty give an affirmative answer, "yes" or "in progress," the survey asks for evidence, or for specific examples of activities indicative of the presence of certain practices. Should the faculty give a negative response, the survey asks a question about the program's plans for changes in the future. For example, do you see your program implementing this practice in the future? If so, how? And when? Later in this chapter, sample tables of responses illustrate the process.

Research Process 4: Administer the Best Practices Interviews

The research process is described here as a protocol for most campus interviews. Additional insights about these processes can be found in chapters 7 and 10.

To administer the interview protocol, Educational Effectiveness Committee members visited each department during a regularly scheduled department meeting. In order to have a significant level of faculty involvement and reflection, the committee recommended that all faculty (tenured, tenure track, and part-time) participate in the interview sessions. Each committee member was provided support and instructions for facilitating faculty response to the best practices questions:

Begin with something like, "We hope that the response tables will also serve as a useful tool for self-assessment and reflection . . . to affirm your current practices, to identify needs for future planning. We appreciate your participation and contributions to the documentation of our Educational Effectiveness for accreditation."

1. Describe the *purpose* of the survey and response tables, a process of gathering consistent information across campus, gathering snapshots of information rather than detailed information.
2. Assure the *anonymity* of the department in the dissemination of results. Results will be displayed in a campuswide snapshot or profile. There will be no comparisons—no identification of individual departments.
3. Stress the *authenticity* of responses so that we are prepared for any probing and need for evidence in our accreditation process.
4. Describe the *first section* of the survey as a set of questions about the department's degree program; urge faculty to think of the program, not courses.
5. The *second section* of the interview will ask faculty to consider individual courses—their own teaching.
6. Assure faculty that there are *no "correct" answers*, no need for consensus, and that data may not be complete.
7. If *issues or discussion-type questions* arise, suggest a process of recording those for future department dialogue.

The interview sessions were highly interactive with much discussion and engagement of faculty. Interviewers asked faculty to assess whether the department's major programs of study demonstrated each of the best practices in assessment, and to describe evidence available to support their response. Program participation was comprehensive and inclusive of the university's 11 undergraduate majors, one master's program, and one teacher education credential program. The interviewers were able to involve 110 of the 199 faculty who attend monthly department meetings. Of those 110 faculty, 67 were tenure track or tenured (of a possible 74) and 43 were temporary (part-time or full-time) lecturers (of a possible 125). Without identifying individual departments or comparing one against another, the qualitative responses from faculty in each department were sorted and translated into a best-practices-in-assessment campus profile, which is discussed in the next section of this chapter.

The previous section of this chapter describes a scholarly approach to developing a survey of best practices and collecting evidence of assessment practices at our campus. The following section provides a set of guidelines for effective assessment that serves as a theoretical frame for the analysis of faculty responses to the 19 best practices survey questions in our evaluation study.

Evidence of Best Practices in Campus Assessment Profile

This section of the chapter is a discussion of the campus profile that emerged from the best practices survey questions and interviews. One intent of this chapter is to translate our internal research into understandable, transparent information that interested stakeholders and other campuses might consider as they review or replicate our processes.

The survey questions and faculty's responses will be useful to campuses in ways that go beyond survey items. They encourage campuses to move toward using the survey results to improve teaching, learning, and assessment on their campuses. Similarly, our campus presents this survey data on an annual basis to department chairs as a reminder to departments to continue their efforts in assessment. The intent is that departments use the data to self-assess. The basic substance of these items is a central part of program review.

Discussion Format

The analysis and discussion of the survey data is formatted in three components. First, each analysis section begins with an assessment guideline. It provides a theoretical context for the survey question or questions that follow. This will help campuses that are interested in replicating our processes to understand the significance of the research to our processes and best practices on campus. As stated earlier, each assessment guideline is based on the wealth of research in assessment for long-term improvement. Thus, following each statement of an assessment guideline is a brief discussion of the assessment literature that supports or gives significance to the assessment guideline.

The second component in the analysis is a summary of the data or responses from faculty. Each assessment guideline is followed by a discussion of the survey question and a summary of the faculty's responses. The intent here is to provide readers with a general picture of best practices in assessment on our campus. A few tables of responses are presented later in this chapter to illustrate the format of the campus profile report. Space limitations prohibit presentation of the entire campus profile. Faculty responses are summarized as evidence of the variety of ways teaching, learning, and assessment on our campus align with best practices in assessment for long-term improvement.

The third component is a discussion of the implications for other campuses of the research and best practice survey approach to assessment-for-improvement. What follows in the next section of this chapter are explications of the three components—assessment guidelines and research significance, discussion of responses relevant to each survey question, and implications and summary. These components are formatted to guide other institutions in assessing best practices.

Assessment Guideline 1: Define and clarify program goals and outcomes for long-term improvement

The significance of this section of questions is expressed well by Astin et al. (1992): "Assessment is a goal-oriented process" (p. 2). Having clearly defined program goals and outcomes is critical to effective assessment and long-term improvement. Clarity of intentions moves a program closer to effective articulation of the values that matter most to the program and its students, faculty, staff, and external communities and stakeholders it serves. This best practices survey approach can play a key role in a program's decision to define its intentions for long-term improvement. It may prompt faculty and administrators to refine and clarify existing goals and outcomes. Survey questions 1 through 5 are relevant to guideline 1.

Discussion of Responses: Questions 1 Through 5

Survey Question 1: Does the program have clear major learning outcomes (MLOs)?

Survey question 1 (table 8-1) asks about the clarity of each program's major learning outcomes (MLOs), which on our campus are a program's description of desired learning—namely, skills, abilities, dispositions—that students are expected to demonstrate upon completion of the major. Faculty in the 13 academic programs responded yes to this question; 3 of the 13 departments elaborated on their future plans to revisit and refine their program goals, course outcomes, criteria, and standards of performance. A few of the 13 departments were already in the process of reviewing and refining their MLOs, and were expecting to complete the revisions later in the academic year.

After reflection and close examination of the survey reports, two departments arranged with the Center for Teaching, Learning, and Assessment to continue the work of revising their major learning outcomes for clarity and modification. Annually, a few departments continue to use the survey profile to reexamine their strengths and weaknesses and plan for improvement where necessary.

TABLE 8-1
Best Practices in Assessment—Campus Profile

Question 1: Does the program have clear major learning outcomes (MLOs)?

Yes	No	Evidence	In Progress	Future Plans
13 departments		• In major ProSeminar • CSUMB catalog • Program fact sheet • Syllabi • Web site • Capstone portfolios • Advising guide	• "Not all of our learning outcomes have been fleshed out completely." • "Outcomes are being revised in response to state standards, program review and to improve articulation with community colleges."	• Departments will revisit outcomes to reduce the number of outcomes, and to refine the language in their standards of performance.

Survey Question 2: Rate the degree to which faculty have common
understanding of the major learning outcomes (MLOs)

(1 = low; 5 = high)

One cannot assume that all faculty have the same understanding of program outcomes. Therefore, it is important to build a common understanding
within a department. When departments were asked to rate the degree of
common understanding among faculty of the MLOs, six departments rated
themselves at level 4, one department at level 4.5, one at level 3.88, two at
level 3, and two at level 5. Reasons for such diversity became clear with further discussion.

A number of departments could not come to agreement on this rating.
In one department, the response was "This varies widely among our faculty.
About one-third of our program is being taught by part-time faculty who
may not be aware that courses are structured around learning outcomes." In
another department, there was some frustration expressed by part-time faculty. Because they want to be more helpful to students, they need better
understanding of the program goals and outcomes.

In contrast, two departments rated their understanding at level 5, and
described a "huge investment" and "lots of ownership" among faculty because of the inclusion of all faculty in the process of developing outcomes.
Maki (2004) confirms the value of establishing principles of a collective commitment to assessment, beginning with assurance of faculty understanding
and buy-in. One implication here is that this level of consensual understanding and buy-in among faculty is essential also to good course development
to improve student learning. Collective understanding fosters a culture of
inquiry for continuous renewal.

Survey Question 3: Does the department provide opportunities for
students to develop common understanding of the MLOs?

Twelve of the thirteen departments reported that they provide opportunities
for students to develop common understanding of the program outcomes
(MLOs). While Major ProSeminar (the introductory course to the major)
was cited across all majors as the primary source of information about program outcomes, other sources included course syllabi, peer advising, Web
pages, and capstone courses and material. Such a variety of faculty responses
demonstrates that departments provide multiple opportunities for students
to develop common understanding of the learning expected of them.

Students on the Educational Effectiveness Committee conducted similar interviews of a sampling of students across academic levels. Their findings corroborated faculty's responses regarding the variety of venues and opportunities for students to understand the MLOs. While faculty buy-in is essential to effective assessment, assessment-for-improvement cannot be fully addressed without student understanding of the learning expected of them.

Survey Question 4: Are outcomes public and visible? How?

When departments were asked whether their outcomes were public and visible, and to provide evidence thereof, they described multiple sources of evidence: the university catalog, fact sheets, student guidebook, Web pages, syllabi, student portfolio formats, brochures, Capstone materials and descriptions, and faculty advising. While the mediums will certainly vary on different campuses, the key implication here is that campuses must consider providing a variety of opportunities for both internal constituencies and external stakeholders to view and understand the goals and outcomes of their majors or degree programs. The objective is to achieve wider and better-informed attention to student learning by all stakeholders with potential for improving student learning and educational effectiveness.

*Survey Question 5: Are courses in the degree program aligned
with MLOs?*

While survey question 2 illustrates apparent variations in the degree of understanding among part-time faculty of respective program outcomes, responses to survey question 5 illustrate that all departments align their courses with program outcomes. The explanations from faculty indicated a mix of sequences in which courses were developed. In most departments, program outcomes preceded course development. In a few cases, "courses came first; the MLOs followed." The Center for Teaching, Learning, and Assessment conducted the first alignment project in spring 1999. One department reported that faculty who participated in the campus Course Alignment Project all rewrote their course syllabus to better align with the MLOs.

Faculty were asked to give evidence of course alignment with MLOs. They reported that evidence could be found in course syllabi, advising guides, fact sheets, individual student learning plans, course alignment sheets, common lesson plan rubrics, and documents from their strategic planning meetings where they reviewed each course for integrity to program MLOs.

Implications and Summary: Questions 1 Through 5

Program goals are achieved primarily at the course level. Through the Center for Teaching, Learning, and Assessment, faculty annually participate in the Course Alignment Project. They either analyze new courses or refine existing courses for alignment of course learning outcomes, assessment criteria, learning experiences, and course assessment with program outcomes. An important implication here is that when faculty and students understand their program goals and outcomes, buy-in and commitment to achievement at the course level are heightened. So is the probability for improved student learning.

While all faculty were aware that the accreditation requirements were driving the timing of this survey, some responses from department faculty provided valuable evidence for both accreditation documentation and improvement in specific areas in respective programs. Faculty responses clearly showed that some faculty viewed this assessment process as an opportunity to improve certain areas in their programs.

Assessment is a goal-oriented process. Campuses that have adopted an assessment-for-improvement approach, define and reexamine program goals and outcomes for continuous renewal and improvement. Whether the goal is to change, improve, replace, or merely clarify intentional learning in a program, evidence of clarity in goals and outcomes across programs, common understanding among faculty and students of program goals and outcomes, and public visibility via a variety of mediums are good practices that build a foundation for meaningful assessment and long-term improvement.

Assessment Guideline 2: Make assessment-for-improvement a team effort

Banta, Lund, Black, and Oblander (1996) support the significance of this guideline well: "There is, perhaps, no more important principle in the assessment literature than this: successful assessment requires collaborative efforts" (p. 35). Designing and implementing assessment-as-learning is a complex task requiring team effort. In the case of our campus, department teams were made up of faculty (tenured, tenure track, and part-time) and students. Faculty play the most important role in curricular and programmatic assessment. They also, more often than other campus constituencies, are involved in training and development activities in assessment. On many campuses, as on our campus, part-time faculty teach a significant number of courses in some departments, and thus have a critical effect on student learning. Therefore, the involvement and participation of part-time faculty and students in educational improvement is equally valuable in building a sustainable commitment across the department.

The value of a collaborative endeavor across the institution in assessment-for-improvement is multifold. In addition to its value in curricular and programmatic improvement, it can enhance the probability of the involvement and participation of campus stakeholders in sustained assessment for long-term improvement. Maki (2004) provides detailed guidance as well as hands-on directions and materials for developing a collective institutional commitment to assessment. Survey questions 6 and 7 address practices aimed at making assessment-for-improvement a team effort.

Discussion of Responses

Survey Question 6: How are MLOs developed? How many faculty participated?

Survey Question 7: Have students been involved in the development and review of MLO assessment?

Following the discussion of common understanding among faculty, interviewers asked, "How are MLOs developed?" and "How many faculty participated?" The most representative response:

> By a few faculty at first, but they [the MLOs] are now in their fourth rendition. Faculty have spent a great deal of retreat time refining these. As new faculty came on, they contributed to the process. To date, almost all of the faculty have contributed, with fewer of the part timers involved.

That fewer faculty participated at first in the development of MLOs can be attributed to the relatively short time range between CSUMB's opening (1995) and the minimal number of faculty constituting some departments at the time. The range of faculty involvement in MLO development was from 14 to 1, depending on the composition of faculty in a department. Over the seven-year period prior to accreditation, faculty involvement increased substantially. Two departments reported the involvement of students as well.

Implications and Summary: Questions 6 and 7

Our best practices survey results align with assumptions that characterize the research in collaborative approaches to assessment. Other campuses, in developing their assessment protocols, should consider the lessons learned in our process and build assessment planning around teamwork and collaboration across all program constituencies. The aim of inclusive involvement is a sustained commitment to assessment and "wider, better-informed attention to student learning by all parties with a stake in its improvement" (Astin et al., 1992, p. 2).

Assessment Guideline 3: Embed assessment into campus conversations about learning

To embed assessment into campus conversations about learning is to place assessment at the center of the learning process, thus the significance of this set of questions. Knowing about human learning and cognition frames the way faculty define learning outcomes, create effective pedagogies, and design assessment approaches and program improvement. Assessment on our campus reflects an understanding of learning as a complex phenomenon involving multidimensional and integrative processes. Our beliefs about learning attend to cognitive theories and research about human cognition, adult learning, and the integration of instruction and assessment that permeate the literature. Bringing together advances in assessment and in the understanding of human learning, these theories compel us to develop curriculum, instruction, and assessment that foster a variety of active, applied, and collaborative learning processes; teach and assess for long-term retention and transfer; and ensure alignment between outcomes and methods of assessment. They also urge us to establish validity and reliability across multiple dimensions of the teaching and learning process by using multiple sources of information about student learning and achievement across outcomes (see Resource List Number 2, appendix 8.A).

Questions 8 through 10 address processes that embed assessment in knowledge about learning and cognition. Faculty responses to these questions reflect our value for and understanding of teaching, learning, and assessment as "multidimensional, integrated, and revealed in performance over time" (Astin et al., 1992, p. 2).

Discussion of Responses: Survey Questions 8 Through 12

Survey Question 8: Does assessment in your courses provide opportunities for active and engaged learning?

Responses to question 8 illustrate departments' use of good practices in providing a range of opportunities for students to be active and engaged learners. Students demonstrate knowledge and understanding through *performance evidence* (such as role playing and project-based learning labs), *product evidence* (such as case studies, Web-based productions, and various written forms), and *experiential evidence* (such as service learning and mentorship), which serves as a source of information about students' applied learning in new and different contexts. Peer critiquing, group projects, and other collaborative assignments are among strategies employed to facilitate students' active engagement in and ownership of learning experiences. Self-assessment and weekly evaluations with direct feedback from faculty to students form a system of monitoring and review of progress that both faculty and students maintain. Thus, students' understanding of program MLOs and related course learning outcomes is expanded as a result of combining assessment with faculty feedback.

Survey Question 9: Is there a match between method of assessment and intended outcomes?

Departments reporting direct linkage of assessment to outcomes and learning activities do so using *process evidence* such as research, analysis and presentation of research, and essay and portfolio development. In these types of assignments, outcomes and assessment are based on the process of production.

Responses to questions 8 and 9 illustrate a variety of best practices in assessment that provide multiple sources of information about students' performance and achievement of outcomes. Additional strategic approaches to achieving reliability and validity are represented in question 10.

Survey Question 10: How has the department addressed bias, validity, and reliability, related to assessment of MLOs?

Several researchers offer simplified approaches to achieving reliability and validity of our assessments (see Resource List Number 3, appendix 8.A). Questions of validity and reliability generally focus on building confidence in assessment findings by assuring (a) agreement among a number of judges, (b) accuracy and consistency, (c) transferability of student performance, and (d) variety and sufficiency in assessing the same outcome in diverse contexts. Understanding learning as a complex process that is revealed in performance over time requires us to consider the reliability and validity of our assessment methods. Two practices that surfaced frequently under faculty responses to question 10 were the use of multiple assessors to read and judge capstone portfolios, and the general practice of using secondary readers for students' papers.

Implications and Summary: Questions 8 Through 10

Overall, the evidence suggests the primacy of student learning and optimal conditions for learning on our campus. The rich list of processes and learning conditions that are evident across most departments align with the wealth of research in learning, cognition, and optimal learning conditions. Through multiple and diverse approaches to assessment, the academic majors on our campus demonstrate adherence to research-based theories and models of learning as a complex and dynamic process.

While other campuses might benefit from the research on learning and cognition, as addressed in this section, each campus is urged to define (or clarify) its perspectives on learning and learning processes, preferably before developing an assessment protocol. Campuses might also consider multiple ways of collecting and evaluating information about students' performance and achievement of outcomes.

Attention to learning, cognition, and related assessment measures also requires attention to the needs of learners and the effects of learning experiences on them. Responses to survey questions 11 and 12, under guideline 4, address optimal teaching practices that support learners and their diverse learning abilities and preferences.

Assessment Guideline 4: Use assessment to support diverse learning abilities and to understand conditions under which students learn best

William Perry urges us to consider that "A fundamental belief in students is more important than anything else. This fundamental belief is not a sentimental matter of realistically conceiving the student where he or she is, and at the same time never losing sight of where he or she can be" (as cited in Knefelkamp, 2003, p. 11). Perry's description is a clear indication of the significance of this set of questions.

Other research studies identify instructional conditions that facilitate diverse learning needs of students. Those conditions include (a) active student engagement in learning and development, (b) facilitation of student understanding of outcomes and standards for student performance, (c) ongoing or regular assessment and prompt feedback to students, (d) student involvement in meaningful, collaborative contexts, (e) substantive student-faculty contact, and (f) respect for diverse ways of knowing and for the assets that students bring to learning situations (see Resource List Number 4, appendix 8.A). Faculty responses to questions 11 and 12 reflect these perspectives about learning.

Discussion of Responses: Survey Questions 11 and 12

Survey Question 11: Does assessment in the major support
diverse learners?

When asked whether assessment in the major supports diversity among learners, faculty across the 13 departments responded yes, citing bilingual cooperative learning teams, collaborative learning groups, and different graduation tracks as common learning support processes. Additional strategies cited as support for diverse learning abilities include portfolios for formative assessment, capstone projects and oral presentations for summative assessment, and various forms of group assignments and assessments. A few departments reported their success in using prompt feedback to students as well as immediate feedback about student performance on exams as ways to support diverse learning abilities. Another value of these strategies is that they help faculty to know what experiences students are having during, as opposed to after, the learning activities.

Survey Question 12: What forms of feedback do students receive from
assessment of MLOs (capstone, portfolios, etc.)?

When asked about the forms of feedback that faculty use to provide students with information about their performance, several departments reported using the capstone project evaluation as a form of feedback, oral feedback from advisors, portfolio assessment and feedback, and assignment-specific feedback mechanisms. Departments that use the portfolio approach emphasized the value of the faculty as advisor, the ongoing and meaningful dialogue between faculty and student, and the immediate feedback that faculty can offer students as they develop their portfolios.

Other departments explained their use of the "rater spreadsheet" in which three readers rate and comment on students' capstone performance. The portfolio and rater spreadsheet process includes comments from faculty, external reviewers, and a required self-assessment section for students.

Implications and Summary: Questions 11 and 12

Faculty responses portray strong interests in knowing about the effects of curriculum and teaching approaches on student learning, and the kind of student effort that results in achievement of outcomes. The rich list of processes and learning conditions evident across most departments suggest optimal learning conditions and assessment practices that lead to student achievement and ultimately program effectiveness.

Assessment Guideline 5: Connect assessment processes to questions or concerns that program decision makers or internal stakeholders really care about

"Assessment makes a difference when it begins with issues of use and illuminates questions that people really care about" (Astin et al., 1992, p. 2). The significance of the next set of questions is about relevance, use, and commitments. What issues are critical to the programs, departments, and/or the institution on your campus? This would be an interesting question to ask on your campus. Assessment experts urge campuses to give careful consideration to collecting information and data that are meaningful and satisfy concrete needs within a program, stimulate faculty discussions that lead to consensual change efforts, and can be transformed into policies that foster the integration of teaching, learning, and assessment (see Resource List Number 5, appendix 8.A).

Results of our best practices survey suggest that CSUMB faculty care about learner-centered pedagogies, collaborative and systematic analysis of student work for feedback, improvement of instruction for student success and ultimately programmatic effectiveness, assessment for improvement, and continuous renewal and improvement. Responses to questions 13 through 17 reflect these curricula and instructional values.

Discussion of Responses: Questions 13 through 17 and Tables 8-2, 8-3, and 8-4

Question 13: Is student work collected systematically for review of program effectiveness?

Question 14: Do faculty collaborate to review/analyze student work for feedback to program effectiveness?

Responses to questions 13 and 14 suggest that faculty across most departments (9 of 13 departments) make program changes based on their systematic collection and analysis of student work. Their collective analysis segue into discussions and decisions to change critical curricular structures, including primarily portfolio and capstone preparation and assessment. The purpose is to ensure student success in achieving course and program outcomes.

Question 15: Has assessment of student work resulted in reflection and action related to individual practices?

Table 8-2 illustrates a variety of effects of students' assessment performance on the individual reflection and practices of faculty. The evidence suggests that faculty are so concerned about student achievement that they are willing to employ practices such as scaffolding large assignments in order to assure student incremental success in coursework. They have strengthened project-based and field-based learning by focusing them on student interests. And, based on assessment of previous student work, faculty change or adjust syllabi, course design, and assignments to support student success. The implication here is clear that assessment-for-improvement and student success have significant effects on individual practices of faculty.

Question 16: Has the feedback from student work promoted any program change(s)? For example?

Equally important as changes in individual practices are programmatic changes resulting from assessment of student work. An array of program-

TABLE 8-2
Best Practices in Assessment—Campus Profile

Question 15: Has assessment of student work resulted in reflection and action related to individual practices?

Yes	No	Evidence of Reflection and Action
12 departments	1 department	• Performance criteria built into assignments • Single assignments broken into four different assignments • Change/adjustment in syllabi • Opened up acting class to field productions • Projects strengthened, based on student interests • Faculty constantly refining courses • Changes in teaching and assessments • Weekly and biweekly feedback sheets and implementation recommended changes immediately • Assessment of previous student work gets reflected into redesigning of course

matic changes is reflected in table 8-3. However, two critical examples high-light specific categories of instructional and student success elements that faculty recognized as needing special attention for on-campus performance and beyond. In some instances, faculty analysis of capstone portfolios re-vealed inadequate instructional attention to outcomes in cross-cultural com-petency and technical skills. Consequently, new courses were designed to address these missing competencies. When faculty also learned that students completing their degree program were having some difficulties gaining ad-mission to master's level programs because of insufficient learning in the his-tory of the discipline, they strengthened this component of the degree program.

Another practice in departments is to assess their major learning out-

TABLE 8-3
Best Practices in Assessment—Campus Profile

Question 16: Has the feedback from student work promoted any program change(s)? For example?

Yes	No	Evidence	In Progress	Future Plans
11 departments	2 departments	• Changes in curriculum, syllabi, lesson planning, new courses • New prerequisites established • New human development program • Students help with hiring • Changes in program & capstone • Use anon. surveys for program strengths and weaknesses • Hiring of faculty for area of program weakness • Revisions in mission statement and major learning outcomes	• One department is piloting a process in which teams of faculty will review capstone and portfolios and will summarize program recommendations at the end of the process.	

comes (program outcomes) for clarity, quality, and alignment with instructional and assessment practices. Question 17 addresses MLO assessment.

Question 17: Has program assessment of MLOs resulted in reflection and action related to individual practices?

When asked about the effects of MLO assessment on individual faculty practices, several results were described. Table 8-4 reflects some of the primary changes, and highlights "good" curriculum and instructional practices that lead to educational effectiveness and ultimately program improvement.

Implications and Summary: Questions 13 through 17

Responses to questions 13 through 17 suggest that best practices in assessment-for-improvement on our campus align closely with the rich research in this area. Whether the goal is to change individual faculty practices or programs, "the point of assessment is not to gather data and return results; it is a process that starts with the questions of decision-makers, that involves

TABLE 8-4
Best Practices in Assessment—Campus Profile

Question 17: Has program assessment of MLOs resulted in reflection and action related to individual practices?

Yes	No	Evidence	In Progress	Future Plans
12 departments	1 department	• Faculty teaching skill-based courses changed the curriculum and pedagogy • Changes in advising for students during capstone • More globalism in courses • Multiculturalism and reflection in courses • Change capstone & syllabi • More attention to student profiles • New approaches to teaching • Reinforce writing throughout program		

them in the gathering and interpreting of data, and that informs and helps guide continuous improvement" (Astin et al., 1992, p. 2).

Assessment Guideline 6: Make assessment protocols and results meaningful and available to internal and external stakeholders for feedback and ultimately improvement

Assessment Guideline 6—given its focus on improvement and accountability—appropriately recycles this chapter to the significance described in the introductory discussion of the two perspectives that frame this chapter:

1. Pascarella's (2001) assumption of institutional excellence or collegiate quality as effective educational practices
2. Gelmon's thesis that "intentional improvement" can result from the "deliberate linkage of assessment and accreditation" (1997, p. 51)

The use of best practices in assessment and dissemination of results internally and externally are essential steps in a larger context of institutional change. Gelmon argues for assessment as a global process that can be also be applied to faculty, program, and institutional improvement (1997, p. 54). Responses to question 18 highlight evidence of best practices in dissemination of educational goals and assessment results to internal stakeholders on campus, as well as external stakeholders, for feedback and improvement for faculty, programs, and ultimately the institution. It follows then that accountability—as follow-up to assessment—plays a significant role in assessment-as-learning and improvement.

Discussion of Responses

Survey Question 18: Are program reports of effectiveness based on student evidence made public and disseminated?

CSUMB, as a learning organization motivated by a culture of inquiry and continuous improvement, has been, and continues to be, responsive to various stakeholders in multiple ways. The dissemination and reporting of evidence of student achievement of program goals and expectations occurs in a variety of modalities across eight departments: student capstone presentations to audiences, program review activities that occur every five to seven years, and student scores on state-based and professional certification agencies. Although five departments reported that student evidence of achievement is not disseminated, at least one of the five reported plans to establish a Web site and a newsletter as avenues to report student achievement and program changes that result from feedback about student work.

Implications and Summary: Survey Question 18

As discussed above, the practices of gathering assessment data, using the results to measure program quality, and reporting results and changes to stakeholders occur in several venues on our campus. Other campuses might find our approaches helpful, or even familiar, and thus adaptable to their campus culture.

The use of best practices in assessment and dissemination of results internally and externally are essential steps in a larger context of institutional effectiveness and change. Maki's research (2004) supports the value of dissemination:

> As institutions develop systemic and systematic core processes of inquiry, they will also increasingly be able to represent their students' achievement to external audiences in ways that reflect educational practices, institutional values, and the diverse ways in which students represent and demonstrate their learning. (2004, p. xix)

Assessment Guideline 7: Design an assessment model that aligns with the institutional capacity to support it

Assessment is most effective when undertaken in an environment that is receptive, supportive, and enabling. Those qualities are significant considerations for the next question. Successful assessment requires an environment characterized by effective leadership, administrative commitment, adequate resources (for example, clerical support and money), faculty and staff development opportunities, funding, and time (Banta et al., 1996, pp. 62–63) so that institutional capacity can support assessment. An institution is advised to measure its capacity to support assessment in monetary realities as well as by its capacity to support ongoing faculty and staff development opportunities, long-term commitment across campus stakeholders to an assessment-as-learning model, and a belief in the inextricable link between teaching, learning, and assessment. In sum, as other campuses will discover, resources assume a variety of forms and involve efforts of internal and external communities. The results of institutional inquiry, research, and data collection should be used to establish priorities at different levels of the institution, and to revise institutional purposes, structures, and approaches to teaching, learning, and assessment.

Discussion of Responses: Question 19

Survey Question 19: Do you think that the department has sufficient resources to carry out effective assessment? If no, how are you dealing with the limitations?

Only 4 of the 13 departments responded yes to question 19; 9 departments responded no. Faculty described the need for more funding, more faculty, more release time for faculty to continue work on best practices assessment, and new resources. For example, many of the best practices probed in the interviews require extensive time and expertise on the part of faculty, and as such are significant capacity issues.

Our campus has addressed issues around faculty time and capacity to engage in assessment by compensating faculty to conduct collaborative reviews of students' portfolios, emphasizing outcomes-based assessment strategies, and rewarding faculty in the area of scholarship of teaching.

Implications and Summary: Question 19

Adequate resources are essential to successful assessment approaches on any campus. Just as effective assessment-for-improvement requires team effort (Assessment Guideline 2), adequate resources for successful assessment require collaborative planning between faculty and administration, and possibly external sources of funds.

Institutions must examine early in the planning stage their individual capacity to fund certain assessment approaches. Adequate resources assume various forms within a campus, and each campus has to determine which forms of resources are most beneficial to its campus. Without a supportive environment, institutional commitment, and resources that align with an institution's financial and personnel capacity, successful assessment cannot be realized.

Conclusion

Does our institution use best practices to assess student learning? What are those best practices? How do we use assessment results to improve individual instruction and programs? Is our process visible and public? And, is it replicable? This chapter answered these questions, starting with the rich research that informed our development of the survey used to examine best practices on our campus. Because the purpose of this chapter was to make our process visible, public, and replicable, the how-to approach provides an explication of a four-step research process and seven guidelines or recommendations that other campuses might consider when developing their survey of best practices. Although the guidelines are designed for best practices in assessment, they can be used for guiding best practices in other educational approaches, for example, in civic engagement or technologically mediated instruction.

Summarily, the guidelines (or recommendations) stipulate that best practices in assessment (1) define and clarify program goals and outcomes for long-term improvement, (2) make assessment-as-learning a team effort, (3) embed assessment into campus conversations about learning, (4) use assessment to support diverse learning abilities and to understand conditions under which students learn best, (5) connect assessment processes to questions and concerns that program decision makers really care about, (6) make assessment protocols and results meaningful and available to stakeholders, and (7) design assessment models that align with institutional capacity to support them.

The four-step research process and seven guidelines described in this chapter could benefit other campuses that are implementing assessment for accreditation or for programmatic improvement. Using the process and following the guidelines will promote inquiry, self-reflection, and direction for improvement—ultimately encouraging institutional learning.

References

Astin, A. W., Banta, T. W., Cross, K. P., El-khawas, E., Ewell, P. T., Hutchings, P., Marchese, T. J., McClenney, K. M., Mentkowski, M., Miller, M. A., Moran, E. T., & Wright, B. D. (1992). *Principles of good practice for assessing student learning*. Washington, DC: American Association for Higher Education.

Banta, T. W., Lund, J. P., Black, K. E., & Oblander, F. W. (Eds.). (1996). *Assessment in practice: Putting principles to work on college campuses*. San Francisco: Jossey-Bass.

Gelmon, S. B. (1997). Intentional improvement. In *Assessing impact: Evidence and action* (pp. 51–65). Washington, DC: AAHE.

Knefelkamp, L. L. (2003, Summer). The influence of a classic. *Liberal Education*, *89*(3), 11–15.

Maki, P. L. (2004). *Assessing for learning: Building a sustainable commitment across the institution*. Sterling, VA: Stylus.

Pascarella, E. T. (2001). Identifying excellence in undergraduate education: Are we even close? *Change*, *33*(3), 19–23.

RESOURCE LISTS

Resource List Number 1: Principles of Effective Assessment

Astin, A. W. (1985). *Achieving educational excellence: A critical assessment of priorities and practices in higher education.* San Francisco: Jossey-Bass.

Astin, A. W. (1991). *Assessment for excellence: The philosophy and practice of assessment and evaluation in higher education.* New York: American Council on Education & Macmillan.

Banta, T. W. (1993). Toward a plan for using national assessment to ensure continuous improvement of higher education. *Journal of General Education, 42,* 33–58.

Borden, V. M. H., & Banta, T. W.(1994). *Using performance indicators to guide strategic decision making.* San Francisco: Jossey-Bass.

Brown, S., & Glasner, A. (1999). *Assessment matters in higher education: Choosing and using diverse approaches.* London: Society for Research into Higher Education and Open University Press.

Erwin, T. D. (1991). *Assessing student learning and development: A guide to the principles, goals, and methods of determining college outcomes.* San Francisco: Jossey-Bass.

Hutchings, P. (1993). Principles of good practice for assessing student learning. *Assessment Update, 5*(1), 6–7.

Loacker, G., & Mentkowski, M. (1993). Creating a culture where assessment improves learning. In T. W. Banta & Associates (Eds.), *Making a difference: Outcomes of a decade of assessment in higher education* (pp. 5–24), San Francisco: Jossey-Bass.

Mentkowski, M., & Associates. (2000). *Learning that lasts: Integrating learning, development, and performance in college and beyond.* San Francisco: Jossey- Bass.

Palomba, C. A., & Banta, T. W. (1999). *Assessment essentials: Planning, implementing, and improving assessment in higher education.* San Francisco: Jossey-Bass.

Resource List Number 2: Cognitive Theories on Learning and Assessment

Alverno College Faculty. (1994). *Student assessment-as-learning at Alverno College.* Milwaukee, WI: Alverno College Department.

Baxter Magolda, M. B. (Ed.). (2000). *Teaching to promote intellectual and personal maturity: Incorporating students' worldviews and identities into the learning process.* San Francisco: Jossey-Bass.

Bransford, J. D., Brown, A. L., & Cocking, R. R. (Eds.). (2000). *How people learn: Brain, mind, experience, and school.* Washington, DC: National Academy Press.

Halpern, D. F., & Hakel, M. D. (2003). Applying the science of learning to the university and beyond: Teaching for long-term retention and transfer. *Change, 35*(4), 36–41.

Mezirow, J., & Associates. (Eds.). (2000). *Learning as transformation: Critical perspectives on a theory in progress.* San Francisco: Jossey-Bass.

Pellegrino, J. W., Chudowsky, N., & Glaser, R. (Eds.). (2001). *Knowing what students know: The science and design of educational assessment.* Washington, DC: National Academic Press.

Resource List Number 3: Establishing Validity and Reliability in Assessment Methods

Brown, S., & Knight, P. (1998). *Assessing learners in higher education.* London, U.K.: Kogan Page.

Miller, A. H., Imrie, B.W., & Cox, K. (1998). *Student assessment in higher education: A handbook for assessing performance.* London, U.K.: Kogan Page.

Resource List Number 4: Support for Diverse Learning Abilities

Angelo, T. A. (1999). Doing assessment as if learning matters most: Three steps to transformative practice. *American Association of Higher Education Bulletin, 51*(9), 3–6.

Astin, A. W. (1993). *What matters in college? Four critical years revisited.* San Francisco: Jossey-Bass.

Banta, T. W., & Associates. (Eds.). (1993). *Making a difference: Outcomes of a decade of assessment in higher education.* San Francisco: Jossey-Bass.

Chickering, A. W., & Gamson, Z. F. (1987). Seven principles for good practice in undergraduate education. *AAHE Bulletin, 39*(7), 3–7.

Resource List Number 5: Connecting Assessment to Decision Makers

Ewell, P. T. (1987). Establishing a campus-based assessment program. In D. F. Halpern (Ed.), *Student outcomes assessment: What institutions stand to gain: New Directions for Higher Education, 59* (pp. 9–24). San Francisco: Jossey-Bass.

Ewell, P. T. (1991). Assessment and public accountability: Back to the future. *Change, 23*(6), 12–17.

Ewell, P. T. (1997). Organizing for learning: A new imperative. *AAHE Bulletin, 50*(4), 3–6.

NINE PRINCIPLES OF GOOD PRACTICE FOR ASSESSING STUDENT LEARNING

1. **The assessment of student learning begins with educational values.** Assessment is not an end in itself but a vehicle for educational improvement. Its effective practice, then, begins with and enacts a vision of the kinds of learning we most value for students and strive to help them achieve. Educational values should drive not only *what* we choose to assess but also *how* we do so. Where questions about educational mission and values are skipped over, assessment threatens to be an exercise in measuring what's easy, rather than a process of improving what we really care about.

2. **Assessment is most effective when it reflects an understanding of learning as multidimensional, integrated, and revealed in performance over time.** Learning is a complex process. It entails not only what students know but what they can do with what they know; it involves not only knowledge and abilities but values, attitudes, and habits of mind that affect both academic success and performance beyond the classroom. Assessment should reflect these understandings by employing a diverse array of methods, including those that call for actual performance, using them over time so as to reveal change, growth, and increasing degrees of integration. Such an approach aims for a more complete and accurate picture of learning, and therefore firmer bases for improving our students' educational experience.

3. **Assessment works best when the programs it seeks to improve have clear, explicitly stated purposes.** Assessment is a goal-oriented process. It entails comparing educational performance with educational purposes and expectations—those derived from the institution's mission, from faculty intentions in program and course design, and from knowledge of students' own goals. Where program purposes lack specificity or agreement, assessment as a process pushes a campus toward clarity about where to aim and what standards to apply; assessment also prompts attention to

where and how program goals will be taught and learned. Clear, shared, implementable goals are the cornerstone for assessment that is focused and useful.

4. **Assessment requires attention to outcomes but also and equally to the experiences that lead to those outcomes.** Information about outcomes is of high importance; where students "end up" matters greatly. But to improve outcomes, we need to know about student experience along the way—about the curricula, teaching, and kind of student effort that lead to particular outcomes. Assessment can help us understand which students learn best under what conditions; with such knowledge comes the capacity to improve the whole of their learning.

5. **Assessment works best when it is ongoing not episodic.** Assessment is a process whose power is cumulative. Though isolated, "one-shot" assessment can be better than none, improvement is best fostered when assessment entails a linked series of activities undertaken over time. This may mean tracking the process of individual students, or of cohorts of students; it may mean collecting the same examples of student performance or using the same instrument semester after semester. The point is to monitor progress toward intended goals in a spirit of continuous improvement. Along the way, the assessment process itself should be evaluated and refined in light of emerging insights.

6. **Assessment fosters wider improvement when representatives from across the educational community are involved.** Student learning is a campus-wide responsibility, and assessment is a way of enacting that responsibility. Thus, while assessment efforts may start small, the aim over time is to involve people from across the educational community. Faculty play an especially important role, but assessment's questions can't be fully addressed without participation by student-affairs educators, librarians, administrators, and students. Assessment may also involve individuals from beyond the campus (alumni/ae, trustees, employers) whose experience can enrich the sense of appropriate aims and standards for learning. Thus understood, assessment is not a task for small groups of experts but a collaborative activity; its aim is wider, better-informed attention to student learning by all parties with a stake in its improvement.

7. **Assessment makes a difference when it begins with issues of use and illuminates questions that people really care about.** Assessment recognizes the value of information in the process of improvement. But to be useful, information must be connected to issues or questions that people really care about. This implies assessment approaches that produce evi-

dence that relevant parties will find credible, suggestive, and applicable to decisions that need to be made. It means thinking in advance about how the information will be used, and by whom. The point of assessment is not to gather data and return "results"; it is a process that starts with the questions of decision-makers, that involves them in the gathering and interpreting of data, and that informs and helps guide continuous improvement.

8. **Assessment is most likely to lead to improvement when it is part of a larger set of conditions that promote change.** Assessment alone changes little. Its greatest contribution comes on campuses where the quality of teaching and learning is visibly valued and worked at. On such campuses, the push to improve educational performance is a visible and primary goal of leadership; improving the quality of undergraduate education is central to the institution's planning, budgeting, and personnel decisions. On such campuses, information about learning outcomes is seen as an integral part of decision making, and avidly sought.

9. **Through assessment, educators meet responsibilities to students and to the public.** There is a compelling public stake in education. As educators, we have a responsibility to the publics that support or depend on us to provide information about the ways in which our students meet goals and expectations. But that responsibility goes beyond the reporting of such information; our deeper obligation—to ourselves, our students, and society—is to improve. Those to whom educators are accountable have a corresponding obligation to support such attempts at improvement.

Authors: Alexander W. Astin; Trudy W. Banta; K. Patricia Cross; Elaine El-Khawas; Peter T. Ewell; Pat Hutchings; Theodore J. Marchese; Kay M. McClenney; Marcia Mentkowski; Margaret A. Miller; E. Thomas Moran; Barbara D. Wright

This document was developed under the auspices of the AAHE Assessment Forum with support from the Fund for the Improvement of Postsecondary Education with additional support for publication and dissemination from the Exxon Education Foundation. Copies may be made without restriction.

9

ONE DEPARTMENT'S ASSESSMENT STORY

Processes and Lessons

Brian Simmons

This chapter describes the work of one of CSUMB's degree programs to create an in-house assessment protocol. The program's early history, including the very rough beginning of its earliest assessment efforts, is presented, as are the developmental stages the program experienced in producing the protocol. The protocol itself is discussed, as are reflections on some lessons learned that may be generalizable from this experience.

The Collaborative Health and Human Services Program: Background and History

This section presents a brief history of the Collaborative Health and Human Services (CHHS) degree program and its early experiences with outcomes-based education and assessment. The author hopes readers will recognize something of themselves and their own situations in this narrative: faculty called upon to develop an outcomes-oriented program with very little time and even less experience and expertise with assessing student learning. In

The author acknowledges the financial support of the Stuart Foundation of San Francisco for the work described in this chapter and the collaborative work of the CHHS faculty that created the assessment protocol.

addition to whatever consolation one might draw from the experience of one who has been there, lessons for moving forward are also suggested.

The CHHS program is an interdisciplinary preprofessional major designed to prepare students for entry-level positions and/or graduate-level education in the traditional helping professions. The major offers formal concentrations in social work and community health and also offers a strong grounding in public policy and public administration. Like all of CSUMB's programs, it is focused on providing students with competence in several predefined learning outcomes (major learning outcomes, or MLOs). Students engage in a variety of learning experiences to achieve the requisite knowledge, skills, and attitudes (KSAs), including mandatory internships totaling a minimum of 400 hours. The latter is consistent with CSUMB's fundamental commitment to applied learning, but also with long-standing traditions in the education of social work and public health students.

First Outcomes and Assessment Efforts

Like most of the early CSUMB faculty, CHHS's first professors had little understanding of what an "outcomes-based approach to education" meant and the implications for curriculum building, pedagogy, and assessment. Rather, the faculty simply knew that they were assigned to build an outcomes-based program. To establish the first set of learning outcomes for the major, the first department chair conducted an informal survey of the social service and public health agencies in the tricounty area served by CSUMB. The thrust of the survey's questions was very basic: what did they want a recently graduated, entry-level employee to know and know how to do? The survey was included in a newsletter that went out to local agencies on a mailing list. No formal records were kept regarding the number of surveys distributed or the number returned. That notwithstanding, based on the responses and the professional judgment of the department faculty, a list of learning outcomes and their corresponding definitions was generated. There were no standards, no assessment criteria, and no examples of acceptable evidence. Indeed, the connections between the courses offered and the MLOs were not always clear: as the faculty later discovered, at least one "required" course did not address any of the defined MLOs. Neither were faculty always sure that they were providing sufficient learning experiences across the curriculum that enabled students to generate evidence needed to graduate (not that the faculty were absolutely certain what that level of evidence was).

Early Lessons

The first effort to assess the students in their fieldwork experiences is illustrative of the faculty's inexperience with assessing outcomes-based learning. The program's founding faculty did appropriately mandate behaviorally oriented learning contracts between the students and the agencies that were mentoring them. The student and her or his mentor defined activities and work products to coincide with MLOs identified by the student to work on that term. However, at the end of the semester, the mentors were given only a sheet of paper with the name and definition of each MLO they and the student had agreed to address and were asked to write an assessment of the student's KSAs in that area. The fieldwork mentors had nothing more in the way of assessment criteria or standards than did the classroom-based faculty.

First efforts to evaluate the students' graduation portfolios did not demonstrate any higher level of sophistication. Given that students were generating evidence in support of their KSAs for each of the various MLOs in a variety of learning experiences, no single learning experience provided an adequate opportunity to fully assess any one of them. Thus the graduation portfolio was adopted. Students gather their accumulated evidence from various sources (e.g., prior learning, classroom, field, individual independent studies, group independent studies and projects) into a portfolio that becomes the summary of their upper division learning for the MLOs. Three evaluators read and must pass each portfolio.

Again, however, reviewers received very little guidance for their reading: no real standards or criteria. They were asked only to use their best judgment to assess whether, in their professional opinion, the student demonstrated what an entry-level employee with a bachelor's degree should know and know how to do in each area. For obvious reasons, obtaining any kind of meaningful kind of inter-rater reliability was not possible. Although all the students in the first few cohorts satisfactorily passed the portfolio review, program faculty had no idea if the readers were reaching that conclusion for anything resembling the same reasons.

Thus was the state of the art for the first few years of the program: unsophisticated and subjective. Students routinely asked how much evidence was required for each section; the routine answer was "enough."

Program assessment was likewise fairly unsophisticated and unsystematic. Granted, in the earliest years, few data existed to analyze. In part, that was also due to minimal or nonexistent efforts to collect them. Some efforts were made to glean lessons from the portfolio reviews if student work revealed patterns of a lack of evidence in some areas. Likewise, an occasional comment or observation from an external portfolio reviewer might have led to adjustments in one part of the program or another, but there was no systematic effort to solicit such input. Additional measures of program efficacy were sorely needed.

The program's faculty were plainly uncomfortable with this state of affairs, but also recognized they lacked the expertise to make needed changes and the resources to acquire that expertise.

The Path to Skillful Assessment Practice

This section delineates the steps the program's faculty took to establish a culture of assessment within the department and to create a proficient assessment protocol for the faculty's use. These processes can be easily adapted for use by other programs regardless of discipline, but should especially be of interest to professionally oriented degree programs.

Redetermining the Validity of the MLOs

The CHHS faculty wanted to reestablish that the MLOs the students' learning experiences were being geared to in fact had validity in the professional field. That is, were the students really learning what they needed to know and know how to be successful, entry-level, helping professionals upon graduation?

Toward that end, the program faculty, with the support of a grant from the Stuart Foundation, and using a common Delphi process, surveyed health and human service agencies in the local area; 75 agencies were part of the initial response group and formed the core of the remaining Delphi cycles. In the first cycle, the respondents were provided with each of the current MLOs and were asked to suggest additional learning outcomes. Department staff from those responses generated an aggregate list of possible learning outcomes. In the second cycle, respondents were asked to rank the relative importance of the potential learning outcomes. (In a third cycle, respondents then identified which MLOs they believed they could offer field-based instruction to the students. This information would serve later to enhance the program's capacity to assist students who wanted to increase their knowledge and skills in specific areas with the identification of field placement sites that were able to address their needs).

The Delphi process affirmed the 11 MLOs that existed at the time. While a few respondents made some suggestions for additions, there was either no systematic pattern to the responses that warranted adding an additional learning outcome, or the CHHS faculty deemed that the suggestions were covered by existing MLOs.

Redefining and Refining the MLOs

With a validated list of learning outcomes in hand, the more difficult task began: specifying what was meant by each MLO. Toward that end, drawing from the work of Forte and Matthews (1994), local health and human services professionals again provided input and validation. For each MLO, a department faculty member with subject matter expertise in that area convened a focus group comprising several health and human services practitioners (broadly defined to include law enforcement) and student representatives from the program (consistent with one of the best practices identified by Palomba and Banta [1999]). Each group met a minimum of three times and was charged with defining the respective MLO in a way that would be meaningful to student, fieldwork mentor, and course instructor. Additionally, each group was asked to define general competencies for each MLO's KSAs. Finally, each group was charged with developing what were called supporting competencies: specific examples of evidence that the student could offer in support of the claim of being adequately competent in each area to warrant the awarding of a degree.

In defining the competencies, focus group members made use of the well-known Bloom's taxonomy (Bloom, 1956). Doing so helped the group members focus their own thinking and concretize the examples. This work in turn helped course instructors and fieldwork mentors design learning experiences to match the thinking of the professionals from the field.

As a result, each MLO was reformulated using a common structure: a broad definition, a less broad but still foundational defining set of KSA statements, and then an even more specifically defined set of supporting competencies. The latter, it should be noted, were intended to be suggestive, not exclusive, of the kinds of evidence that students could submit in their portfolios for a satisfactory review. An example is provided in figure 9-1. The complete list of MLOs, their definitions, KSA statements, and supporting competencies can be viewed on the Health, Human Services, and Public Policy (HHSPP) Web site (CHHS, 2004).

Realignment of the Curriculum

The CHHS faculty then started a concerted effort to ensure that (1) the courses and other learning experiences offered addressed the MLOs, and (2)

FIGURE 9-1
CHHS's Cross-Cultural Competence MLO

Definition: Demonstrate the ability to be comfortable with differences between self and others, to engage in a process characterized by mutual respect and sensitivity, to assess the needs and capabilities of culturally diverse populations, and communicate effectively across cultural groups to deliver appropriate health and human services.

Core Competencies:

Knowledge: Cross-culturally competent workers in the health and human services know the basic issues associated with cultural competence, know their own culture and the impact it has on professional practice, and have knowledge of the specific beliefs and practices of the different cultural groups (broadly defined) with whom they will be working.

Skills: Cross-culturally competent workers in the health and human services know how to access available information and resources to improve services to the groups they are working with and how to adopt professional practices to meet culturally unique needs.

Attitudes: Cross-culturally competent workers in the health and human services acknowledge the importance of culture and maintain vigilance toward the dynamics of cultural differences.

Supporting Competencies:

Entry-level cross-culturally competent workers in the health and human services have the ability to:
- Recognize the limits of their own knowledge, competencies, and expertise and how those limits affect interactions with people from other cultural backgrounds
- Demonstrate a positive attitude and approach to learning about the characteristics of different cultural communities and the resources available to serve them
- Demonstrate an understanding of their racially and culturally bound values and attitudes and seek to cultivate a nonracist worldview
- Challenge assumptions, stereotypes, and paradigms of others
- Demonstrate a basic knowledge of how oppression, racism, discrimination, and stereotyping affect all people, including a history of the oppression of some groups by the dominant culture and the role of internalized oppression
- Claim their own cultural identities; have a working knowledge of that culture, including an awareness of how it affects their own beliefs, values, and behaviors; and present that culture to others

- Contrast their own beliefs and attitudes with those from other cultures and challenge their own biases and practices
- Demonstrate an understanding of communication style differences
- Establish an approach that actively seeks out educational and social experiences that foster their own knowledge, understanding, and cross-cultural skills
- Adapt practice to different cultural situations
- Acknowledge that one individual need not have all the answers, and to be open to themselves and others taking risks, reaching out across cultures, and learning from their mistakes
- Acknowledge the role of indigenous helping practices and respect intrinsic help-giving networks in the community
- Seek professional experiences (e.g., training, education, consultation) to improve effectiveness in working with others who differ culturally
- Think critically on matters of cultural diversity

---

that the opportunity to achieve all the MLOs was in fact present somewhere in the curriculum. This process began at a faculty retreat with the creation of a list of all the courses offered by the program. The faculty member primarily responsible for a given course then discussed what actually took place in the course, including what was done to address the MLOs. In that way, the faculty had a common understanding of what was actually being delivered in the curriculum.

The faculty identified one class that, while offering what was thought to be important content, was not actually directed toward any of the MLOs, while others approximated the MLOs but did not provide students the opportunity to generate the kinds of evidence deemed necessary to graduate. This lead to the elimination and consolidation of classes and a closer alignment between assigned student class work and the MLOs. Likewise, CHHS faculty consolidated and reorganized those classes so that the material addressing the MLOs could be completed in a more efficient manner.

Realigning the Assessment of Field-Based Learning

Making realistic learning contracts and assessment forms for the students and their fieldwork mentors has been one of the most challenging parts of the process. The goal of making the forms as user friendly and manageable as possible conflicted with the goal of making them meaningful for both student and mentor. The forms have gone through several iterations since the program's inception. As noted previously, the initial assessment forms had a single page per MLO with very little structure and guidance for the student and mentor (see appendix 9.A). The present system again has a single page for each MLO, but now the form contains both the learning contract and the assessment form. This remains a work in progress. Examples of the current version of the forms appear in figures 9-2 and 9-3.

Developing Criteria and Standards and Increasing Internal Program Consistency

Following the conclusion of the Stuart Foundation project, department staff received a grant from CSUMB's Center for Teaching, Learning, and Assessment to continue development of the assessment protocol. The first task was to develop a common assessment framework that could be used across a variety of teaching and learning settings. The second major task was to define standards and criteria and to establish other means of standardization. While this may sound sequential in a temporal sense, in reality the framework and the standards and criteria were created in tandem.

After several attempts, a framework was successfully developed that named and defined each learning outcome and provided space for grading the student in that given area. With the addition of a "grade" for having no evidence at all, students are assessed on a four-point scale: *outstanding, commendable, adequate,* and *needs improvement.* An example of how the framework was modified specifically or used in our fieldwork program was presented in figure 9-2.

Rather than develop specific criteria related to each learning outcome, department faculty instead developed a universal set of criteria that could be used for those four standards for any assignment, project, paper, or fieldwork experience. The criteria appear in appendix 9.B, CHHS Common Grading Rubric. The standards and criteria are provided to the students in each course syllabus. While generic in nature, they have proven to be specific enough to provide students with guidance about the level of work that is expected and how grades are assigned. Course instructors and fieldwork mentors have found them useful in determining how to assess student performance.

In addition to the creation of standards and criteria, department faculty also established other processes and mechanisms for standardizing the in-house assessment work:

- A common syllabus format. Each course follows essentially the same format, providing background for the course, course learning out-

FIGURE 9-2
Mentor Field Assessment Progress

MLO 1—Collaboration: Demonstrate the ability to work in teams in interprofessional settings across traditional lines of programs, agencies, disciplines, and diverse communities to establish common missions and purposes; and to collaborate with others in decision making, learning, completing tasks, and applying knowledge of group processes and group interaction.

Circle the number that best reflects the students' level of competence at the beginning and end of the field experience

Collaboration Competencies	Planned Assignments and Projects	Progress on Projects and Evaluation of Student		Assessment of Entering & Exiting Level of Competency					
					None/N/A	Limited	Adequate	Commendable	Outstanding
Knowledge: Demonstrate what collaboration means, why it is important, and how community conditions can be improved by employing the collaborative process.			Entering		0	1	2	3	4
			Exiting		0	1	2	3	4
Skills: The ability to build consensus and sustain participation with an interprofessional group solving problems and resolving conflict using different decision-making processes relevant for collaborative groups.			Entering		0	1	2	3	4
			Exiting		0	1	2	3	4
Attitudes: Demonstrate the ability to share resources, expertise and responsibility to achieve a common goal in a collaborative setting.			Entering		0	1	2	3	4
			Exiting		0	1	2	3	4

Required Comments on Student Performance for this MLO:

This evaluation has been reviewed and discussed with the student

Agency Mentor	Date	Student	Date	CHHS Faculty Advisor	Date

FIGURE 9-3
Mentor Field Assessment Completed

MLO 1—Collaboration: Demonstrate the ability to work in teams in interprofessional settings across traditional lines of programs, agencies, disciplines, and diverse communities to establish common missions and purposes; and to collaborate with others in decision making, learning, completing tasks, and applying knowledge of group processes and group interaction.

Circle the number that best reflects the students' level of competence at the beginning and end of the field experience

Collaboration Competencies	Planned Assignments and Activities	Completed Assignments and Evidence for Portfolio		Assessment of Entering & Exiting Level of Competency				
				None/N/A	Limited	Adequate	Commendable	Outstanding
Knowledge: Demonstrate what collaboration means, why it is important, and how community conditions can be improved by employing the collaborative process.			Entering	0	1	2	3	4
			Exiting	0	1	2	3	4
Skills: The ability to build consensus and sustain participation with an interprofessional group solving problems and resolving conflict using different decision-making processes relevant for collaborative groups.			Entering	0	1	2	3	4
			Exiting	0	1	2	3	4
Attitudes: Demonstrate the ability to share resources, expertise and responsibility to achieve a common goal in a collaborative setting.			Entering	0	1	2	3	4
			Exiting	0	1	2	3	4

Required Comments on Student Performance for this MLO:

This evaluation has been reviewed and discussed with the student

Agency Mentor _____ Date _____ Student _____ Date _____ CHHS Faculty Advisor _____ Date _____ comes (categorized by the different types of outcomes found at CSUMB), and the standards and criteria for grading.

- A common grading rubric. The faculty found inconsistencies among the instructors regarding the value of a given grade. For example, for a student who achieved a 90% score, some instructors assigned an A, others an A minus, and others, still, a B plus. Instructors now assign letter grades based on a common rubric (see appendix 9.B).

The CHHS Assessment Protocol

The product of over four years' work, the CHHS Assessment Protocol provides a dynamic set of tools for assessing both student learning and program effectiveness. This section presents the individual tools in the protocol, the questions they are designed to answer, and how they are used. A version of the protocol's full table of contents, adapted from Simmons and Judson (2004), appears in appendix 9.C.

Assessment of the MLOs

Assessment of the student's KSAs occurs at several points throughout the student's time in the program. The following identifies and describes those points in time and the process of assessment:

Entering Student Self-Assessment

Where do the students stand relative to the MLOs when they first enter the program? Students, especially reentry students, are not proverbial blank slates when they begin their degree program. They bring with them a wide range of previous learning experiences (e.g., prior coursework, employment, and volunteer work). These experiences equip them with some knowledge and skill that are germane to the MLOs. Establishing a baseline measure of this knowledge and skill provides a means to gauge student progress through the program.

Ideally, the program would have valid and reliable instruments to measure the KSAs for each MLO at the time of entry. That level of sophistication has yet to come. Instead, the program relies on student self-assessments.

Students are introduced to the MLOs and the KSAs in a course taken during their first semester in the program, whose goals include familiarizing students with the requirements and processes of the major, the campus, and the pedagogical approach. When discussing the MLOs, an emphasis is placed on the need for actual evidence that can support the student's claim to be at a certain level of competence. Undocumented subjective impressions are to be avoided. Once conversant with the MLOs and how to assess them, the students assess themselves on all 12 of the MLOs, using the standard assessment form. (This is the same form that is in appendix 9.B.)

While this does meet the goal of providing something of a baseline to compare student competence in the MLOs, the faculty remain uncertain of the value of this particular assessment opportunity. Student self-assessments, especially this early in the program, tend to be somewhat inflated and thus tend to provide unreliable measures of actual student competence. The process does provide students with exposure to the assessment tool and the procedure, so it does retain some value from that perspective.

Field Learning Agreement and Student Assessment Matrix

How well do students progress in their command of the KSAs while participating in their internships? Generally speaking, a student is in the field every semester he or she is in the program. With each new placement (or sometimes at the start of a new semester at the same placement), the student and her or his mentor complete a learning agreement. The learning agreement form is based on the standard assessment form, but has some modifications to allow for an assessment of both entering and departing competencies and a description of the tasks the student is to work on during the semester to advance his or her KSAs. Only those MLOs that the student and the mentor have agreed to work on during the period covered are actually assessed. By the time the student graduates, he or she will have documented fieldwork evidence for most, if not all, of the MLOs to supplement the classroom-based evidence. Most will have evidence from more than one site.

Exiting Student Self-Assessment

Did the student's competence in the MLOs improve during her or his time in the program? The first of the two ways the program seeks to determine that is to have the students complete an exiting self-assessment. During the student's final semester in the program, she or he once again completes a version of the standard assessment form, evaluating herself or himself on all of the MLOs. The faculty consider this to be a more realistic snapshot of the student's view of where he or she stands. The student is more conversant with the MLOs and their requirements and (perhaps) a bit more humble about his or her own limits. Given the tendency to inflate the initial self-assessment, some of the indicators may even be lower than they were two years (or more) earlier.

Portfolio Review

Given the varying possible learning opportunities available to each student to accumulate KSAs for each MLO (i.e., the student may be working on given MLOs in a course, in a field placement, in a capstone project, or in some other learning experience), a single assessment point (e.g., a given course) is not possible until the student actually completes the program. Thus the program calls for students to create a graduation portfolio that is the compilation of the best evidence of their KSAs for all of the MLOs. This was described earlier and has been a constant since the program's inception.

The portfolio serves as the second means for conducting an exiting assessment of the student's progress toward competence in the MLOs. In its totality, it is the student's statement that she or he has completed the program.

The protocol currently calls for each portfolio to be examined and approved by three reviewers: two members of the faculty and a practitioner from the field whose profession is consistent with the student's declared concentration within the major. The reviewers use a version of the standard assessment format and evaluate the student on all of the MLOs. As part of the protocol, an orientation for new readers was developed to familiarize them with the assessment form and the MLOs' standards and criteria. A common set of instructions was also to enhance additional interreader reliability of the portfolio assessments.

The outside reader, who does not know the student whose portfolio she or he is reading, serves to counteract whatever bias (favorable or negative) that the faculty readers (who do know the student) may have. The external readers also provide a program quality control check, a point discussed below. The instructions to the external readers is contained in appendix 9.D.

Postgraduate Self-Assessment: One-Year Postgraduation

The ultimate outcome of any program is the postgraduation success of its alumni. What, if any, contribution did the MLOs make toward the accomplishments of the program's graduates? The protocol calls for alumni to be surveyed one year after graduation to assess which of the MLOs they have found most useful in their postprogram careers. It also calls for a survey of their employers to see what, if any, differential impact they are able to discern from having hired a student educated in an outcomes-based system. Due to resource limitations, these sections of the protocol have not yet been implemented. The department does maintain a database of permanent contact information on the alumni so that these sections can be implemented when resources become available.

Program Assessment Elements

Besides assessing student performance, department faculty were also interested in assessing program performance. With that goal in mind, several program assessment elements were created as part of the protocol:

Student Assessment of Agency and Mentor

What was the student's experience in the agency as an intern? Would the student recommend this site for a future student? As noted above, the field practice program is an integral piece of the CHHS program, with students documenting a minimum of 400 fieldwork hours during their time in the program. With such an investment of resources, department faculty and staff wanted a more sophisticated information loop about the strengths and weaknesses of the field practice program. The first tool created for the protocol was the Student Assessment of the Agency and Mentor. As suggested by the title, at the end of the field placement, the student completes an assessment form about her or his experience regarding both the agency and the mentor. Staff in the field track these assessments and make them available for new students to review prior to selecting a placement site. Feedback is also provided to the agencies should corrective action be necessary.

Mentor Assessment of CHHS Field Practice Program

From the view of the mentor, how is the field practice program working? To round out the information on the field program, the mentors are also asked to assess their experience with the program. Mentors rate their interactions with the department staff, the training they receive, and staff responsiveness to their needs. Results are incorporated into the field program's annual report to the faculty and used for program improvement. This is yet another example of the program's reliance on the community's expertise to assess the program's functioning.

Additional Program Assessment Elements

Finally, three more measures of program effectiveness are tracked, one involving learning outcomes and the other involving what students do upon their departure from the program.

Student Portfolio Review

The portfolio review process is described above. In addition to reviewing student work, the external portfolio readers watch for and identify any perceived gaps in the curriculum, especially for any recent changes in professional philosophy and practice that the program's pedagogy does not reflect. The program faculty then discuss these comments during the semiannual retreats geared toward program revision. In addition, these readers provide a "reality check" on the program. They are frequently people who hire or evaluate entry-level employees and are able to provide immediate feedback regarding the preparation their potential employees are receiving.

Student Competency Summary Matrix

Part of the work of the Stuart Interprofessional Education Consortium (2001) was to define a set of interprofessional learning outcomes. Not surprisingly, there was some overlap with the CHHS MLOs, but some dissimilarity as well. To provide something of a cross-check on the effectiveness of the program, graduating students complete a second self-assessment using the Stuart Interprofessional Competencies. While there is no 1:1 correspondence with the CHHS competencies, enough similarities exist to detect areas of program strength and areas in need of improvement.

Student Graduate School Rate of Acceptance

In its earliest program documents, the department declared that one of its goals would be to prepare students for entry into graduate-education programs. The goal remains unchanged. Since the first cohort, program faculty have tracked not only the number of students who apply and are accepted into graduate programs, but also which programs and which universities accept them. As of this writing (September 2004), the program enjoys a 94% success rate of applicants being accepted into graduate programs. Of additional interest is the wide range of fields that the program's graduates have chosen to study. While social work remains by far the discipline the majority of the students pursue, other alumni have chosen public health, criminal justice, counseling, business administration, public administration, education, law, nursing, and public policy. Department faculty members offer this as evidence of the efficacy of the interdisciplinary approach used in preparing the students.

Lessons Learned

The CHHS assessment experience has provided a number of important conceptual and process insights for those considering embarking on their own assessment journey. They provide a list of elements critical to the successful development of the CHHS Assessment Protocol. The author's reflections on these elements are contained in this section.

Collaboration Among Interdisciplinary Faculty and Community Professionals

Clients of the various health and human services systems face complex sets of issues. The faculty believe that one of the strengths of the program is the belief that practitioners cannot rely upon the approach of a single profession to assess client situations and design appropriate interventions. Collaboration among professionals with a variety of skills and sets of knowledge is essential. Doing so is one of the assessment best practices identified by Palomba and Banta (1999). Students must be prepared to implement this collaborative approach upon graduation. The program faculty likewise believe that the preparation for this approach to practice likewise should not be left to academicians from a single discipline, nor, in fact, just to academicians. Working with faculty from a variety of disciplinary backgrounds and practitioners from those systems that clients are likely to encounter not only defines the nature of the program's learning outcomes but also provides the program's students with a rich educational experience they would not have otherwise had.

The external members of the professional community likewise can play an important role in program assessment as well as in the assessment of student learning. Their expertise, grounded in the reality of everyday policy demands and practice issues, is an important resource for ensuring that the program stays attuned to professional needs and program demands. The building of collaborative relationships with these "community partners" is an essential element of the CHHS protocol.

Being Committed to Integration of Academic and Practice Settings

Each MLO has elements best taught in the classroom and others best taught in the field. The goal, the achievement of the KSAs associated with the whole outcome, cannot be reached without an approach to teaching and learning that integrates both field-based and classroom-based learning. Assessment must likewise take place in the classroom and the field, thus providing another role for our community partners.

Having the Ability to Tolerate Ambiguity and Uncertainty

Adopting an outcomes-based approach to teaching and learning will be a new experience for most faculty who, by definition, are accustomed to being experts in their respective fields. Most faculty are *not* experts in assessing student work. Adopting the approach of a learner rather than an expert will be key. There will be much trial and error and continual revision of approaches and assessment formats based on experience. Many things will not be as precise (at least initially) as one might like. Processes, terms, and concepts that were once thought agreed upon will need to be revisited (probably more than once) as experience raises questions not previously considered. Thus, the more program faculty can tolerate ambiguity and uncertainty, the greater the likelihood of ultimate success.

Keeping the Professorial Ego in Check

Faculty members are not generally known for their humility. Attempting to adopt an outcomes-based approach to teaching and learning will undoubtedly identify significant "turf" issues for many programs, as faculty are asked to change the way they think about how they teach and assess. During the program realignment, certain members of the faculty gave up or significantly reorganized favorite classes when it became clear that doing so would serve the students more efficiently. Likewise, there are multiple "right" approaches to assessing student outcomes. Insisting upon one approach or another is a sure recipe for disaster. Remaining flexible and open to the perspectives of others is essential.

Letting go of turf involves risk and moving people beyond their levels of comfort. It may be necessary to create incentives to help motivate some faculty to actively engage in the assessment process. Maximizing student learning and having concrete evidence of having done so in itself will be highly (and sufficiently) encouraging for some. Other inducements may be necessary for others. These will obviously vary from program to program and individual to individual, as will the ability to offer them.

Taking a long-term view may also be necessary. As faculty vacancies occur, hiring committees should take great care to ensure that new hires will be at least compatible, if not comfortable, working in an organizational culture of assessment.

Being Committed to Ongoing Program Renewal/Improvement

The faculty in the CHHS program are all committed to a continuous process of assessment, reflection, and program improvement. An outcomes-based approach to teaching and learning provides the opportunity to attend to that commitment. For example, the portfolio review process described above has on more than one occasion revealed gaps in instruction: certain outcomes were not being addressed as thoroughly as the faculty thought, or as courses evolved over time, the desired emphasis on certain outcomes had shifted. The program faculty have used these and other opportunities to make changes in specific courses and in the program itself.

Being Committed to Producing Well-Prepared Entry-Level Professionals

Most academic programs are created from the perspective of teaching "what should be taught." For example, every MSW program has one or more courses on policy, research methods, and human behavior. Business programs routinely have courses on accounting and organizational behavior. An outcomes-based approach reverses the question and asks, "What should be learned?" What is it that one wants a social worker or a businessperson to know and know how to do? That question is best answered by looking to the fields of practice in which the students will find themselves after graduating, and curricula are best designed with the responses to those questions in mind.

Increasing Accountability

Students, parents, future employers, governing boards, legislative bodies, and taxpayers all have the right to expect the resources they are investing in the educational process will be put to good use. Having an outcomes-based approach and the requisite assessment methods increases those expectations because the program has actually named ahead of time what knowledge and skills the students will have when they depart. But this approach also enhances the program's ability to respond to the challenge of accountability.

What comes with the culture of assessment is the ability to document the success of one's efforts. The assortment of assessment instruments collected over the student's time in the program and the student's own graduation portfolio provide concrete evidence that the program is producing the promised preprofessional. They also reveal program gaps, which in turn become opportunities for reexamining the curriculum and its delivery and making necessary corrections. Sound outcomes and sound self-correcting mechanisms will allow the constituent groups to be quite satisfied with the stewardship of their resources.

Conclusion

Successful implementation of an outcomes-based curriculum and its accompanying assessment protocol can be a lesson in humility. While academicians are trained experts in their respective fields of knowledge, most received very little training in teaching, learning, and assessment. Acknowledging the limits of one's own knowledge and abilities and having the willingness to expose oneself to a different view of pedagogy is essential. So too is the willingness to yield traditional turf issues and other symbols the professorial identity is attached to: the author and his colleagues found being able to give up cherished classes and to acknowledge the expertise of nonacademicians to be critical elements of the process. Last, program faculty acknowledge that there is no final "completion" of the work of creating the assessment protocol. At the risk of using an overworked phrase, adhering to a philosophy of continuous renewal keeps the program and the teaching and learning within it vibrant and exciting.

References

Bloom, B. S. (Ed.). (1956). *Taxonomy of educational objectives: The classification of educational goals: Handbook I, cognitive domain.* New York: Longman.

Collaborative Health and Human Services (2004). Program major learning outcomes. Retrieved September 15, 2004, from http://hhspp.csumb.edu/academic/CHHS/mlo.htm.

Forte, J. A., & Mathews, C. (1994). Potential employers' views of the ideal undergraduate social work curriculum. *Journal of Social Work Education, 30,* 228–240.

Interprofessional Education Consortium. (2001). *Defining the knowledgebase for interprofessional education.* San Francisco: Stuart Foundation.

Palomba, C. A., & Banta, T. W. (1999). *Assessment essentials: Planning, implementing, and improving assessment in higher education.* San Francisco: Jossey-Bass.

Simmons, B., & Judson, K. (2004, March). Assessing student learning: Lessons from an outcomes-based health and human services program. Paper presented at the 50th Annual Program Meeting of the Council on Social Work Education, Anaheim, CA.

EXAMPLE OF PREVIOUS FIELD-BASED LEARNING ASSESSMENT

Collaboration: Demonstrate the ability to work in teams in inter-professional settings across traditional lines of programs, agencies, disciplines, and diverse communities to establish common missions and purposes; and to collaborate with others in decision making, learning, completing tasks, and applying knowledge of group processes and group interaction.

_____   _____
Student's Signature & Date   Mentor's Signature & Date

CHHS COMMON GRADING RUBRIC

The form on pages 194–198 contains the common grading rubric used by all CHHS course instructors and contains the standards and criteria instructors in all learning experiences use to assess student performance.

Department of Health, Human Services & Public Policy
Collaborative Health and Human Services
Standards and Criteria for Ranking/Grading Competency Levels

STANDARDS FOR QUALITY OF WORK

	Ranking	Score	Grade	Academic Criteria	Field Criteria
Outstanding/ Excellent	4	90–100	A – to A +	**The work (oral and written) is excellent.**	**The work (oral and written) is excellent.**
				It shows creative and critical thinking, original responses to the material; strong analytical skills; strong descriptive and bibliographic skills; and the ability to synthesize material.	*Takes responsibility for own professional development (including Field Learning Agreement) *Eager to learn—seeks and utilizes training *Enthusiasm for the work
				The work draws critical connections between research materials and their historical, cultural, political, social and economic contexts and uses an excellent level of detail to demonstrate knowledge and skills.	*Written work is publishable within the agency, e.g., reports, brochures, court reports, etc. *Ability to synthesize information and apply to the job
				The work draws on multiple sources and shows excellent bibliographic, annotation and synthesizing skills.	*Understands political and professional culture *Incorporates feedback
				Written and oral work shows logical and clear thought and expression, unity and coherence of analysis and creativity.	*Works beyond expectations, which includes the following: —Stays beyond the scheduled hours as needed —Goes the "extra mile" to help out when needed —Ability to work independently —Demonstrates leadership

3	80–89	B − to B +	Commendable/ Very good	**The work is better than average.**	Excellent spelling, punctuation and grammar are evident.	*Understanding of micro and macro systems
				There is some original thought and response to the material.	Student is always prepared and strongly contributes to the group learning process.	*Ability to collaborate with broad range of clients and coworkers
				The work demonstrates good interpretive, descriptive and synthesizing skills.	Presentations are professional, original and engaging.	*High level of self-awareness as a developing professional
				The work shows the ability to make critical connections between the historical, cultural, political, social and economic contexts.	**The work is better than average.**	**The work is better than average.**
				It provides an appropriate level of detail to demonstrate knowledge and skills development.		*On time—punctual and reliable
				The work draws on multiple research sources and shows good bibliographic, annotation and synthesizing skills.		*Dresses appropriately
				Written and oral work shows logical and clear thought and expression, unity and coherence of analysis and creativity.		*Produces high quality work, both written and oral
						*No spelling, punctuation or grammar problems
						*Ability to work with minimal supervision to complete assignments
						*Dependable, consistently follows through on assignments
						*Takes responsibility for on-the-job training

	Ranking	Score	Grade	Academic Criteria	Field Criteria
Commendable/ Very good	3	80–89	B − to B +	**The work is better than average.**	**The work is better than average.**
				There are a few spelling, punctuation and grammar errors, but they do not seriously interfere with meaning or reading.	*Ability to respond to constructive feedback
				Presentations are generally professional and somewhat original.	*Ability and willingness to ask for assistance and information as needed
				Student is usually prepared and contributes to the group learning process.	
Adequate *(Note: C − is not a passing grade.)*	2	70–79	C − to C +	**The work is average.**	**The work is average.**
				It remains at a surface level and is more descriptive than analytical.	*Fulfills contractual requirements for learning agreements and job duties at minimum levels
				It does not make use of original thought or response to the material.	*Ability to complete entry-level tasks and assignments
				There is evidence of difficulty in synthesizing material and reflecting critically its context.	
				The work draws on limited (one or two) research sources and is lacking in bibliographic completeness and accuracy.	

Unsatisfactory	1	60–69	D– to D+	Written and oral presentations lack sufficient clarity or accuracy. Sufficient errors in spelling, punctuation and grammar interfere with meaning and reading. Presentation of the work is incomplete, minimal or unclear. The student is sometimes unprepared and often unable to contribute to the group learning process.	**The work is significantly below average.** The work lacks organization, thoughtfulness and shows difficulty in understanding the readings and expressing ideas. There is evidence of an inability to interpret the material beyond a minimal description. There is an inability to critically interpret materials and analyze connections between materials. Multiple errors in bibliographic sources, spelling, punctuation and grammar seriously interfere with meaning and reading.	**The work is significantly below average.** *Not able to synthesize information and apply to job *Difficulty maintaining consistent schedule, not dependable *Unethical practice *Does not complete required paperwork within scheduled due dates

	Ranking	Score	Grade	Academic Criteria	Field Criteria
Unsatisfactory	1	60–69	D– to D+	**The work is significantly below average.** The work is not presented with originality or care. The student is frequently unprepared and unable to engage in the group learning process.	**The work is significantly below average.** *Does not respond to training *Does not take responsibility for learning experience
None	0	59–0	F	**The work is unacceptable or not submitted within established deadlines.**	**The work is unacceptable or not submitted within established deadlines.**

THE COLLABORATIVE HEALTH AND HUMAN SERVICES ASSESSMENT PROTOCOL

1. Assessment of CHHS Major Learning Outcomes (MLOs)
   - Entering Student Self-Assessment: First Semester Junior
   - Exiting Student Self-Assessment: Last Semester Senior
   - Portfolio Review: Graduation Assessment by faculty and mentor
   - Postgraduate Self-Assessment: One year post graduation

2. Assessment of CHHS MLOs in Field Placements
   - Field Learning Agreement and Student Assessment Matrix
   - Student Assessment of Agency and Mentor
   - Mentor Assessment of CHHS Field Practice Program

3. Pathway Options and Instructions for Assessment
   - MLO Academic and Field Evidence
   - MLO Pathway Guidelines
   - Criteria for Assessment/Ranking: Academic and Field
   - Standard syllabus format
   - Portfolio Assessment instruction for reviewers

4. Student Contact and Data Collection
   - Entering student information
   - Exiting student locator

5. Program Summary Data
   - Student competency summary matrix
   - Postgraduate status summary: graduate school acceptance and employment trends

Note: From *Assessing student learning: Lessons from an outcomes-based health and human services program*, by B. Simmons and K. Judson, 2004, Anaheim, CA. Presented at the 50th Annual Program Meeting of the Council on Social Work Education

COVER LETTER TO EXTERNAL
READERS OF THE PORTFOLIO

CALIFORNIA STATE UNIVERSITY MONTEREY BAY
INSTITUTE FOR COMMUNITY COLLABORATIVE STUDIES
100 Campus Center Seaside, California 93955-8001
Phone (831)582-3565 Fax (831)582-3899 http://iccs.csumb.edu

Dear Portfolio Reviewer:

Thank you for agreeing to review the portfolio of one of our graduating seniors. This is an important piece in the assessment cycle that our students experience during their time here.

In reality, however, your participation serves two functions. The first and most obvious is your feedback on the student's collection of evidence in support of a minimally acceptable level of knowledge, skill, and attitude in the twelve areas that we have defined as learning outcomes. The second function is to provide feedback to the CHHS faculty regarding the program itself. I'll say more about that in a moment.

Assessing the Student's Work

While reading the portfolio, we strongly encourage you to be in front of a computer that is opened to the "MLO Pie" on the CHHS website. There you will find the definition that CHHS uses for each learning outcome, the "Knowledge-Skill-Attitude" (KSA) statements for each MLO, and what we call the "supporting competencies" for each MLO. Ultimately what we are looking for from each student is evidence that is "Adequate" or better for each MLO as defined by the KSA statements. The supporting competencies are meant to be suggestive (not exhaustive) of the kinds of evidence the student might put into the portfolio.

You will receive a hardcopy of an assessment form and a sheet that defines the standards that CHHS uses. The assessment form uses a Likert-like scale. We ask that you read enough of each portfolio section to get a good sense of the student's level of work and circle the number that represents your assessment of the work for that MLO. We have also provided space for you to offer feedback to the student.

You will undoubtedly find that the student is using a piece of evidence in support of more than one MLO. The explanation of how the evidence supports the respective MLO should be found on the table of contents for each MLO. We have asked the students NOT to reproduce multiple copies of the evidence. Rather, you will find instructions where to find the evidence if it is being used in more than one section.

Programmatic Feedback

The second function served by the outside reader is to provide feedback to the CHHS faculty regarding the program itself. In many ways, we rely on the outside portfolio reviewers to provide a quality control check on the program. We want to collect in a systematic way your thoughts, observations, reflections, and wisdoms gathered from your experience as a portfolio reader. The purpose of this exercise is to take your feedback and use it to improve our curriculum, assignments, pedagogy, field program, etc.

So, as you read through each portfolio, we would appreciate your recording your questions, thoughts, and observations on this form. For example, if you conclude that a student's evidence is minimally sufficient to pass the MLO, but that you think more evidence in a certain area or of a certain type would have strengthened the student's case, jot that down. Perhaps the evidence of knowledge or attitude is more implicit than explicit; you are comfortable that the student knows what needs to be known, but wish that something more concrete had been presented. Note that. If there seems to be a disconnect between the student's written work and the observations of the field work mentor(s), note that. If you have a question about how something was presented or wonder how something is being taught, put that down too. If you found a particular assignment to be useful or intriguing (or not so useful), let us know that. If you think the content being presented to the students is dated or otherwise not useful, feel free to say so.

You need NOT record the name of the student on this form. We are more interested in your reactions that might be representative of systematic issues or things that need to be addressed. If you are reading more than one portfolio, you need keep only one set of notes and turn that in when you are finished. You also should not feel the need to record things if you have no questions or observations that you would like to share.

The form is broken down simply by MLOs for you to record whatever observations you might have for that particular section. Additionally, there is space on the back for general questions or comments. If this particular structure does not fit how you would like to pose your question(s) or state your observation(s), feel free to do it however you would like and we will figure it out. Use additional sheets as needed.

We hope during the next year to use your responses to this rather open-ended exercise to create a more structured, closed-ended (but not entirely so) form that will make this a little easier in years to come.

We are the only academic unit on campus that uses external community reviewers for the graduation portfolios and have been acknowledged by our peers for taking this approach. We do so to honor our commitment to our community partners, but in turn we recognize that your taking the time and making the effort to be part of this process reflects your own commitment to CHHS and CSUMB. We thank you.

Be sure to pick up your complimentary hat or t-shirt when you turn in your portfolio. Thanks again for this important contribution to the teaching and learning that we do at CHHS.

Brian Simmons and Jerry Endres
Capstone Advisors

FACULTY INTERVIEWS

A Strategy for Deepening Engagement in Inquiry

Swarup Wood

I've been teaching twenty years and this is probably as deep as I've gone into my own thinking, evaluation, and rethinking of my teaching. And it's been the most meaningful time too.

The benefit of assessment is that you get to see where you went wrong. You see the mistakes. And if you don't take the time to reflect on them, then you'll never improve in those areas. I really can't overstate how valuable I found this work.

Although these quotes are not from a pep talk by an expert on accreditation or by an administrator pushing assessment, but from one of my faculty interview subjects, they are emblematic of the value of interview studies in examining the worth and efficacy of campus activities. They also illustrate how and why CSUMB faculty valued two faculty development processes that focused on assessment. This chapter draws upon the data from two interview studies I conducted to understand the efficacy of these faculty development processes. The chapter further examines the use of interview studies to understand and document the effects of campus activities and processes.

Rationale and Chapter Organization

I had the privilege to serve on our Educational Effectiveness Committee as our institution prepared for accreditation. In addition, I was intensely involved in two processes significant to our documentation and demonstration of educational effectiveness. These experiences made me keenly aware of how campuses can effectively use interview studies to capture and document evidence for use in their accreditation portfolios, and use the powerful insights of interview data for long-term improvement.

A traditional approach to documenting effectiveness is to report some kind of campus activity that constitutes a best practice and show that it promotes student learning. We had several examples of such educational effectiveness processes, and we could have stopped and successfully achieved accreditation. However, as discussed in chapter 2, we were committed to making our accreditation process a learning experience and an impetus for ongoing improvement of our work. This chapter is about the use of interviews as a tool for probing, for deeper self-study, for reflection and discovery beyond the surface-level assessment, and for reporting of an activity or process. Using this kind of study, institutions can analyze, understand, critique, and appreciate the benefits and challenges of the activity to promote long-term improvement.

This chapter describes the methodology and findings of two interview studies I conducted to understand what faculty learned from their participation in two faculty development processes that both focused on assessment. The first process was directed to the development of examples of evidence, criteria, and standards for CSUMB's general education learning outcomes. The second process was directed to the collaborative review and analysis of student evidence demonstrating mastery of learning outcomes. While typical faculty development consists of workshops or presentations with content delivered to faculty, these faculty development processes were constructivist, as they built on faculty expertise, and mirrored what CSUMB faculty value and use in their own thinking related to pedagogy and the CSUMB vision. The questions that framed both interview studies asked, what did faculty learn from their assessment work, and how did it influence their thinking and practice with respect to teaching, learning, and assessment? These kinds of questions could and should be asked of any campus process.

I developed these interview studies as a piece of my own scholarship because the faculty development processes had such a significant impact on my teaching. The chapter thus is written from the perspective of a faculty participant with a personal voice and tone that reflects the engagement of the author. The studies were subsequently used as evidence in CSUMB's accreditation portfolio.[1] More important, the interview studies illustrate the potential of such documentation processes in understanding the efficacy of various faculty development practices or other institution-wide processes, of gathering evidence in preparation for accreditation, and of being an impetus for ongoing institutional improvement.

First I present the two interview studies and draw on them to showcase the potential value of interview studies in documenting educational effectiveness. I then describe the benefits of interviews for both institutional improvement and ongoing study, suggest how-tos both technical and practical, and recommend possibilities for use of interviews. The meaning of these interview studies for CSUMB, and potentially for other institutions, goes beyond their initial role in documenting effectiveness of professional development on campus. Their meaning provides impetus to ongoing improvement for the campus.

Campus and Researcher Context

General Education Faculty Learning Communities

Before I describe the interview studies it is important for the reader to become familiar with the faculty processes that were studied. As previously stated, the processes and the documentation of them were excellent examples of educational effectiveness. Thus my elaboration of those processes will provide insights and possibilities for our readers.

At its inception our university committed to outcomes-based education (OBE), and did so with the intention of focusing its curriculum/instruction on student learning outcomes, fostering continuous attention to student learning, and enhancing institutional accountability. The first curriculum area to receive attention in the development of OBE approaches was our comprehensive and contextually designed general education (GE) program and curriculum. In the course of the development work, a supportive infrastructure was initiated by the faculty learning communities. These faculty learning communities meet once a month and are charged with developing and maintaining the GE outcomes, criteria, and standards; developing and sharing effective pedagogies for teaching to the various GE learning outcomes; and reviewing courses that serve the specific GE area. Faculty who

[1] A full analysis of these data has been submitted for publication in the *Journal of General Education.*

teach GE courses participate in GE faculty learning communities. There are 13 faculty learning communities, one for each GE area, for example, ethics, science, and creative and artistic expression. Tenure-track faculty are expected to attend GE faculty learning community meetings as a function of their workload. Part-time faculty are expected to attend and receive a stipend for their participation. The two processes that follow were conducted within the context of faculty participation in learning communities.

The First Process: Developing Criteria and Standards for Learning Outcomes

GE learning outcomes were developed by the GE faculty learning communities and were in place for several years before faculty began the work to be described. As an outcomes-based institution our university needed to make assessment public and transparent to all of CSUMB's constituencies. Faculty had individual understanding of the learning outcomes, and what students had to do in order to meet those outcomes in their own courses, and it was assumed that faculty had a shared understanding of what the outcomes meant. In 1999 faculty were approached with a question that pushed them more deeply into assessment and OBE: how is it a student would know, and be able to demonstrate, that she'd mastered a given learning outcome? In response, the faculty learning communities developed a process of inquiry by which they collaboratively discussed, developed, and articulated the ideas that faculty used in their personal assessment of student work and made them public and visible. The process was supported by our Center for Teaching, Learning, and Assessment, and focused on developing the following for each of their learning outcomes:

- *Examples of evidence:* student work that demonstrates mastery of an outcome
- *Criteria:* qualities or attributes required of the evidence
- *Standards:* different levels of achieving the criteria

The process emphasized inquiry as faculty grappled with what they wanted students to know and be able to do (Maki, 2002). For many of my interview subjects, this process was a very significant learning experience and drove them to reflect on learning outcomes in different ways and in considerably more depth than they'd done previously. In most cases the learning outcomes were modified as a result of this work. After further refinement of the learning outcomes, examples of evidence, criteria, and standards were then made public on a Web site, in course syllabi, and later in the university catalogue.

The Second Process: Collaborative Peer Review of Student Evidence

After developing examples of student evidence, criteria, and standards for the GE outcomes, and implementing these in courses over three semesters, GE learning community faculty were approached with another question: How do we *know* that students are achieving the learning outcomes in GE courses and that courses were actually making good on their commitment to hold students to the learning outcomes? To respond, faculty who taught GE courses collected examples of student work; assignments were designed to demonstrate student achievement of one or more GE outcomes. These included examples of work that were exemplary and satisfactory, and work that did not meet the outcomes.

The student evidence was analyzed through a three-step process similar to that used in qualitative research. The analysis was done collaboratively in small groups of four to eight faculty. Copies of identical pieces of evidence were given to each faculty, and the whole group worked on only one piece of evidence at a time. Faculty read the same piece of student evidence three times, focusing on a different purpose with each reading.

The purpose of the first reading was to develop a broad understanding of the student's work, and determine holistically whether the student had met the outcome. This served as a kind of reliability check as well as a basis for the second reading. In many cases there was excellent agreement on the quality of the student work (both within the group of faculty and with the original evaluation), and in many cases there was considerable disagreement. These disagreements tended to arise over use of language and interpretation of what the outcome actually meant; they frequently lead to substantive discussions.

The second reading served as a kind of validity check to study and substantiate the evaluation made in the first reading. If a piece of work demonstrated mastery of a given outcome, then anyone evaluating the work should be able to point to examples of the criteria and standards within the work. Faculty again read the student work, this time using highlighters to document examples of the criteria and standards. Conversations following the second reading tended to be very rich as faculty documented the presence or absence of the criteria and standards. In many cases faculty had to struggle with the meaning of various terms, for example, defining exactly what was meant by "complexity, depth, accuracy" and various other terms used in the outcomes, criteria, and standards.

In the third reading faculty looked for what might be learned about the pedagogy from the student work. This was perhaps the most subtle aspect of the process, yet much was made obvious in some of the evidence. For instance, in some student work the student felt safe enough to strongly disagree with the instructor in his/her written work, illustrating the instructor's success in creating a classroom environment in which there was room for more than the instructor's "truth."

Researcher Motivation

I participated in these processes as chair of the science GE learning community. It was thought provoking, while developing criteria and standards for learning outcomes, to sit with five PhD scientists from different disciplines and argue heatedly over the meaning of the word "fact." Furthermore, it was evident that if we were not in complete agreement, we could hardly include the concept in one of our learning outcomes. The discussions focused on teaching and learning as we examined both exactly what we wanted to students to know and be able to do, *and* how to structure outcomes and teaching activities so that students actually master the outcomes. The differences in our use of language came up again and again, and it became clear that though we were reading the same words in our outcomes, we were teaching to different ideas. I began to wonder if the science GE learning community's experiences were unique or if the work had been rich for other faculty learning communities as well. My provocative experience with the science GE learning community led me to develop the first interview study.

The collaborative review of student work a year and half later was even richer than developing examples of evidence, criteria, and standards. My colleagues and I were confronted with much more bias in our evaluation of student work than we expected, such as being distracted from the assessment criteria by excellent writing, or being influenced by a student's growth over the semester. Furthermore, the process brought to our attention some worrisome and significant disconnects between what we asked of students and what we actually assessed. After what were very exciting results from the first interview study, and my own experience of collaborative review and analysis of student work, I was compelled to conduct a second and more rigorous interview study of what other faculty learned from their collaborative review of student evidence.

First Interview Study

This research is best described as two ethnographic interview studies, as I was a participant as well as an observer (Esterberg, 2002). Certainly my interpretation of the interview data was influenced by my experience as a participant. Interviews were selected for data collection rather than surveys because I didn't believe a survey would capture what I experienced as a participant. It was important to hear and to probe faculty voices and faculty thinking. Answering the research questions required in-depth exploration of faculties' insights, perceptions, and evaluation of the assessment experiences. The interviews were semistructured (in depth) and thus allowed me to probe the meaning of my subjects' assessment experience. This approach truly offered the self-study, reflection, and discovery we intended for our accreditation work.

Methods

For the first interview, study data were gathered from interviews of faculty (9 of 40) who participated in developing examples of evidence, criteria, and standards for their GE learning outcomes. Those 9 faculty were selected by the researcher to represent 9 different learning communities, and their selection may have influenced the validity. The data were collected through semistructured (in-depth) interviews. Interviews were tape-recorded and recordings were transcribed. Interviews were conducted in person, in subjects' offices. Interview questions reflected the author's experience.

Subjects were asked the following questions:

- What did you learn from the process?
- What did you like best about the process?
- What was your biggest epiphany?
- Was any part of the process painful?
- Is there anything else you would like to add?

The entire set of transcripts were read twice and coded to determine themes that arose in more than four interviews. Transcripts were then read a third time and scored for the presence of the different themes and for the identification of examples as recommended in the ethnographic literature (Esterberg, 2002; Johnson & Christensen, 2000).

The Potential of Interview Studies: Reflections on the First Study

In assessing the value of these interview studies with respect to documenting the efficacy of the first faculty development processes, institutional improvement, and long-term change, it might be useful to contrast faculty's insights with what we would know (and been able to use as evidence) without them. We would have been able to report that many GE area faculty engaged in the first faculty development process. As a result of the first process faculty modified most of the GE learning outcomes, and developed criteria and standards for these outcomes. In addition, from notes and reports of sessions with faculty, we would have been able to document that the first session facilitated significant discussions that helped develop a common understanding of the learning outcomes among learning community faculty. From informal conversations it would have been clear that faculty enjoyed and were deeply engaged in the first process. With the interview data, we learned that the faculty placed high value on the process and had begun to think differently about outcomes and their teaching. So, the interview data described the impact of the process on individual faculty

All of the issues above are important; however, by comparing the superficial knowledge of the meaning these processes had for our faculty and campus, illustrated in the preceding paragraph, with the themes that emerged from analysis of both interview studies, one begins to understand the potential of interview studies to unearth and bring to light both the effectiveness of these institutional processes and how they can be used to promote long-term improvement. As I present the themes from both studies, I'll discuss their importance with respect to documenting effectiveness, and how they might be used to promote long-term change and institutional improvement.

Findings: First Interview Study

Five different themes emerged from the first interview study following the GE faculty learning communities' work on developing examples of evidence, criteria, and standards for their learning outcomes. The first three themes were also present in the second interview study, so they will be addressed later with the results of the second study.

- Value(s) of the assessment work
- Building consensus on what learning outcomes mean to faculty
- Concerns about the agenda of OBE

- Consideration of learning outcomes from a student's perspective
- Influence of faculty status on participation

Student Perspective

Several faculty said that the process forced them to address learning outcomes from a student's perspective and that it was a very valuable aspect of the work. For example:

> I think it is extraordinarily valuable for faculty to do this work because it focuses people to talk about what they are doing in their classes and it makes us look at things much more from a student's perspective.

One faculty said that even though she considered herself very student centered, this process drove her to rethink learning outcomes from a student's point of view. By approaching their learning outcomes from the perspective of "What do these outcomes really mean, and how can students demonstrate competence?" faculty were forced to shift from the perspective of one who does the teaching, to that of one who does the learning (and has to demonstrate mastery of that learning). I believe this student-centered approach of having to experience learning outcomes from a student's perspective is very valuable with respect to improvement because it facilitates a deeper connection between faculty, their teaching activities, and the learning outcomes. It also gives insight into how well students may or may not be able to use teaching and learning activities to master learning outcomes.

Faculty Status

Faculty status was a theme in the first interview study (one third of the interview subjects, and included both part-timers as well as tenure-track faculty) but not in the second. It is interesting that while many understand in the abstract that higher education is inherently classed, few in the upper classes (tenure track and tenured) experience it deeply enough to anticipate it. Like all systematic inequities, this is a frequently hidden aspect of academic culture, and it takes a glaring example for those in the dominant, powerful, upper class to connect with the experience of those in the lower class.

For example, one tenured faculty said, "My biggest epiphany was that the degree to which faculty participated, and their perspective, was shaped by their status." She went on to say that this had not been apparent during the work meetings, but had come up in conversations around the water cooler, and so on. The following quotes by lecturers illustrate what some of these faculty felt during the process. "As a lecturer, I became very concerned about my own retention." "I often felt the tension of not being able to disagree. I was reserved." In light of this, it is important to address these issues in faculty development, and to acknowledge openly the differences in power of the respective faculty groups.

Implications

CSUMB claims to be a student-learner-centered institution, and our faculty have actually done the work of articulating learning outcomes, examples of evidence, and the qualities required of that evidence (criteria). Many faculty described how this work forced them to approach what they require from students from their students' perspective. This result provides strong support that CSUMB is in fact a learner-centered institution, but that this is an ongoing process necessary to maintain and improve our GE program. Furthermore, any process that prompts faculty to consider and to focus on teaching from a student perspective will ultimately support the kind of learning and growth intended for most faculty development processes.

The literature on the extensive use of part-time faculty in higher education discusses problems both on maintaining program coherence, as well as how marginalization of part-time faculty affects both faculty and student learning (Caprio, Leslie, Warasila, Cheatwood, & Costa, 1999; Gappa & Dubowsky, 1997). At CSUMB and many other campuses, part-time faculty teach the majority of GE courses. Some part-timers who've been here long term have substantial experience with the GE learning outcomes. Thus there is potential for faculty who have the most experience with the learning outcomes to have a disproportionately small voice in the evolution and maintenance of the outcomes over time. In this instance the issue is that the university is unable to benefit fully from part-timer experience, rather than making sure they are "on board" with respect to program objectives.

Toward documenting effectiveness and promoting improvement, understanding this disconnect between part-time faculty and their experience in our GE faculty learning communities is very important. This finding allows us to showcase what we currently do to include part-time faculty (pay them for attending faculty learning community meetings) and develop and implement strategies for developing more inclusive environments within these learning communities. An important consideration in any long-term change or improvement process is the inclusion of part-time faculty.

Second Interview Study

The second interview study took place after the faculty learning communities completed extensive work sessions focused on analyzing student work. The student work was selected to demonstrate achievement of the outcomes and criteria.

Methods

The second interview study focused on faculty experience and learning during their collaborative review of student evidence. Methods of this study differed slightly from the first study in that a larger percentage of faculty participants were interviewed (17 of 53), that all of the faculty learning communities were represented in the study, and that interview questions were developed in consultation with the Center for Teaching, Learning, and Assessment. Interview subject selection was directed again to attain broad representation of the perspectives beyond those of my experience.

Interviews consisted of the following eight questions:

- What was the purpose of the peer review of student work—what were you trying to achieve?
- What did you learn about teaching and learning from this process? What did you learn about assessment from this process?
- What did it affirm or reinforce about your thinking or practice of teaching and learning?
- Are there any changes you'll make in your work as a result of this process?
- What did you learn about our general education outcomes, criteria, and standards?
- Did this work affect or influence your thinking, or how you feel, about outcomes-based education?
- Were you surprised about anything that came up during the process?
- Is there anything else you'd like to add about the process?

The entire set of transcripts were read twice and coded to determine themes that arose in more than four interviews. Transcripts were then read a third time and scored for the presence the different themes and for the identification of examples (Esterberg, 2002; Johnson & Christensen, 2000).

In addition to the interviews, independent of this study, and as part of a recent program review of our general education program, learning community members wrote a brief summary and analysis of what they learned from the peer review of student work. I analyzed these summaries as well as transcripts of the interviews.

The Potential of Interview Studies: Reflections on Second Study

Again it is useful to contrast the faculty development processes as evidence with the interview study data as evidence. Without the interviews, we would have been able to report that students met the outcomes and criteria, and that the analysis process resulted in further refinement of learning outcomes, criteria, and standards. We would not have been able to report that the collaborative review of student work facilitated significant discussions regarding implementation of the criteria and standards, as they form the basis of grading rubrics. We also would have missed the fact that faculty enjoyed and were deeply engaged in the process. We would not have heard their descriptions of how valued the process was for their teaching.

Findings: Second Interview Study

Eight different themes emerged in transcripts of interviews of what faculty learned from the collaborative review of student work. Several of these themes were identical to or overlapped considerably with themes from the first study.

- Benefits and value
- Building consensus on what learning outcomes mean to faculty
- Fear and vulnerability
- Bias
- Aligning teaching and assessment with learning outcomes, criteria, and standards
- Changes in teaching, assessment, and reflection on pedagogy
- Peer review and collaboration
- The value of outcomes-based education

Benefits and Value

As with the first study, one of the most striking themes apparent in the interviews was how faculty perceived their experience especially in terms of its value to their work. Eighty-eight percent of those interviewed indicated directly that they appreciated the work. Faculty routinely used words and phrases like "excellent, great, fantastic, exciting, enjoyed, fascinating, absolutely wonderful" in describing their experience, not typical faculty responses to assessment work.

Several faculty indicated being worried initially that the work would end up being just one more burden. All of those who were worried at first came away feeling very positive. In fact no one spoke negatively about the process or product, and more than half of those interviewed expressed gratitude for the opportunity. This is again in sharp contrast to the typical views of assessment work.

As in the first interview study, the power of their experience and why faculty valued it varied considerably and will be explored in subsequent themes. Some faculty, especially those whose students' work was reviewed, found it validating. Reflecting on the experience one faculty said:

> It was very validating . . . and to hear my colleagues say, "Oh, what a good idea. Now I know how to talk about what I do in my class." I suddenly realized I was serving as a good role model. I hadn't expected that.

For other faculty their excitement was driven by seeing how they could apply collaborative review of student work to other aspects of their teaching or programs. One said, "I got so excited about this that I wanted to extend it to the whole department so we could go through the same process for the major learning outcomes." Subsequently excitement over the work with the GE learning communities has led several of the degree programs on campus to begin collaborative review and analysis of student evidence.

Another faculty spoke of the power of the process that prompted her to reflect deeply on her own practice of teaching and assessment, saying:

"The benefit of assessment is that you get to see where you went wrong. You see the mistakes. And if you don't take the time to reflect on them then you'll never improve in those areas. I really can't overstate how valuable I found it."

Another subject said: "I've been teaching 20 years and this is probably as deep as I've gone into my own thinking, evaluation and rethinking of my teaching. And it's been the most meaningful time too."

In addition to appreciating and valuing the work, faculty said the work was important. Eighty-two percent of those interviewed said that the process should be repeated periodically, and many felt the process was essential for the success of OBE. Subsequently the GE learning communities voted unanimously to create policy to repeat the collaborative review of student work with the Center for Teaching, Learning, and Assessment on a biannual basis.

These findings are critical in that they do not portray the stereotypical resentment and resistance of faculty to assessment, but rather an appreciation and enthusiasm for these assessment processes because of their value and meaningful connection to teaching and learning. Here again, the constructivist process provided faculty with control of the work and the capacity to make their own meaning.

With respect to institutional change and improvement these are very important results. On many campuses, faculty development processes that decreased faculty resistance to assessment would be considered significant news. These interview studies allowed us to document this shift in faculty attitudes toward assessment; similar studies could be easily deployed to study significant faculty development activities on other campuses.

Building Consensus on What Learning Outcomes Mean to Faculty

The process of developing examples of evidence, criteria, and standards required faculty to build a shared understanding of their learning outcomes by forcing many assumptions regarding language, philosophy, and academic discipline out in the open. Each interview subject in the first interview study indicated that though they assumed a common understanding of the outcomes, they then realized that different faculty had very different interpretations. This theme was also present in the second interview study (almost 60% of the subjects in the second study indicated that the collaborative review of student work helped build a common understanding of what the learning outcomes mean to learning community faculty) and is a particularly important finding for CSUMB as an outcomes-based institution. Faculty assume that they are "speaking the same language" as they develop and discuss learning outcomes. However, these results indicate that single outcomes can mean very different things to different faculty. These findings can be used to support institutional improvement because they illustrate the importance of ongoing discussions of what our learning outcomes mean, and the importance of maintaining our faculty learning communities or other venues to promote these discussions (Maki, 2002, 2004).

Fear and Vulnerability

If most teaching, as Shulman (1993) describes, is done behind closed doors, then I warrant that much assessment takes place under lock and key. Most of us know it as a very private endeavor, and the reasons for this privacy likely derive from a mixture of expediency as well as from the fear of risk and exposure. Most (83%) of the faculty whose student work was reviewed experienced fear and felt vulnerable. Fear brings on a heightened experience, and these interviews were some of the more interesting and poignant. Almost all of those who spoke of their discomfort also spoke of the benefit of their work being made public. For example, one faculty said, "I was actually fearful to have people from other departments listening in on my teaching process." She then went on to detail how validating the experience was. "I really felt like part of the group after that happened. These were probably some of the best moments I've had with faculty across the campus."

Predictably, the fear wasn't necessarily rational. One faculty who said, "the level of vulnerability was stunning," also acknowledged that she was a tenured professor with little or nothing to lose. It was more a matter of making public something that was intensely personal, private, and in which she'd invested a tremendous amount of herself. That faculty member likened her fear to the apprehension of having a child return after 30 years to detail the worst of her parenting.

The conditions of evaluating student work with a group of peers are very different than evaluating it in the context of our busy faculty lives (late at night, after grading 30 other papers, etc.). Sometimes student work looked considerably different, when evaluated by a group, than it had when it was evaluated originally by the faculty member who submitted it. One person, for whom this was true, reflected, "But the funny thing is that if I hadn't been embarrassed I probably wouldn't have learned as much."

Although it did not surface as a theme, several subjects spoke about the constant tension of not knowing how their evaluation of student work compared to other faculty. Were they harder, or easier? Were they consistent? These subjects also spoke about the relief of seeing how other faculty evaluated a particular piece of student work, and that their evaluation was similar to that of their colleagues. I believe this kind of apprehension is common among faculty. Johnstone, Ewell, and Paulson (2002) talk about this absence of discussion and consensus when they acknowledge the lack of academic currency in higher education. The collaborative review of student evidence served to decrease this kind of anxiety and to build a consensus of expectations. Interview studies provide a kind of secure context for faculty to reveal typically private thoughts and concerns. They can give access to information that is sensitive and not typically gained through surveys or other information-gathering techniques.

In spite of the fact that many interview subjects spoke of their fear, I believe one of the things that made these faculty development processes so successful is that faculty were willing to take risks, and this willingness actually derived from considerable trust among the faculty. Tom Angelo (1999) discusses developing shared trust as a precondition for faculty learning communities, and it is certainly clear to me that this kind of work cannot happen without shared trust. However, learning communities themselves seem an excellent venue for developing shared trust among faculty and administrators who focus on assessment, and I believe that was the case at CSUMB. The substantial time faculty spent together in their respective learning communities developing our GE program allowed faculty to build rapport and considerable shared trust, which paved the way for the success of our assessment processes. In addition, the assessment processes deepened the trust within the learning communities. The assessment processes implemented here might have been valuable for faculty who were strangers; however, I believe the familiarity and trust built in the faculty learning communities paved the way for a deeper experience. I also believe that the results presented here speak strongly about the potential of using faculty learning communities to support assessment activities on other campuses.

Bias

Three quarters of the subjects said that the collaborative review of student work revealed some aspect of their bias. When analyzed collaboratively with colleagues, student work frequently read very differently than when individual faculty evaluated it during the course. Faculty typically attributed this difference to personal bias, and several were caught off guard by the experience. "I'm more biased than I thought, candidly," one faculty said. Other faculty saw how qualities of the student work, other than the criteria being evaluated, influenced their grading. Another faculty was taken aback when she saw that she'd taken the educational distance the student had traveled into account in her original evaluation of the student's work, and that quality of the work in and of itself was considerably less than what was indicated in the original score. In at least one case the collaborative review of student work allowed faculty to see how the quality of the writing influenced their evaluation—even though writing quality was not being assessed. One said, "In some cases we were dazzled by excellent writing to the point that we actually missed holes in the evidence."

The fact that this work surfaced so much bias brings to light the consistency, or lack thereof, regarding faculty judgment in evaluating student work. It again highlights the need for very clear standards or grading rubrics (Johnstone et al., 2002) and the value of this kind of collaboration among faculty. In an age where universities are moving from seat time and credits to student learning as academic currency, these results underscore the need for consistent faculty judgment and describe the kinds of activities campuses may engage in to help achieve this goal.

Aligning Teaching and Assessment with Learning Outcomes, Criteria, and Standards

With respect to the utility of the collaborative review of student work, one of the most important results was that it illustrates disconnects in the alignment of teaching, learning, assessment, and learning outcomes. Some faculty identified disconnects between what was being taught, and the stated learning outcomes. One said, "I think we were all a little horrified at what came out—here it is, big as life, one of our outcomes and we're not even really addressing it in any significant way."

Illustrating disconnects between assignments and learning outcomes, some faculty observed that students really had followed directions and accomplished what they had been asked for—it was just that the faculty had really wanted (and graded for) something else. This quote, "We really wanted them to do one thing, but we were asking them to do a different thing—and they gave us what we asked for . . . and gee what a revelation," exemplifies disconnects between learning outcomes and assignments. Other faculty witnessed disconnects between assignments and grading rubrics. One faculty had given an exam in which he asked students to "list the points of an argument" that had been discussed in class. The faculty member then unwittingly graded the work as though he'd asked students to discuss the argument. Even more alarming was that other instructors participating in the review of the students also failed to catch the disconnect (it was brought to our attention by our director of teaching, learning, and assessment).

Several faculty echoed what one faculty said: "This process underscored how critical it is to align assessment standards and criteria with the resources and learning that is facilitated in the class." There were many more who noted how the process impressed upon them the importance of carefully crafting questions used in assessment.

My experiences in these processes have very much changed the way I look at my own assessments. When I begin to see a trend in incorrect answers on my assessments, I begin to scrutinize my question or the directions very carefully. I also use how well my students perform on a given aspect of an assessment to reflect on how well I've taught that piece of the curriculum, how much opportunity my students had to practice those skills, and how well I scaffolded my instruction.

Many of the changes that faculty made in their teaching and assessment as a result of this work were geared toward better alignment. Again and again, faculty indicated how the process facilitated a deep reflection on what was working and what wasn't, and that what we want students to learn, learning outcomes, must be aligned with our teaching activities. Overall, 82% of my interview subjects indicated that the process revealed at least one of the preceding disconnects.

The importance of this result is not so much the individual issues that that were raised, but the fact that this collaborative review of student work gave faculty a tool, a lens, for looking into their teaching and assessment, for discovering and addressing things that did not work, and in many instances, for celebrating the things that did. If my interviewees represented the participating faculty, then it is possible that more than 50 (or one fifth) of our faculty are now closely checking the alignment between their teaching and learning activities and learning outcomes.

Changes in Teaching, Assessment, and Reflection on Pedagogy

Along with using the review process as a lens for reflection on their practice, the fact that 88% of those interviewed said that they'd made changes in their teaching must be viewed as one of the most significant products of the assessment processes and results of the interview studies.

Many of the changes faculty made involved rewriting assignments to clarify language, and better connect them to learning outcomes. Several indicated they were building better scaffolding into their teaching to promote cumulative learning to reach the outcomes. Others noted that they would shift toward more regular and iterative assessments. One faculty, after making several unsuccessful attempts to help her students connect with and understand the language of the learning outcomes and criteria, took the process she used with her colleagues in the collaborative review of student evidence and used it with her students. She brought examples of past student work for her current students to critique. The students evaluated the work according to the learning outcomes, criteria, and standards. The students did not have to agree with the instructor's original evaluation, but they did have to explain the basis of their evaluations. In contrast to her many prior attempts she felt this proved to be a very effective means of connecting students to the learning outcomes.

Sixty-five percent of those interviewed indicated that the process was useful as a tool for reflecting on pedagogy. Some appreciated the fact that the review forced them to look critically at their own pedagogy, while others, who had been using assessment solely as an evaluation tool, came to see assessment as a valuable teaching tool.

With respect to institutional improvement, these last two themes are particularly important to note. These interviews shine as a method for excavating beneath these faculty development processes and illustrating the impact the processes had on faculty teaching. The data on aligning teaching practice with outcomes and changes faculty made in their practice of teaching and assessment speak volumes about a campus culture that is responsive to student evidence and to the efficacy of these faculty development processes. These kinds of data make clear why faculty voted to institutionalize the collaborative review of student evidence, why the campus had to prioritize funding to pay for the work, and about our ongoing commitment to institutional improvement.

Peer Review and Collaboration

At its heart, peer review is a collaborative process, one in which multiple pairs of eyes and perspectives help force assumptions out in the open, and refine ideas toward maturer and clearer ends. Ever since Boyer's landmark *Scholarship Reconsidered* (1990), academics have been rethinking the role of peer review in the academic process. Faculty who conduct *Scholarship of Teaching* research have articulated well the value of peer review in traditional academic research. For similar reasons, peer review is a key criterion for scholarship of teaching research (Hutchings & Shulman, 1999).

It has been said that university faculty are more likely to collaborate with colleagues across the globe than with those down the hall. One of the things that stands out here is that as a result of these assessment processes, not only did faculty learn from each other and make changes in their teaching and assessment activities, these faculty really enjoyed and valued collaborating with "colleagues down the hall." As with all of the trends, there was a spectrum of comments regarding the value of collaboration. Similar to the first study, some faculty spoke effusively of how valuable and powerful it was to work with colleagues in this way, how we frequently get to collaborate with students like this but rarely with faculty colleagues. Overall, 82% of the subjects interviewed spoke positively about the collaborative aspect of the experience. Since collaboration is truly the hub in a collaborative peer review process, the number of subjects for whom it was important stands out as significant. This implies that one of the ways we can support institutional improvement is to create and maintain venues for faculty to collaborate with each other on teaching, learning, and assessment.

The Value of Outcomes-Based Education

In the first interview study, several of the subjects began this work nervous about an assumed agenda of outcomes-based education.

"I was afraid I was being asked to run humanities courses [an understanding of the human experience] through a business model."

"We had been worried that outcomes would be used to endorse a particular style of measurement that we were very much against."

Both of these quotes illustrate the tenor of much of the concern over OBE before we developed examples of evidence, criteria, and standards for our learning outcomes. It was very interesting that as a result of the work, the subjects felt like they'd used OBE to further their own agenda, better instruction toward their GE outcomes, rather than being driven by a supposed OBE agenda.

"The process of developing standards and criteria alleviated our concerns. We saw that our outcomes still upheld the values of the CSUMB Vision."

"We were able to develop the outcomes to meet our agenda rather than having the outcomes-based model develop us."

Evidence gathered in the interviews following the collaborative review of student work (second interview study) was interesting with respect to how this process influenced faculty perception of OBE. It was clear that, for the most part, faculty had moved well past their concerns regarding OBE. Twenty-nine percent of those interviewed indicated that the process reinforced (positively) their perception of OBE. For another 65%, the value of OBE increased as a result. Some said the process improved their ability to implement and to actually achieve outcomes-based education; for others the process has allowed their teaching to become much more intentional. A few went so far as to say that it was the collaborative review of student work that has enabled us to actualize OBE on campus. The fact that the value of OBE increased in almost two thirds of the interview subjects as a result of these faculty development processes implies that the work had a profound impact on faculty attitudes toward OBE and probably on assessment.

The implications of this for CSUMB are remarkable. CSUMB has made the claim of being an outcomes-based institution, and thus it is reasonable to assume an accreditation agency ought to be very interested in how we support that claim. This evidence goes well beyond documenting our having developed learning outcomes (what we would have done without the interview studies) by illustrating that our faculty have actually taken ownership of OBE and are using it to develop more effective pedagogies.

Implications

Each of these themes illustrates the success of these interview studies at unearthing information valuable both to CSUMB's documentation of educational effectiveness and its ongoing efforts to promote long-term improvement. Changes in teaching and assessment, in faculty behavior, and in faculty attitudes toward assessment and OBE documented here speak volumes about the efficacy of the two faculty development processes, about what the campus has done well, but also what kinds of other activities the campus will want to initiate and support in its commitment to long-term improvement.

The Value of Interview Studies

In addition to the importance of the interview studies in illustrating what faculty learned, the interviews themselves also promoted continued growth from the faculty development processes in that they required faculty to reflect on their experiences. They reminded people of the power of the experiences, of the changes they were going to make in their teaching, and assessment. They are completely analogous to what many faculty strive for in their classrooms by forcing faculty to think about what they'd learned, to revisit the ideas and mental images they'd formed during the sessions. These are exactly the reasons we use reflection as a pedagogy. In addition to all that may be learned from these two interview studies, it is very clear that the actual interviews were probably useful learning experiences for my interview subjects. They certainly were for me. In addition to being excellent learning experiences, it was an honor to interview colleagues from across campus. Many of the interviews involved a very personal exchange. I felt in some interviews as though I were allowed into a very personal and private aspect of these faculty's professional lives, and it was very gratifying to make meaningful connections with colleagues across campus.

Planning for Interview Studies

Interviews are a well-established method used in qualitative research. They are very labor intensive, but can provide a very effective and penetrating means of collecting information. The purpose of this chapter is to describe the value of interviews and to encourage other institutions to consider using interviews for in-depth self-study. Because of the time and labor involved in interview studies as well as the importance of this kind of self-study, several issues should be considered in the use of interviews.

The composition of accreditation teams has changed in recent years to include a good balance between administration and faculty. This secures good connections between areas where most of the exciting teaching and learning occurs (between and among faculty and students), and the upper administration, and gives accreditation teams better access to the kinds of projects and activities a campus may wish to study. It is essential that the team first develop a comprehensive list of candidate projects/activities that will illustrate the campus's growth toward stated goals, and then decide how to capture the impact of these activities. Of course the primary reason for any self-study is that a campus wants to understand the efficacy (or lack thereof) of various kinds of faculty development and student learning/enrichment programs. Use of this kind of self-study in the accreditation process allows a campus to showcase its successes and respond to how it is learning from its mistakes.

Why an Interview Study?

I hope the preceding pages have truly answered this question. From a how-to perspective, semistructured (in-depth) interviews allowed me to probe deeply into faculty experience and to follow my questions in ways that a survey could not. They allowed me to ask open-ended questions. It is important to note that interviews make room for unanticipated data to emerge, and that these data are often quite informative. What emerged from the transcripts was a very rich understanding of the faculty's experience. The above quotes illustrate the power these two faculty development processes had on many faculty. The faculty language is powerfully convincing of the impact of the faculty development processes on faculty affinity toward OBE, and assessment in general. It illustrates how and why faculty changed their teaching and assessment practice, the success of the faculty learning communities, and, ultimately, the impact of these processes on changing campus culture. From the quotes it is also easily understood why faculty valued the processes so highly. The numerical data illustrate a great deal about what faculty learned, while the quotes really underscore poignancy—that these faculty learned something new and valuable about their teaching. In this way the studies provided excellent evidence of an engaged faculty who were challenged by and responsive to these deeply engaging faculty development processes. It is easy to see how a campus would use this information as evidence of educational effectiveness and how it would respond to promote long-term improvement.

Issues to Consider

Because of the time and energy required for a successful interview study several criteria should be taken into account in selecting an appropriate project, including visibility and timing.

Projects considered for study via interviews should be large enough that they have good visibility across campus. Conducting an interview study on a small project limits potential interest in the study, as well as interest in the results and application (how useful it might be on other parts of campus) of the study. At CSUMB, the design of examples of evidence, criteria, and standards for our general education learning outcomes, as well as the collaborative review of student evidence, involved roughly 35% of all faculty. Because of the interdisciplinary nature of our GE model, both processes drew from a broad cross-section of the faculty. Faculty were very willing to serve as interview subjects. (Only one person declined by never returning my phone calls.) There was enough subsequent interest in the results of the study that I've presented the study to two different groups on campus.

As in all original research, timing is critical and will influence greatly what is learned from interviews. I'm sure that most campuses have many exciting projects and events (various faculty development activities, teaching cooperatives, learning communities, book clubs, etc.) that are relevant and have real impact on faculty and educational effectiveness. However, unless the campus is primed to study how the projects influenced faculty teaching/ learning, student learning, or the campus culture, the effects of the projects can't be documented for either accreditation or use on other parts of the campus. Subjects should be interviewed while the experiences are still fresh, so planning the interview study, developing questions, and scheduling interviews should be done as early as possible—certainly no later than during the last phase of the project.

My interview studies were very much an ethnography as the study germinated from my participation. It is conceivable that an accreditation team might want to conduct an interview study of a program it did not know much about. Under these circumstances, consultation with the program directors and several participants to help design interview questions would be essential and invaluable.

Conclusion

Interview studies are labor intensive and would be neither appropriate nor desirable as a sole method of gathering evidence. They do however have great potential for allowing an accreditation team to study a campus project or process deeply, for reflection and discovery beyond the surface-level assessment and reporting of an activity or process. They can facilitate extracting potentially extraordinary experiences that might easily be missed in other forms of data collection. The studies presented here showcase what CSUMB faculty learned from two faculty development processes. They highlight the potential of interview studies in the analysis, critique, and appreciation of campus projects; facilitate the documentation of educational effectiveness; and promote institutional improvement.

References

Angelo, T. (1999, May). Doing assessment as if learning matters most. *AAHE Bulletin*. Retrieved June 16, 2002 from http://aahe.org/Bulletin/angelomay99.htm.

Boyer, E. L. (1990). *Scholarship reconsidered: Priorities of the professoriate*. Princeton, NJ: Carnegie Foundation for the Advancement of Teaching.

Caprio, M. W., Dubowsky, N. Warasila, R. L., Cheatwood, D. D., & F. T. Costa. (1999). Adjunct faculty: A multidimensional perspective on the important work of part-time faculty. *Journal of College Science Teaching, 28*(3), 166–173.

Esterberg, K. (2002). *Qualitative methods in social research*. Boston: McGraw-Hill Higher Education.

Gappa, J. M., & Leslie, D. W. (1997). *Two faculties or one? The conundrum of part-timers in a bifurcated work force*. Washington DC: Forum on Faculty Roles & Rewards, American Association for Higher Education.

Hutchings, P., & Shulman, L. (1999). The scholarship of teaching: New elaborations, new developments. *Change, 31*(5) 11–15.

Johnson, B., & Christensen, L. (2000). *Educational research: Quantitative and qualitative approaches*. Needham Heights, MA: Allyn & Bacon.

Johnstone, S. M., Ewell, P., & Paulson, K. (2002). *Student learning as academic currency*. American Council on Education/Educause Series on Distributed Education: Challenges, Choices, and a New Environment. Washington DC: American Council on Education.

Maki, P. (2002, May). Moving from Paperwork to Pedagogy. *AAHE Bulletin*. Retrieved June 16, 2002 from http://aahebulletin.com/public/archive/paperwork.asp.

Maki, P. (2004). *Assessing for learning: Building a sustainable commitment across the institution*. Sterling, VA: Stylus.

Shulman, L. (1993) *Teaching as community property: Putting an end to pedagogical solitude. Change, 25*(6) 6–7.

11

ADMINISTRATIVE ALIGNMENT
AND ACCOUNTABILITY

Diane Cordero de Noriega and Salina Diiorio

One of the current buzzwords in higher education is *alignment*—another *A* word. It usually can be found in the company of *accountability* and *assessment*, and of course, it has found its way into *accreditation*. Fortunately, it hasn't caused the stir that the other *A* words provoked in their early use, and that's probably because alignment immediately makes sense to us. It's one of those concepts that is so logical and seems so basic that we can't imagine having to think about it. If asked, we would almost be offended, "Of course, we align our planning, or our budgets, or our decision making with their impact on student learning." Such alignment is the content of one of the principles of good practice in assessment (American Association for Higher Education, 1992).

What we discovered with increasingly complex understandings at CSUMB in the course of our first eight years of development was that alignment is critical at multiple levels. From our beginning we focused on aligning our plans and developments with our vision, as described in chapter 3. Years later we discovered that we needed other levels of alignment. We needed internal alignment within each of our planning processes, and we needed alignment among our institution-wide processes. In this chapter we share our initial efforts, our reflections, and our restructuring toward total alignment for accountability. We've arrived at a decision-making model that ultimately aligns our priorities, our processes, and our structures with each other, as well as with our goals for student learning. Thanks to our preparation for accreditation, we've refined our alignment thinking and the decisions that emerge from that thinking.

Early Alignment Attempts

In the flurry of developing a new campus, much of our planning began in isolation of other planning. One thread remained constant throughout the planning—the university Vision Statement. Once developed, that vision was an appropriate filter for our early attempts at alignment. Otherwise, much of the planning and initial decision making was conducted simultaneously and without connections. This may be attributed to the stresses and enormity of planning necessary for a new campus; however, experienced and more mature campuses may also find the same lack of connection between major processes of planning and decision making. Typically, the one connection that consistently appears is the connection between budgets and other decision-making processes—it's a practical necessity. As described in chapter 1, the one connection that we have just begun to prioritize in higher education is the connection between our planning and decision making and student learning. With the influence of accreditation, campuses have begun to emphasize that relationship, and to direct queries of alignment to that end. This chapter is directed to that same priority, as well as to giving attention to the need for alignment between processes. Without that second level of alignment, student learning is not well served.

To achieve the overall alignment that we will describe and prescribe strategies for, we have found that three components were essential:

- Infrastructure
- Process focus
- Alignment thinking

Those three components frame this chapter for our own reflections and self-assessment, as well as for use by other campuses. Much of our internal reflection was motivated and nurtured by our accreditation review. Once it was made public, continued reflection in our culture of inquiry will promote the long-term improvement we are committed to.

Alignment and Accountability

In the midst of our burgeoning campus beginnings, there was little awareness of the need for an infrastructure to oversee decision making and planning.

We looked to the President's Cabinet as a kind of planning body, but as we grew and the need for more in-depth planning expanded, we realized the need for a larger, more representative group.

The Administrative Council: Infrastructure for Alignment

The Administrative Council was formed initially as an expansion of the cabinet, but quickly served more of an oversight function at a grassroots level. The intention was for the council to be as inclusive as possible in terms of leadership, and that was quite appropriate for our beginning campus. The council membership included the provost, vice presidents and associate vice presidents of each division, deans, directors of campus programs (library, Center for Teaching, Learning, and Assessment, institutional assessment and research, etc.), and the Faculty Senate chair. Early in its deliberations, the council achieved an awareness that emerged from alignment with student learning and the vision. That awareness gave impetus to a commitment to collaboration between academic affairs and student affairs, and the associate vice president for student affairs joined the council.

Search for Direction: Focusing Process on Alignment

With well-developed representation, the council began to function in a fairly expansive manner. Throughout its early operations, the group kept a focus on student learning, assured that such alignment would suffice to direct the council's agenda. However, after just a few years of such broad focusing, the council was forced to conduct an internal search of purpose and function. Its attention and queries probed for a kind of definition and direction for the council. After several years of agendas that included almost anything anyone wanted to bring to the attention of the council, the group began to ask questions. Why are we here? How do we define ourselves? Where should we focus our attention? Hours and hours of deliberations, typically unfinished weekly agendas, and a sense of being spread too thin accelerated the process of focusing. As the campus approached accreditation processes, it became clear that the group needed to reorganize, or more accurately, organize, around campus priorities. This awareness of the need for another level of focus beyond student learning was also the beginning of another level of alignment.

The Administrative Council identified three areas of focus that would direct and align future agendas and related planning and decision making, including

- Alignment of new and existing campus plans with the newly adopted strategic plan (planning alignment)

- Determining the cost of our unique model (costing the model)
- Assessing and documenting our performance toward the goals and outcomes of the strategic plan (institutional effectiveness)

To those ends, the planning alignment, costing the model, and institutional effectiveness groups were formed. Initially these groups were independent. We were slow learners! Once they were constituted and barely began to meet, it became evident that their members represented the Academic Council and the major areas of planning and decision making as intended. We quickly acknowledged that they needed to be carefully aligned in their functioning. From these groups, their connections, and their "reporting line" to the council, a clearly defined purpose intentionally emerged for the council. That purpose was the implementation and assessment of the strategic plan, and the assurance of alignment and integration of all other campus plans. The three council groups became new threads to weave with student learning for a more complex alignment across campus. We describe each in our reflection on progress and for future planning. We intend for these very honest reflections to encourage and support the efforts of other campuses. But first, a discussion of the strategic plan and its inception will lay a foundation for the threads that were woven between the three focus areas.

The Strategic Plan: A Living, Working Document

The strategic plan was immediately seen as a tool for accountability, even before its development. Strategic plans are usually meant to be broad, guiding documents that set direction and focus for an institution. Some are working documents; some wind up on the shelf. Strategic plans are sometimes long wish lists, or a laundry list of to-dos. We all know we need to have one, just like a mission statement or a vision, but are they really a tool that the institution uses to regularly check on how it is doing?

As the campus prepared to draft a strategic plan, there was a commitment for the plan to be a living, working document. That commitment became a kind of filter for the content of the plan—a serious and intentional way to strategize for what really mattered on campus.

As discussed in chapter 3, the strategic plan at CSUMB was intentionally designed to align with the University Vision and the academic core values. The strategic themes of the plan describe the values, outcomes, and context for achieving the vision and ultimately educational effectiveness. It was written specifically to operationalize the vision, and to hold the institution accountable for achieving its vision.

To ensure that the strategic plan was informed by the vision, the provost led a series of "visioning" sessions with the campus community, in order to reaffirm the campus commitment to the vision. The Strategic Planning Committee, consisting of students, faculty, staff, administrators, and community members, was then formed. It undertook a two-year process of developing the themes, outcomes, and indicators that would synthesize the vision and core values, and become the strategic plan.

The four themes the strategic plan was developed around are

- Pluralistic academic community
- Student learning
- Support for learning
- Engaged campus

Each year the Administrative Council decides on a theme that provides the focus for the campus, helps departments to set priorities, and drives the budget development process. It was agreed early on that the outcomes under the chosen theme are the things that we want to hold ourselves accountable for; these are the indicators that will answer the question of whether we are being faithful to our vision. This annual progress assessment process became one of our most important pieces of evidence for accreditation. In addition, an overall progress assessment of each of the themes has since been instituted as part of a five-year review and renewal of the strategic plan.

Planning Alignment and Integration: Thinking Alignment Across Plans

The strategic plan was not drafted until the fourth year of campus development. In the meantime, the initial capital construction/master plan and the initial five-year financial plan had already been drafted. Enrollment planning was under way, and the process to develop a comprehensive academic plan had just been initiated. Because they were all being developed in relative isolation of each other, and were in various stages of completion, none of the plans appeared to be aligned with each other, even though each was aligned with student learning. Nor were they aligned with the strategic plan in a way that would allow the strategic plan to be the overarching, guiding document for all planning at CSUMB. The questions we began to ask were, how do we know that all of our plans are going to get us where we want to go? and, will we all arrive at the desired outcome if we have not agreed in advance what that outcome is to be? The questions prompted a new awareness of the need for complex internal alignment that had not been anticipated or acknowledged in our early and ongoing ambitious planning.

CSUMB seemed to excel, out of necessity, at "building a bicycle while riding it." In fact, it may be that we became so experienced and proficient at such development that we kept it as our mode of operation. It was time to be more intentional, and the process of plan development and planning alignment allowed us to rethink and to become more aligned and intentional. This is an awareness that we can now share—in order to be aligned, intentionality is a requisite characteristic of planning. Without it, alignment is hit-or-miss. And without it, the connection with student learning may be weakened.

Since the campus plans were all in various stages of development and implementation, and clearly we could not stop and start all over again, we decided that as the strategic plan emerged it would become the touchstone all other plans would align to. It was probably the path of least resistance. The campus understood that as plans were completed, alignment with the strategic plan would have to occur before a plan could be fully endorsed and implemented. In the case of the enrollment and academic plans, they were still in the developmental state and could be aligned in progress. In contrast, we worked to align the capital construction/master plan and the financial plan retroactively and retrospectively, because the plans were already complete.

Plan alignment was extremely important to CSUMB as a new, developing campus, but it may be even more important for well-developed and experienced campuses to attend to such alignment. To that end, we share the thinking that accompanied our attempts to become internally aligned.

One realization that directed our efforts was a conceptualization of the campus plans as the implementation methods for the strategic plan. With that understanding, the first task was to determine the common assumptions that would serve as the "hooks" for aligning our plans. The common underlying assumptions we agreed to were

- The strategic plan themes: The strategic themes were the first point of alignment for all major plans on campus. We needed to demonstrate that the major plans were, in fact, tactical implementation plans for the strategic plan. In this way we could assure ourselves that the strategic plan outcomes were, indeed, being implemented and that we would be able to assess our progress on a regular basis. The assumptions served as a contextual frame for our strategic plan themes and implementation.

- Growth: As a new campus within the CSU system, we are expected to maintain a steep growth trajectory for the foreseeable future. This rapid and sustained growth presents considerable challenges for the campus with regard to space, faculty and staff hiring, dorm construction, student services, and so on. It is extremely difficult to keep pace with expected growth of between 400 to 500 full-time equivalent students (FTE) per year.

- The constraints related to converting a military base into a university: While some of the buildings inherited by the university were used as instructional space, others needed to be dramatically refurbished and repurposed. In addition, there were buildings that dated from World War II and had lead paint and asbestos problems. Furthermore, none of the buildings were compliant with the Americans with Disabilities Act (ADA). In fact, what we found is that after a certain point it was more expensive to convert buildings than to build new ones.

- Continuous improvement: In its vision, CSUMB made a commitment to continuous improvement, to becoming a true learning organization. This means that all policies and plans have renewal dates that require us to review and assess them periodically. We are committed to gathering data regularly to check on how we are doing on all processes, and then making changes as appropriate. In order to keep faithful to this commitment, we had to institutionalize this commitment through our planning.

- CSUMB as a residential campus: We are unique in the CSU system in that we are 60% residential. We require students who live beyond a 25-mile radius to be in residence for two years. As a result, we had to consciously decide to maintain this level of residency, since it would seriously affect our plans for the build-out of the campus. The campus is residential for students, as well as for faculty and staff. As we grow we need to be mindful of planning for learning space and living space as well.

We also agreed that, at a minimum, the plans that needed to be aligned with the strategic plan included the academic plan, the enrollment plan, the financial plan, and the capital construction plan/master plan. Such prioritizing kept us from being overwhelmed in our alignment attempts. That may be important for other campuses to keep in mind, in order to avoid attempting such unlimited levels of alignment so that everything bogs down.

As the work progressed, it became clear to the group again that alignment with the strategic plan was not sufficient. The assortment of major plans needed to also be integrated in such a way that, if any one of the common underlying assumptions were to change, then all other plans would recognize the change and realign accordingly. A test of this integration came with the budget crisis in California. Enrollment targets were reduced as a result of the decreased funding the California State University system was receiving. Immediately, the campus leadership through the Administrative Council recognized the impact on all of the plans. Dorms that we planned to build needed occupants, and we had to make adjustments to make sure beds were filled (capital construction/master plan). With fewer students anticipated, our academic plans for developing new majors had to be slowed down (academic plan). Our financial projection also had to be adjusted given that fees and the subsidy that the state provides would both be less than originally expected (financial plan).

This work was not done in isolation, but in an integrated way using the Administrative Council as the vehicle. The overall long-term change that resulted for the campus is that all plans continue to reflect the common assumptions that were identified, and further, that all plans serve as the tactical implementation of the strategic plan. The test for our planning alignment came much sooner than expected, but it gave us an opportunity to apply the assumptions as triggers for realignment. It will take time to ensure that these processes are fully institutionalized and expected as an annual readjustment, but having an early test gave us evidence that the process was on track. We also see these processes as important for our ongoing self-assessment and impetus for improvement.

The second group for our prioritizing model was the costing the model group. This is not a focus of many campuses because the model is traditional or well accepted and its costs are generally accepted as a fait accompli. Because CSUMB decided from its beginning to educate students in a different way, as spelled out in its vision, the issue of cost was a nagging concern. The concern could be put aside in the beginning but could not be ignored when early financial support ended.

Costing the Model: Thinking Alignment and Student Learning

The model in this discussion is the academic model, but it has repercussions across all the units on campus. For example, you cannot talk about student learning without considering the support for student development from student affairs. Another acknowledgment must preface the discussion that follows; that is, this topic of costing the model served very positive and productive purposes, unlike typical budgetary conversations.

CSUMB was committed to serving its targeted students in ways that built on assets, that actively engaged students in their own learning, and assessed their learning in terms of outcomes they would achieve and take from the campus. Questions of cost came up time and again in our own conversations as a reflective exercise. Those cost concerns also came up repeatedly in previous initial accreditation processes and became a kind of "call to action" beyond reflection. It was clear that we had to have answers, and that we needed to have clarity about those answers. As we grappled with questions of cost, our first task was to define for ourselves and for others including WASC the key components or elements of our academic model. Until we had those well defined, it was impossible to answer queries of cost.

Our academic model consisted of these important components: a First Year Experience, general education requirements called University Learning Requirements, service learning, requirements in each academic major program of study (Major Learning Outcomes), and our senior capstone program. A careful examination of each of these reveals an admirable alignment with the vision, campus values, and the mission. By now, our readers are well aware of each of these components and their commitment to the campus intentions.

With that check on initial alignment, the next step was to examine the kind of support needed to implement and maintain those components at a high quality level in terms of educational effectiveness. The core supports for the model included the following:

- Administrative support services including institutional research, academic budgeting, grants and contracts, and the deans' offices
- Technology support with faculty, student, staff e-mail accounts, basic software load sets, wireless access, technology help desk, and instructional technology software
- Faculty support including shared governance processes; retention, tenure, and promotion (RTP) processes; professional development grants and programs; and focused recruitment
- Student support with advising, financial aid, health and counseling, disability resources, faculty mentoring program, and a specialized and successful peer tutoring program.

Once we were clear about the components of our model, several huge questions loomed for our responses:

Does our academic model actually cost more (and more than what)?
What components or aspects of the model cost more?
What changes will be necessary if the cost cannot be funded?

We answered the first and most essential question with data comparing cost per full-time equivalent student from the campus, state, and university system (FTE is the funding formula the CSU System uses—annual FTE equals total annual semester student credit hours for the college divided by 30). We also compared campus data with national data from the National Association of College and University Business Officers (NACUBO). In doing these comparisons, we found that our cost was indeed higher than traditional campuses, but that we were achieving economies of scale. That is, as we moved beyond the start-up phase and enrollments increased, costs per student began to decrease.

With that "cost more" issue addressed, we set about to identify the source(s) of extra cost. Most of the components added additional costs to the usual cost of educating students. For example our general education requirements were a costly component of our academic model. We paid a coordinator responsible for the overall coordination of the university learning requirement program. We also paid a coordinator for each faculty learning community, paid part-time faculty to participate in the communities, and paid faculty for analysis of student work during the summer. Each of the expenses supported critical components of the University Learning Requirements in terms of achieving the vision, the pedagogy intended for our students' learning, for accountability of our general education outcomes, and for consistency in assessment of general education.

Our costs for some of our unique programs did not differ from other campuses, specifically CSU campuses. Our difference was our number of students compared to those institutions. Ultimately, that difference would be diminished with rising student enrollments, so our answer was a current yes but with intentions of reducing the costs per student.

Strategic Plan Review and Renewal: Bringing Assessment, Alignment, and Accountability Together

The institutional effectiveness group was charged with establishing an assessment and renewal process for the campus strategic plan. Although it was originally envisioned that the plan would be renewed in five-year cycles, we decided to begin with a sort of midway review three years into the five-year process in order to get a snapshot of our progress to date. The institutional effectiveness group worked closely with the Office of Institutional Assessment and Research (IAR) to develop strategic plan progress reports on each of the four strategic plan themes: pluralistic academic community, student learning, support for learning, and engaged campus.

First, the group reviewed the goals, outcomes, and indicators for each theme and identified those individuals and/or departments that were logically responsible for (1) acting on the outcomes, (2) tracking the specific data needed to assess the indicators, and (3) the actual evidence that would need to be collected and analyzed (CSUMB, 2002). For example, under the theme pluralistic academic community, outcome 1.2 is "Gender equilibrium exists within staff, faculty, and administration ranks reflecting the gender demographics of our CSUMB student body." The indicator for this outcome is "At all levels across all departments, gender demographics of all campus constituencies (student body, staff, faculty, and administration) are within 10 percent of student gender distribution" (p. 6). The institutional effectiveness group identified IAR as the office responsible for tracking the student data, and human resources for the staff, faculty, and administrative data for this indicator. The group then identified those functions on campus that would be both directly and indirectly responsible for acting on the data provided— those that would have "ownership" of this outcome, so to speak. These included student affairs through its enrollment management planning, human resources through employment services and the equal opportunity office, the president, vice president, provost, and deans. The evidence of achievement of this outcome would be a report on gender data that would need to be produced and analyzed by IAR and human resources.

Once this process was complete, IAR then consulted with other units across campus, including the provost's office, deans, and student affairs in order to refine the evidence selection and analyze it against the indicators and outcomes. Once the evidence was collected, IAR produced a report for each of the four themes sequentially. The entire process took approximately one year, from first report to last. The reports were presented to the full Administrative Council, which was asked for feedback on the process, and suggestions for additional evidence that may not have been identified in the report.

This process of assessment occurred on multiple levels. First, it was meant to assess institutional attainment of stated goals. Each of the theme reports reported on institutional progress, and identified "assessment gaps" where evidence was missing or insufficient to assess. But this process also offered an opportunity to assess the strategic plan itself. "Indicator gaps" were also identified where outcomes and indicators needed clarification or revision because they were too vague, or they didn't seem to quite get at the questions we wanted answered, or the indicators didn't align with the outcomes, and so forth. One example would be under the student learning theme. Outcome 4.1 reads: "Students connect new ideas or skills to prior knowledge and experiences, and they feel that others recognize and value their prior knowledge and experiences" (CSUMB, 2002, p. 13). The corresponding indicator is "Students voluntarily and spontaneously incorporate aspects of their life experiences into coursework." An assessment gap was identified because, although we do have some anecdotal evidence supporting this, we currently do not have any institutionalized, comprehensive analysis of student coursework that measures incorporation of personal life experiences, or determines if students incorporate their life experiences "voluntarily and spontaneously." There are also indicator gaps on two levels here: (1) there is no corresponding indicator to assess whether students "feel that others recognize and value" the life experiences and prior knowledge they bring with them, and (2) the indicator is vague and does not suggest what evidence might be used to assess the outcome (student and faculty surveys, analysis of course syllabi, teaching evaluations, etc.). This and all of the other identified gaps are being considered by the Administrative Council, and will inform the plan's revision and renewal over the coming year.

Through the initial assessment of the strategic plan, the institutional effectiveness group identified several areas that needed to be addressed on an institutional level. First, the group saw a real need for ownership of individual outcomes by appropriate groups and offices on campus to ensure *intentional* planning and budgeting at the outcome level. This would mean that the strategic plan could not simply sit on the shelf, unused and unread. Departments would need to actively align their operations with strategic plan goals, and they would have the responsibility for collecting and reporting on data regarding specific outcomes for the next round of strategic plan assessment reports.

Second, the group identified the need for the renewal and revision of goal, outcome, and indicator language to more accurately reflect what we want to measure. Through the strategic plan assessment reports, we have already begun the process of reviewing the alignment between indicators and outcomes, as well as the alignment between outcomes and the goals of the university so that they remain vital and relevant to a changing institution.

A clearly articulated process for collecting, managing, and compiling strategic plan evidence is needed, with appropriate groups or offices being responsible for managing and collecting indicator data at the outcome level. And finally, for our growing campus we need to establish a process to incorporate additional themes and issues that require action in the strategic plan process as they arise.

The Administrative Council will now take up all of these challenges. The most significant outcome of this first assessment and renewal process for the strategic plan has been to move us forward in becoming a true learning organization, integrating the assessment of institutional effectiveness into our daily business and thereby promoting long-term change.

Reflective Conclusion

We have truly been a learning organization when it comes to alignment of our major planning and decisions with our goal of student learning. We have learned hard and time-consuming lessons, costly lessons in terms of resources, and lessons that have been humbling. From each lesson, we have gained insights and understandings, especially about the need for multiple levels of alignment to be threaded through our campus processes. As a learning organization, we may make more mistakes and hope to gain new insights for future planning and decision making. Most institutions of higher education have realized that learning is essential to change and improvement (Boyce, 2003). As we continue to build infrastructure, expand our thinking, and focus our processes, alignment will be our guidepost for ongoing learning and improvement.

References

American Association for Higher Education. (1992). *Principles of good practice for assessing student learning.* Washington, DC: AAHE.

Boyce, M. E. (2003). Organizational learning is essential to achieving and sustaining change in higher education. *Innovative Higher Education, 28,* 119–136.

California State University Monterey Bay. (2002, January 24). *Strategic plan.* Seaside, CA: CSUMB.

12

POSTSCRIPT AND
REFLECTIONS

Amy Driscoll

As we finished writing our chapters, we realized that we have not been direct about the outcomes of our accreditation review. Not for any deliberate reason! We were just so focused on the theme of our book. Our message to our reader colleagues at other campuses is this:

Conduct your processes of inquiry, documentation, assessment, and review for your own campus use to self-assess for improvement. Don't do it solely for accreditation.

Our readers may have felt nervous about our review with such thinking, with such approaches. We are happy to announce that we received an "extraordinarily favorable report," that our WASC team confirmed the overall CSUMB academic programs and the university capacity to meet current and future needs.

Some of the report narrative will not be surprising if you have read chapters 2 through 11. Among the comments from the visiting team (Ramaley et al., 2002) are:

"The team found a wonderful, engaging, resourceful, energetic, and creative community of people who have clearly established a genuine community guided by a remarkable sense of common vision and purpose" (p. 15).

"CSU Monterey Bay has an exemplary educational model that will provide significant insights for other institutions. The institution has the potential to become a national model as the experience of the institution continues to be documented and assessed, and shared with the higher education community and policy makers" (p. 18).

"At CSU Monterey Bay everything centers on what is best for students. This habit is reflected in how administrators talk about their responsibilities, how faculty maintain student learning as the source of their inspiration and motivations, and how students talk about their experience on campus" (p. 28).

"The Vision statement is central to the CSU Monterey Bay experience. The institution is as much vision-driven as it is outcomes based. The Vision and mission were described in a variety of settings and by a broad range of people to explain their motivations, aspirations, their goals, and the distinctive character of the campus. The Vision is clearly very real and in the past years, it has been made operational in concrete terms" (p. 22).

"The campus has used the stages of the accreditation process effectively as an opportunity for reflection and a way to test basic assumptions upon which the model is based" (p. 16).

"There is a strong culture of continuous improvement that encourages the community to identify issues requiring further work and the willingness to revisit continually, and to develop new approaches that reflect what the campus has learned" (p. 17).

"In the opinion of the team, several of whom have specific expertise in assessment, the campus has one of the best-developed approaches to a continuous process of inquiry and engagement to enhance educational effectiveness of any institution in the nation" (p. 19).

Those affirmations were energizing and rewarding to the campus community especially after years of preparation. They also communicate a strong sense of responsibility to the campus itself and to our colleagues in higher education. The institution is now responsible for the following:

- Staying learner centered in thinking, discussions, and decisions
- Staying true to the vision and mission in both image and actions
- Sustaining our commitment to reflection, inquiry, engagement, and continuous improvement

None of these are minor or easy—they require our vigilance and continued hard work. They definitely leave no room for just maintaining the status quo.

Our responsibility to the larger higher education community is focused on sharing our processes and insights while continuing to document and assess our practices. This book achieved multiple responsibilities. It has provided a way to publicly discuss our strategies and processes, our successes and errors, and our learning. We hope that it initiates and nurtures ongoing conversation and collaborative learning on campus and on a national level.

Lest you think that our future intentions are pure Pollyanna, a campus scan more than a year after our accreditation review finds some of the following:

Tuesday, May 17, 2005, a group of faculty, student affairs representatives, tutors, and administrators meet to begin a comprehensive assessment of the writing support program for our students at the first-year level and at the third-year level (transfer students). Their questions begin with "What difference are our services and resources making for students?" Each of the group members contributes a question of personal interest to expand the inquiry process.

Thursday, May 26, 2005, a group of science faculty has gathered for the day to analyze student work to document achievement of the science University Learning Requirement, a general education requirement. Their conversations focus intensely on improvements of their curriculum and pedagogy.

Friday, May 27, 2005, I meet with Swarup Wood at his request to brainstorm questions for another series of faculty interviews. "After facilitating the assessment work this year, I am motivated again to check faculty perceptions . . . it's important to find out what they are getting out of this process this time" (S. Wood, personal communication, May 27, 2005).

The campus has certainly gone beyond accreditation to assessment processes that promote improvement. It's a good place to be!

Reference

Ramaley, J. A., Bringle, R. G., Freund, S. A., Harding, E., Hengstler, D. D., Hutchings, P. A., & O'Brien, K. (2003, May 5(7). *Report of the Educational Effectiveness Site Visit Team, California State University, Monterey Bay.* Seaside, CA: Authors.

INDEX